American Popular Music

American Popular Music:
Readings from the Popular Press
Volume I:
The Nineteenth Century and
Tin Pan Alley

Edited by
Timothy E. Scheurer

Bowling Green State University Popular Press
Bowling Green, OH 43403

For my wife Pam
with gratitude and love for sharing
the music with me all through the years.

Contents

General Introduction

When we think about the role of music in our American culture, our minds might fancifully go back to the Pilgrims arriving on our shore. As they peered into the darkened thicket of the New World, as William Bradford described it, did they perhaps have a hymn to sustain them and make the passage easier? We know that music in worship would play important roles in the lives of succeeding generations of New England settlers in their efforts to create the New Eden. We know as well that music was important to the slaves in the south, and we know it is so today as we listen to drive-time radio to get us to and from work, and as we listen to either radios or Muzak playing in our work environment. Walk through a new neighborhood subdivision currently under construction and you will hear music coming from inside of houses, from vehicles parked out front, music helping subcontractors in their work. As you take this walk you get a sense of what it must have been like to walk down 28th street in New York circa 1910 when Tin Pan Alley was in its heyday. On a hot summer's day the windows would have been flung open to stave off the stifling heat, and the sounds of dozens of pluggers working in buildings along the street would have drifted out on to the steamy New York street in a cacophony of creativity and commerce.

Music has been, is, and will continue to be an integral part of our daily lives. It is vital to our beliefs, our rituals, our work and our play. It is both a reflection of and a formative part of the fabric and needlepoint of our culture and history. These volumes will examine the stitchery of that fabric and popular music's place in the design. The two volumes that constitute *American Popular Music* feature essays covering a wide variety of subjects of interest to students and scholars of popular music. Extending from the time of Stephen Foster up to our present day and the music of Bruce Springsteen, these essays will look at popular music in the cultural context, exploring the events, the people, and the media that have shaped our popular musical heritage over the last two hundred years. The essays in both volumes are arranged, moreover, to provide not only an historical perspective to the subject but to provide a cross-section of the complex of factors (creative and media oriented) that go into the creation of popular music. It is a rich tapestry, part Bayeux tapestry and part day-glo art, that has much to tell us about our values and history.

One of the major goals of these two volumes, and central to our understanding of the importance and impact of popular music on our values and history, is that mercurial concept of popularity. What does popularity mean? What makes something popular, and what does that tell us about

1

ourselves? How do we account for phenomena like Michael Jackson or an album such as *Saturday Night Fever?* Why, when you go through a room of people in their 50's and 60's (as I did not long ago) and ask what their favorite song is, do a large majority select Hoagy Carmichael's "Stardust"? Popular culture scholars have been dealing with questions like these for over 20 years, and not surprisingly the answers vary. In fact, it is this variety of approaches and responses to popularity which excites the scholars and students of popular culture. The essays contained in these two volumes reflect this variety.

The basic premise of critical analyses of popular music is the assumption that the concept of popularity is important to humanistic studies, that collective appreciation of objects and events says something important about what we value and how we live. Consequently, these volumes exist as an affirmation of the belief that popular music itself is vital to humanistic studies. Too often it seems that critics, when investigating music in America, want to embrace some other form of music (folk, blues, classical, jazz) as the representative music of our culture. Is it embarrassing that such patently commercial stuff such as Harry Von Tilzer, Walter Donaldson, George Gershwin, Neil Sedaka, The Byrds, Fleetwood Mac, or Wham mirrors some of our most cherished beliefs and deeply held values? Whatever the reason, popular music studies, especially those of the Tin Pan Alley years (1880-1950), have been relegated to show business lore, occasional thoughtful biographies (with little musical criticism), or just plain critical disdain. This situation has changed over the last ten to twenty years, aided largely by excellent studies of rock music by people such as Greil Marcus, Simon Frith, and Charlie Gillett, to name just three. That Charles Hamm would write in his excellent history of popular song, *Yesterdays,* "Tin Pan Alley did not draw on traditional music—it created traditional music"[1] is also a measure of how criticism of popular music has improved recently. It is hoped that these volumes will continue the trend of concerted and serious thinking about all aspects of popular music.

Critics and intellectuals may rightly fear that popular music does not reflect the Arnoldian notions of culture as the best of what is written and thought, but to ignore it or dismiss it as mere entertainment does everyone a disservice. That the state of twentieth century music (both serious and popular) has been shaped more by Charles K. Harris than Charles Ives is perhaps a bitter pill to swallow for music lovers and scholars of American culture. The presence, however, of Sondheim's *Sweeney Todd* as part of the New York City Opera's season, or a Rodger's and Hammerstein musical performed by Samuel Ramey or Kiri Te Kanawa is testimony to Charles K. Harris' influence and the impact of Tin Pan alley on all phases of music in America.

Another one of the goals of these two volumes is to show popular music in an historico-cultural context. Consequently, I chose a chronological arrangement in the chapters and, as best I could, within the chapters. A chronological approach, first, allows the reader to understand the role music and/or the people who make the music play in their own time. As we, moreover, come to a better understanding of past time periods, we then can also gain some insight into our own time. This is a premise of the *annales* approach to historical and cultural criticism which is currently in vogue. Although criticized in some quarters, the approach nonetheless has validity in rectifying the notion that *only* great artists and serious literature and art forms played decisive roles in giving certain ages their character and in the creating the drama of history itself. Robert Darnton and Fernand Braudel have demonstrated brilliantly that the seeming minutiae of daily life—including those most disposable of all arts, the popular arts—indeed do shape larger historical issues and events. This, of course, has been the claim of popular culture scholars for the past twenty years, and these volumes will, I hope, give testimony to that position. Indeed, whose voice was more influential in the nineteenth century, Thoreau or the Hutchinson family? Furthermore, what does the public reception of the Hutchinson family's music and stage show tell us about the values of that period? Another instance of this is the average perception that the first great age of consciousness raising in popular music occurred in the 60's. This, I believe, will be dispelled as one reads about the Hutchinson family of the nineteenth century.

Another reason for choosing a chronological approach—and a third goal of these volumes—is to chart developments in the history of popular music and to enable the reader to appreciate changes and influences within the art form itself. Readers, as they make their way through these two volumes, will see a number of intersecting lines that will be essential for understanding the role music plays in our culture. For instance, the development of ragtime was not only a phenomenon of the early twentieth century, but it played an important role in the development of jazz, swing, and, ultimately rock 'n' roll. The hue and cry lifted against ragtime would be lifted at least two more times before 1955 and in smaller forms since the dawn of the age of rock. Ragtime, according to preachers and some pundits, was the devil's music leading western civilization into a hopeless moral morass—and so it would be with jazz in the 20's, swing in the 30's, and rock in the 50's. It continues to today in the Parents Music Resource Center (PMRC). Each form, moreover, was tied to what can only be termed cultural revolution as each played a major role in spearheading new ideas and styles in their respective decades. By illuminating why certain events took place in popular music's past it is hoped we will be able to deal better with the controversies of the present and to anticipate changes that may occur in the future.

A fourth goal of these collections is to provide the student of popular culture and popular music with a cross-sectional analysis of the forces that contribute to the creation of our popular culture. The articles contained in these two volumes deal in varying fashion with the delicate and dynamic interplay of the creative people, the media, and the audience, and how these forces have affected popular music and, consequently, shaped our cultural values. Essays will deal with the central issues of cultural studies: heroes, beliefs and myths, rituals, stereotyping, iconology, institutions, fashions and communication, the building blocks of our cultural consciousness and the elements which help us define who we are and what we value. The very near deification of Elvis on the recent anniversary of his death, and the emotional outpouring that the anniversary elicited, only begins to suggest the powerful impact hero figures have in our culture.

The essays will also examine the role of the media in the creation and perpetuation of cultural values and attitudes. For instance, the Paul Whiteman band was known as one of the major jazz ensemble of its day, but a comparison of his "It Happened in Monterey" and Louis Armstrong's "West End Blues" (made within about two years of one another) reveals two very different perspectives on jazz. Armstrong may have set a standard for future jazz trumpeters, but Whiteman not only set the standard for recording of dance bands but his access to all the media of the day (stage performances, radio, movies, and recordings) made his sound the standard for the period and, for good or ill, probably defined jazz for the general public.

Throughout, the reader is encouraged to ask questions about the relationship between the art and the audience. Ultimately, the study of popular music should, like a study of any of the arts, bring us to a better understanding of who we are, of how we create, think, act, and perpetuate those values which give us our cultural identity. For all our dogged attempts at maintaining our autonomy and individual identities, the drive to belong, to feel a sense of a community embracing a set of shared values, is equally as strong. Popular music has played an important role in the establishment and maintenance of those values. From Stephen Foster's gentle portrait of ante-bellum blacks, to Harry Von Tilzer's and Andrew Sterling's view of the fallen women in "Bird in a Gilded Cage," to Benny Goodman's liberating beat in swing, to Dylan's stewardship of the political values of the baby boom generation, to Bruce's Springsteen's impassioned portrait of Americans ten years "running down the road, nowhere to run nowhere to go," popular music has entertained us, informed us, raised our consciousness, and, in the final analysis, defined us. Just as the medieval tapestry served a number of functions in that society, so the tapestry of American popular music reveals much about our culture; in its music its very soul is laid bare for us to puzzle at and wonder over.

The essays in chapters two and three of Volume I are largely devoted to American popular music before the age of rock. The organization is quite simple, with one chapter devoted to 19th century music and the other devoted to the music of the Tin Pan Alley years (c. 1880-1950). The essays will deal with subjects as wide ranging as minstrelsy, ragtime, images of women, swing, dance bands, the evolution of lyric writing styles, and the evolution of radio. The first chapter in this volume, "Thinking About Music," contains articles dealing with some of the theoretical issues in popular music studies. Music making and consuming is, as most know, an incredibly complex phenomenon. It involves creativity (both musical and verbal), performance, business, audience needs, and these are but the largest most general categories. The purpose of these essays is to orient the reader to the complexities of popular music studies and to offer some theoretical notions to augment the reading of the remaining essays in Volumes I and II. It is intended as an introduction to music theory for both volumes, so readers of Volume II are encouraged to come back to these essays before foraying into the age of rock.

Note

[1]Charles Hamm, *Yesterdays: Popular Song in America* (New York: W.W. Norton, 1979), p. 325.

References

Suggestions for further reading will follow each of the chapters. Here I would like to list some of the general histories and studies of American Popular Music for the period prior to the age of rock. For the purposes of general background to popular music there really are not a lot of journals and/or magazines available that deal in depth with the subject of popular music only. *Popular Music and Society* out of Bowling Green State University's Popular Press is one of the few and thank goodness it is also one of the best. Otherwise, readers will have to scour publications like *American Music, Popular Music, The Journal of Popular Culture, The Journal of American Culture, American Quarterly, Stereo Review, High Fidelity,* and occasional essays in major papers like the *New York Times* to find articles on popular music before the age of rock. Consequently, I will confine myself to listing books unless there is a particularly important essay.

Chase, Gilbert. *America's Music: From the Pilgrims to the Present.* 3rd ed. New York: McGraw-Hill, 1987.

Cooper, B. Lee. *The Popular Music Handbook: A Resource Guide for Teachers, Librarians, and Media Specialists.* Littleton, Colorado: Libraries Unlimited, 1984.

Ewen, David.*All the Years of American Popular Song.* Englewood Cliffs, NJ: Prentice-Hall, 1977.

———. *American Popular Songs From the Revolutionary War to the Present.* New York: Random House, 1966.

———. *Great Men of American Popular Song.* Rev. and enlarged. Englewood Cliffs, NJ: Prentice Hall, 1972.

Hamm, Charles. *Yesterdays: Popular Song in America.* New York: Norton, 1979.

Hitchcock, Wiley and Stanley Sadie. *The New Groves Dictionary of American Music.* 4 Vols. New York: MacMillan, 1986.

Kealy, Edward R. "Conventions and the Production of the Popular Music Aesthetics." *Journal of Popular Culture,* 16 (Fall 1982), 100-115.

Kingman, Daniel. *American Music: A Panorama.* New York: MacMillan, 1979.

Kinkle, Roger. *The Complete Encyclopedia of Popular Music and Jazz, 1900-1950.* 4 Vols. New Rochelle, NY: Arlington House, 1974.

Mattfeld, Julius. *Variety Cavalcade: A Musical-Historical Review, 1620-1969.* 3rd ed. Englewood Cliffs, NJ: Prentice-Hall, 1971.

Mellers, Wilfrid. *Music in a New Found Land: Themes and Developments in the History of American Music.* New York: Hillstone, 1964, 1975.

Palmer, Tony. *All You Need Is Love: The Story of Popular Music.* New York: Grossman Publishers, 1976.

Shapiro, Nat, ed. *Popular Music: An Annotated Index of American Popular Songs.* 6 vols. New York: Adrian Press, 1964-73.

Spaeth, Sigmund. *A History of Popular Music in America.* New York: Random House, 1948.

Whitcomb, Ian. *After the Ball: Pop Music from Rag to Rock.* New York: Simon and Schuster, 1973.

Thinking About Popular Music

The One Dimensional Approach To Popular Music: A Research Note

R. Serge Denisoff and Mark H. Levine

Scholarly treatments of popular music have exhibited two paramount methodological techniques: opinion survey and content analyses of song lyrics. One research procedure consists of polling a sample of adolescents, usually in a classroom setting, as to musical preferences and favorite artists.[1] The other dominant methodology evidenced in popular music studies is the content analysis of songs usually taken from printed sources such as *Hit Parader, Song Hits Magazine, Country Song Round Up, Rhythm and Blues,* and other publications addressed to a teenage market.[2] Several analyses in a similar vein have appeared dealing with propaganda songs in social movements.[3] Given the nature of these approaches one omission becomes readily apparent. The music itself is rarely treated despite the acknowledgement by several students of the important role of tonal and esthetic structures of popular songs. One observer notes, "words are only part of the total sound and are responded to as such."[4] Addressing sociologists, Bernhard places the focus "on both the lyrics and on the sound of the music itself as a medium of communication... the sound is not to be examined but just felt."[5] These admonitions not withstanding, most observers have relied upon printed lyrics to analyse popular music. Using this latter approach we only perceive one dimension of the message communicated by a popular song.

Several recent studies have indicated that content analyses of lyrics from songbooks based on popularity charts may only reflect the sentiments of the songwriter and tastes of program directors and record industry A & R (Artists and Repertoire) executives. Gillett, in his study of rock 'n' roll songs, suggests that the process of "covering," the replication of a song from a sub-group by a major artist, is prevalent. During this process deviant messages and themes are reworded or changed and thus withheld from the Top Forty charts.[6] Hirsch, in treating the structure of the popular music industry pointed to a number of censorious practices present, from the A & R man to the program manager on each local "Big Sound" station.[7] Therefore, we may assume that many so-called "hit songs" may not be reflective of the ideology or taste *per se* of Top

Reprinted with permission from the *Journal of Popular Culture,* Volume 4:4 (Spring 1971), pp. 911-19.

Forty listeners. Reisman and Barzun have argued that popular music does not function on the intellectually meaningful level but rather on the environmental plane.[8] Several recent studies indicate that Top Forty listeners may not, in fact, assimilate the lyrics of popular songs.

Robinson and Hirsch, in a survey of high school students in two Michigan cities, found that most respondents could not provide an adequate description of the message of so-called "protest songs." They reported that, "Over seventy percent of all students sampled wrote that they are attracted more by the 'sound' of a song than by its 'meaning.' "[9] In sampling a college audience's reaction to socio-political themes on the Top Forty, the writers reached a similar conclusion, with some variations.[10] These findings seem to indicate that lyric analysis alone is not reflective of the total musical product or subject matter.

When referring to contemporary music we mean a multitude of musical genres—folk, folk-rock, rock-a-billy, acid-rock, San Francisco acid-rock, country rock, blues traditionalists, blues interpreters, jazz rock—which comprise the idiom termed Top Forty.

Popular music, as defined by the industry, is designed to appeal to the teenage and young adult audience. It would appear that the relative standardization of musical genres represented in past decades rendered content analyses more applicable at that time. This is equally true of folk type protest songs which stress the lyric rather than the instrumentation, e.g., the "talking blues" structure.

A content analysis of Elvis Presley's early hits suggests little of the social significance of his personality or his music. An examination of the lyrics finds his songs traditional love statements as described by Peatman in the early 1940s.[11] Some of Presley's best sellers were "I Want You, I Need You, I Love You," "Let Me Be Your Teddy Bear," "Love Me Tender," "All Shook Up," "Heartbreak Hotel," and "Hound Dog." Excerpts from the last two songs will explicate the traditional character of the songs:

> So, if your baby leaves
> And you have a tale to tell,
> Just take a walk down Lonely Street
> To Heartbreak Hotel,
> Where you'll be so lonely
> That we could die. (Heartbreak Hotel)

> When they said you were high classed
> Well that was just a lie
> You ain't never caught a rabbit
> And you ain't no friend of mine. (Hound Dog)

The deviant aspect of Presley was entirely visual and tied to his hybrid musical genre, rock-a-billy, rather than the lyrical content which did little more than elaborate the sentiments of Shakespeare's youthful rebels, Romeo and Juliet.

Another illustration of some of the limitations of the content analysis of lyrics of rock and roll songs is found in the following lyrics which deal with the difficulties of being an adolescent:

1. Same thing every day,
Gettin up goin to school
No need of me complainin'
My objections overruled...

2. Workin in a fillin station
Too many tasks
Wipe the windows, check the tires
Check the oil—dollar gas...

3. Get sick get well
Hang around an ink well
Ring bell, hard to tell
If anything is goin to sell
Try hard, bet barred
Get back, write braille
Join the army, if you fail...

4. I'm gonna raise a fuss
I'm gonna raise a hollar
About working all summer
Just to try to make a dollar

5. Yeah I'm doing all right in school
They ain't said I've broke no rule,
Don't bother me, leave me alone,
Anyway I'm almost grown.

A cursory reading of the above lines from four different songs will convey a common theme of generational conflict—the trails and tribulations of high school and part-time jobs. Yet the qualitative difference here is elusive. Verses 1, 2, and 5 are from songs written by Chuck Berry, an urban blues guitarist. Verse 3 is from Bob Dylan's "Subterranean Homesick Blues," while verse 4 is from Eddie Cochran's "Summertime Blues." Despite the overt lyrical similarities, neither Berry nor Cochran "songs" were originally viewed as expressing protest. Conversely, Dylan's piece has frequently been cited as a protest song. Equally, the musical genres involved, while exhibiting some similarities, were addressed to totally different publics. Berry's "Monkey Business" was aimed at Negroes specifically, and Top Forty listeners in a very general sense. "Summertime Blues" was written for a white teenage "Big Sound" audience. Dylan's composition was of yet another time and place. Nevertheless, using the content analysis technique alone we could find all of the four songs relegated to the same category.

Rock groups which got started at the Fillmore Auditorium in San Francisco quite often have been unsuccessful on national record sales charts. This lack of success is due to the fact that the lyrics or the music alone is not sufficient for a "total experience" to take place. The Big Brother and the Holding Company band, in person, with emotional contagion, a color show, great volume, and psychedelic lighting, was always well received. Conversely, Big Brother's original two record albums have not been very successful.[12]

Numerous observers of rock 'n' roll music have posited that instrumentation obscures the lyric content. "One finds that young children often have a totally different notion of the lyrics of a song from those actually recorded...."[13] This is equally true of adult analyses in popular music publications. *Crawdaddy*, a major rock magazine, described a majority of performers in a "stream of consciousness" manner relating the feelings of the reviewer more than the music itself.[14] Sociologists, while avoiding the Joycian style, experience some of the problems found in "Dylanology" as Carey reports.[15] One classic exhibition of the isogenetic process in content analyses is found in Robinson and Hirsch's characterization of the Lennon-McCartney composition of "Lucy in the Sky with Diamonds," as a drug song or "deviant."[16] The songwriters have denied that the song was designed to connote hallucinogenic drugs. Paul McCartney outlined the difficulties of interpreting songs in an interview:

...you write a song and you mean it one way, and then someone comes up and says something about it that you didn't think of—you can't deny it. Like 'Lucy in the Sky with Diamonds.' people came up and said, cunningly, 'Right, I get it. L-S-D,' and it was when papers were talking about LSD, but we never thought about it.[17]

Fellow Beatle, Lennon, added, "For instance, the title 'Lucy...' wasn't really about LSD."[18] In a series of interviews and press conferences with rock musicians the senior writer found that most performrs felt their songs were being misconstrued, especially when it came to the subject of illegal drugs.[19] This confusion involved in the interpretation of songs is compounded due to the so-called *in* meanings" which are designed to convey both an exoteric and an esoteric theme. There are generally two forms of these songs; (1) the rhetorical song, and (2) the multiple level song. The first type of lyrical structure is usually an indictment of some aspect of society with a conformist acceptance in the conclusion. "We Gotta Get Out of This Place" by the original Animals is a rock song condemning poverty, but the solution is from Horatio Alger, that is, working one's way out of the slum. Janis Ian's "Society's Child" chronicles the tribulations of inter-racial dating, but ends stating:

Baby, I'm only society's child
When we're older things may change
But for now this is the way they
Must remain...

The ending to this song is parallel to the above five verses, which had little to do with inter-racial dating, with the possible exception of Berry's "Too Much Monkey Business."

The multiple level song is more common and depends greatly upon the sophistication of the listener. Songs like "Mr. Tambourine Man," "Eight Miles High," "Get Off My Cloud," and "Rainy Day Women No. 12 and 35" are all songs *believed* to be drug songs, but have also been critically discussed in other contexts. Unless researchers have a songwriter's or performer's interpretation of these songs, their analysis is no more valid than that of any music critic. It therefore appears highly desirable to first ascertain the original lyrical intent, especially in studies addressing musical tastes and the ability of listeners to interpret songs.

One excellent index of the difficulties of analyzing popular songs appears when teenage respondents are asked to write down what precisely a pop tune means. One striking aspect of the several studies attempting to get at Top Forty listeners' tastes and concentration spans *vis-a-vis* rock 'n' roll is that only a maximum of .30 percent of N have been capable of correctly stating what a given song means.[20] At this writing, the content analysis technique of studying popular songs does not seem to be sufficient beyond the printed word in analyzing young people's ideology. Given the growing interest in popular culture and contemporary music, it seems that social scientists will have to methodologically transcend current means of content analysis and polling.

Several innovations appear warranted in the realm of content analysis of popular music samples. The primary improvement would be to address the entire recording as a *gestalt*. As noted, lyrics suggest a clarity and rational structure which may not be transmitted to Top Forty listeners. The rapid delivery of Bob Dylan's "Subterranean Homesick Blues" blended into an amplified rock arrangement makes the lyrics nearly unintelligible without repeated concentrated efforts to understand all of the words. A reading of the song in Goldstein's *Poetry of Rock* may well classify it as a protest song. On the other hand, "Eve of Destruction," exhibiting more of a lyrical emphasis, is isomorphic to the printed words, but still lacks the accusatory tone of the recorded version.

Another advantage of record sampling is the sensate aspect of the tonal qualities of the song under consideration. Many popular song lyrics, as illustrated by the lyrics of Elvis Presley hits, are misleading. The lyrics of Grace Slick's rendition of "White Rabbit" remained similar in two different recordings, yet the impact of the conclusion in the popular Jefferson Airplane version of "feed your head" allows for no confusion as to the reference to drugs. The earlier Great Society rendition of the song—same lyrics—is most indefinite. The differences in the Charles Calhoun rock classic "Shake, Rattle and Roll," even without some lyrical changes, are significant. The original recording by Joe Turner, a black urban blues singer, was guttural, stressing sexuality in both the singing style and the lyrics, e.g., "You wear low dresses, the sun comes shining through—I can't believe my eyes all of this belongs to you." Even without this verse there is little doubt that Turner's use of the word "roll" as stressed by the arrangement to refer to a dance. Elvis Presley's interpretation of the same song incorporates both qualities, although the "suggestiveness" is basically visual and vocal rather than in the lyric. Pat Boone's recording even more than Haley's stressed the Saturday night hop orientation of "Shake, Rattle and Roll." Each of these versions communicate a different ethos and *gestalt*. The lyrics alone will not distinguish these differentiations. Consequently, it is suggested that present approaches to popular music are necessary but not sufficient to deal with the entire *gestalt* of popular music.

Notes

[1]J.S. Coleman, *The Adolescent Society* (Glencoe: Free Press, 1961), p. 23.

[2]See J. Peatman, "Radio and Popular Music," in *Radio Research:* 1942-43, eds. P. Lazarsfeld and F. Stanton (New York: Duell, Sloan and Pearce, 1944), pp. 335-93; D. Horton, "The Dialogue of Courtship in Popular Songs," *American Journal of Sociology* LXII (May, 1957), 569-78; and J.T. Carey, "Changing Courtship Patterns in the Popular Song," *American Journal of Sociology* LXXIV (May, 1969), 720-31.

[3]J. Greenway, *American Folksongs of Protest* (Philadelphia: University of Pennsylvania Press, 1953); M. Truzzi, "The 100% American Songbag: Conservative Folksongs in America," *Western Folklore* XXVIII (January, 1969), 24-40; and R.S. Denisoff, "Protest Movements: Class Consciousness and the Propaganda Song," *Sociological Quarterly* IX (Spring, 1968), 228-47.

[4]Carey, *op. cit.*, 721. Also see R. Goldstein, ed., *The Poetry of Rock* (New York: Bantam Books, 1968), pp. xi-xii.

[5]A Bernhard, "For What It's Worth: Today's Rock Scene," paper read at annual meetings of the American Sociological Association, San Francisco, 1967, 1-2.

[6]C. Gillett, "Just Let Me Hear Some of That Rock and Roll Music," *Urban Review* (December, 1966), 11-14.

[7]P. Hirsch, "The Structure of the Popular Music Industry," unpublished manuscript (Ann Arbor: University of Michigan, 1969).

[8]D. Riesman, "Listening to Popular Music," in *Individualism Reconsidered* (Glencoe: Free Press, 1954); and J. Barzun, *Music In American Life* (New York: Doubleday, 1958).

[9]J.P. Robinson and P.M. Hirsch, "Teenage Response To Rock and Roll Protest Songs," paper read at the annual meetings of the American Sociological Association, San Francisco, 1969.

[10]R.S. Denisoff and M.H. Levine, "The Popular Protest Song: The Case of the 'Eve of Destruction,' " *Public Opinion Quarterly* (forthcoming). Cynthia Weil, a song writer, suggests "...in some songs you can't even understand the lyrics, but it doesn't matter. The most important things are the melody, the *idea* of the lyrics, the sound of the singers and instruments," quoted in N.S. Woodstone, "The Songwriters," *The New Sound/Yes*, ed., I. Peck (New York: Four Winds Press, 1966), p. 38.

[11]E. Presley, *Elvis' Golden Hits*, RCA-LPM 1701.

[12]R.J. Gleason, *The Jefferson Airplane* (New York: Ballentine Books, 1969).

[13]C.I. Belz, "Popular Music and the Folk Tradition," *Journal of American Folklore* LXXX (April-June, 1967), 134.

[14]The "Dylanology" debate in the pages of *Broadside* (NYC) magazine is but one illustration of the "selective perception" involved in interpreting popular songs.

[15]Carey, *op. cit.*, 722-23.

[16]Robinson and Hirsch, *op. cit.*, 4.

[17]Quoted in A. Aldridge, "Beatles Not All That Turned On," in *The Age of Rock*, ed., J. Eisen (New York: Random House, 1968), p. 142.

[18]L.F. Aarons, "Sgt. Pepper Makes A Pitch For Peace," *Los Angeles Times Calendar*, (June 15, 1969), 14.

[19]While this does not constitute a representative sample, many of the rock musicians contacted have been publically labeled as singers or performers of "drug-oriented" songs such as "Looking For My Man" and "What Condition My Condition."

[20]Robinson and Hirsch, *op. cit.*

Five Constraints on the Production of Culture: Law, Technology, Market, Organizational Structure and Occupational Careers*

Richard A. Peterson

The production of culture perspective takes as its point of departure the observation that the nature and content of symbolic products are shaped by the social, legal and economic milieux in which they are produced. The perspective does not contradict the alternative orientations that examine cultural products with respect to each other, as created by inspired artists, as expressing the views of their consumers, or as reflecting the spirit of the society at large (Griswold 1981a). Properly applied, the production of culture perspective complements and reinforces these other perspectives (Peterson 1976).

A number of excellent monographs have focused on the influence of the milieux in which symbolic elements of culture are created. Think for example of the early studies by Ian Watt, Leo Lowenthall and others which related the evolution of popular literary forms to such extra-artistic factors as the spread of literacy, printing technology, the marketing strategies of publishing and the like.

Only since 1975, however, has the production of culture perspective become a self conscious approach. In addition to this collection of essays, evidence of a growing self-consciousness can be seen in three other special journal issues explicitly devoted to the emerging perspective: the *American Behavioral Scientist* (July, 1976), *Social Research* (Summer, 1978) and the English journal, *Media, Culture and Society* (forthcoming, 1982). In addition, numerous recent works can be cited which employ the perspective without explicitly embracing it. (For a review of this work see Peterson [1979:152-158]).

Since the production of culture perspective can be applied to the explicit development of symbols in the fine arts, science, law and religion, this is not the place for a complete review. The goal here is more modest. Drawing examples from the various domains of popular culture, this article focuses on five factors which alone, or in combination, often constrain or facilitate the evolution of culture. These influences include law, technology, the market, organizational

Reprinted with permission from the *Journal of Popular Culture*, Volume 16:2 (Fall 1982), pp. 143-53.

structure and occupational careers. The operation of each of these will be considered individually, and then all five together will be applied to explaining the emergence of rock and roll music in the mid 1950s.

The Five Constraints Illustrated

The five constraints typically work in concert. It is somewhat arbitrary therefore, as the illustrations will show, to single out any one for special attention. In each of the illustrations which follow, the focus will be on the one constraint which seems to be most important in shaping the popular art form being reviewed.

1. Law

Statute law and government regulation shape the financial and aesthetic conditions within which popular culture develops. For example, copyright law transforms whole classes of creative activity into property that can be bought, sold, stolen and litigated about much like other goods. The extension of the law to cover new classes of creative activity can shape the development of whole art forms (Ryan 1982; Plowman and Hamilton 1980).

Take for example the impact of changing American literary copyright law during the 19th century. Literary critics have often noted that 19th century American novels dealt with quite different subjects than did their English counterparts. While the latter were typically about love, marriage and bourgeois domestic life, American novels were much more often about an isolated male protagonist combating nature, the supernatural, or the evils of organized society. Critics and commentators typically interpret these striking contrasts as deriving from differences in English and American society or character.

Griswold (1981b), however, suggests that the differences may be due in part to the operation of copyright law. Until 1891, she notes, American law protected American writers but not foreign authors. In practice this special "protection" of American writers meant that they were discriminated against by American publishers. It was far cheaper for an American publisher to bring out an American edition of an English novel because it could be had for the taking with no copyright payments being made to the author or English publisher.

In consequence, the American market was flooded with cheap English novels on love and domestic life. In order to tempt a publisher to risk the higher publishing costs, Griswold argues, the American author had to exploit the adventure themes that English authors were not treating.

If this explanation has any weight, then the themes of English and American novels should converge rapidly after 1891 when the United States recognized international copyright agreements thus putting all authors on an equal footing. Just such a convergence has been noted by various commentators. To explain the shift, they refer to global changes such as the closing of the frontier, or the increasingly cosmopolitan nature of the American reading public. The production of culture perspective, however, suggests that the mundane facts of copyright law must be factored into the explanation (Griswold 1981b).

Numerous other examples of the influence of copyright law could be cited. Other sorts of law and government regulation are important as well: for example, anti-trust laws, laws concerning censorship, and the regulation of the media by the Federal Communications Commission.

As with the other four constraints discussed below, laws are not simply imposed from outside, as a more detailed examination of the struggle over the copyright laws would reveal. Rather, the various parties involved in the production process regularly lobby for or against particular laws and regulations. They also work to have statutes strictly enforced or ignored as it fits their own financial interests.

Thus, for example, until the advent of television, the three major broadcasting networks shaped and used the regulations. They also work to have statutes enforced or ignored as it fits their own financial interests.

Thus, for example, until the advent of television, the three major broadcasting networks shaped and used the regulations of the Federal Communications Commission to maintain their domination over radio, prevent the development of other networks, and severely restrict the number of licenses given for independent stations (Barnouw 1968). In a similar fashion, the leading firms of the movie industry in the 1920s and the comic book industry in the 1950s used a public uproar over sex and violence in these media to craft industry-run self-censorship codes that drove most of their competitors out of the business (Randall 1968; Smith 1974). Thus, law is not a neutral structure but is a resource that may be used to gain and consolidate power, shaping the nature and content of the popular arts in the process.

2. Technology

Marshall McLuhan did more than anyone else to dramatize the influence of technology in shaping popular culture. But by asserting that "the medium *is* the message," he focused all the attention on the cognitive impact of the medium so that it is easy to dismiss the influence of technology on shaping the *content* of the popular arts and communication.

Video technologies have radically reshaped world popular culture since World War II. The advent of television changed the demand for, and eventually the content of, both radio and cinema. The high cost of television production together with the low cost of transmission has led to the dissemination of American TV around the world. Video news has transformed the political consciousness of the American policy (Mattellart 1979; Gitlin 1980; Smith 1980), and now the cable and satellite technologies are revolutionizing TV itself.

Rather than focus on the recent changes in popular culture made possible by the new video technologies, however, we will draw on a much earlier example of the impact of a new technology. Mukerji (1979) argues that the development of print-making presses for wood cuts, engravings, and etchings made possible the emergence of mass-produced popular art works in the late 15th century at the same time that the fine-art painters were differentiating themselves from the craft-guild Artisan-painters.

Mukerji shows that a number of printmakers, of whom Marantino and Durer are the best known today, used the new picture-printing technology to develop a new aesthetic and syntax for their works on religious and secular themes that were mass-produced and sold widely throughout Europe. She notes that these mass-market oriented printmakers developed an aesthetic which has characterized popular culture ever since. It was naturalistic, standardized, conservative, and technically slick. Mukerji quotes Durer as saying the intent was to produce works that could be evaluated by the unlearned common folk (Mukerji 1979:259).

3. Market

To talk of markets and marketing is to refer to the audience, consumer, or fan in a very special way as Habermas (1975) has noted. "Market" denotes the audience as it is identified and conceptualized by financial decision-makers within a popular culture industry. When such people say there is "no market" for a particular cultural work, or that the "market" won't accept it, they mean that, in their opinion, not enough of a profit can be realized to justify the production, distribution and promotion of the item (DiMaggio 1977).

Thus, the ways in which potential audiences are defined and measured as markets directly influence what will be produced. The terms "formula" (Cawelti 1976), "convention" (Becker 1982), "audience images" (Gans 1957), and "product image" (Ryan and Peterson 1982) are terms used by researchers to suggest how artistic and financial decision-makers redefine the heterogeneous and unknown mass of potential consumers into a homogeneous and predictable "market" that can be tapped through standard market practices.

Joseph Turow's study of the marketing of children's books...provides an excellent case in point. He finds that books which are intended to be read by children are marketed in two quite different ways. In one, which he calls the "library market," publishers produce books to be sold to librarians who disseminate them to children. In the other, which he terms "the mass market," publishers sell books to stores, which in turn sell them to children and their parents. In practice, publishers orient their sales to one or the other of these two markets, and as a result of doing so, construct very different images of their youthful audience.

Publishers in a library market seek individual books having novelty in plot, character, writing style, and graphic design in the knowledge that these attributes of "innovation" and "quality" will attract library buyers. Such works tend to be relatively expensive and while some become sales hits, many fail to sell well.

Publishers for the mass-market try to build sequences or lines of books that will "sell themselves." These publishers accent explicit titles, bright covers, anthropomorphic animal characters, slick cartoon-like illustrations and writing to fit a formula. The publishers seek out known authors who have a good "track record" in the market. Such standardization facilitates the cost efficient production of books which will have predictable if not spectacular sales.

This illustration of two ways of marketing books for children suggests how important it is to understand the market for which cultural items are produced when one wishes to use cultural objects to make judgments about the creator of popular culture items, the audiences which will consume them, or the society at large.

Stebbins' article suggests the influence of the market on the socialization of magicians in the United States. He shows that young magicians learn to shape their performances to satisfy the demands of several sorts of audiences and performance situations. Sanders (1974) has shown a similar sort of interaction as folk music performers learn to "psyche out" the demands of various types of audiences. In all these, and numerous other studies as well, we see that the audience, consumer, buyer, fan, viewer, reader, or market interact with creators in shaping cultural products (Ryan and Peterson 1982).

4. Organizational Structure

In this context, the term "organizational structure" refers to the routine ways people coordinate their efforts in actualizing a symbolic product or service (DiMaggio and Hirsch 1976). The influence of organizational structure has received relatively little attention. This is in part because the 19th Century idea of a divinely (or madly) inspired lone creative genius has continued to rivet scholarly and popular attention on the creative individual (Becker 1978; Kris and Kurz 1979) at the expense of the complex set of institutions and organizations which seek out, finance, merchandise, and live off the genius (White and White 1967; Walters 1977). Howard Becker and his students have done more than any other group of researchers to redress the imbalance by showing the ways that organizational structure influences the form and content of creative works. (See Becker (1982) for a review of much of this work.)

Eleanor Lyon provides an excellent example of the influence of organizational structure on the work being produced. She describes the stages of rehearsal in theater companies which engage a new set of actors for each production, and briefly contrasts this form of organization with another, the repertory theater, in which a number of actors are hired to work together for an entire season and often stay on for a number of years.

The one-shot system of production brings together a number of strangers who must mesh their talents to put on a credible collective performance with only two weeks of practice. This contingency calls for a form of organization which puts great power in the hands of the director and requires actors to work without complaint in standardized conventional ways. Often they must defer to a star performer who has been hired to attract an audience.

In contrast, the repertory theater is built around a group of actors of comparable levels of talent and reputation. Having worked together through a number of productions, the actors need to rely less on the director and can play to each other more directly rather than through a set of theatrical conventions. In such a case the attraction is the group and its reputation, so individual stardom is de-emphasized.

Based on Lyon's discussion, one would expect that over time these two forms of theatrical organization will develop distinct repertoires and somewhat different markets. Certainly these two forms of organizations have quite different consequences for the job lives of actors. While the actor in the established repertory company can look forward to a relatively stable job life, the actor in the one-shot sort of organization is hired and fired on a production-by-production basis. In such circumstances the actor must continually hustle new work and be free to travel around the country at a moment's notice to find employment. One might conjecture that the organizational differences would mean that the average level of excellence would be higher in a repertory company because of the experience that actors have working together, but that the most critically acclaimed productions would come from the one-shot system when the various elements—director, play, actors, and stars—happen to meld in a dynamic way.

5. Occupational Careers

As the preceding paragraphs suggest, the ways that creative people define their occupations and organize their careers can influence the nature of the work they produce. Perhaps the most thoroughly researched case in point contrasts the occupational careers of painters working within an academic system of art devoted to perpetuating tradition with those working in an avant-gardist market oriented to innovation (White and White 1965; Crain 1976; Rosenblum 1978; Adler 1979; Peterson and White 1979; Becker 1982).

Edward Kealy provides an example of a single task, that of controlling the complex electronic equipment in phonograph recording studios, that has been organized along several quite different occupational career lines. One we will call the "studio engineer," and the other the "sound mixer." The former predominated in the decade following World War II. The latter have emerged with the advent of technologically sophisticated rock music.

The studio engineer defines himself as a craftsman who knows how to manipulate a complex technology in order to recreate a lifelike sound. For him the perfect recording would sound just like live music. Working in a studio owned by a major recording company, the recording engineer belongs to craft union which regulates wages, working conditions, and access to the job. These workers look to other studio engineers for approval of craft work well done. Within this system, they enjoy what Kealy calls a bureaucratic craft union mode of career.

In marked contrast to these studio engineers with their apparently safe stable careers working for a major company, the "sound mixer" defines himself as a "fellow musician" whose instrument is the studio technology. His goal is not to reproduce live music. Rather, it is to "play the studio" in order to produce hit records. Sound mixers do not work within the organizational confines of a large corporation. They work on a free-lance basis in an independent studio or set up a studio of their own. Kealy calls this the entrepreneurial mode, and like all entrepreneurs the sound mixer is completely at the mercy of the competitive market without the career protection afforded by a craft union or secure organizational employment.

Neither one of these two ways of arranging the technical tasks of the recording studio has been able to completely establish its dominance. The technology, market, and organizational structure of the recording industry have all been changing too rapidly for that. But they have had a contrasting influence on non-popular music. While the studio engineer is a conservative force aesthetically, the sound mixer has been at the forefront of aesthetic changes in popular music. They have been responsible for what Kealy calls the "real rock revolution." The differences between "sound mixers" and "studio engineers" have been described in terms of occupational careers, but to develop fully the differences and to chart their consequences for cultural products, it would be necessary to show how all five of the constraints work in concert.

The Constraints in Concert

Derral Cheatwood in his article on the Tarzan films suggests the importance of accounting for the joint influence of all five constraints considered simultaneously. Cheatwood focuses primarily on the influence of the changing organizational structure and the related changes in the definition of the market on symbolic conventions in the Tarzan movies. But, as he notes, aspects of changing occupational careers, technology, and law also have an important influence.

All too often, however, the joint influences of these factors and others are not considered together. One reason is that most scholarly communication is in brief oral presentations and in journal articles so that it is virtually impossible to cover all the relevant influences without being blatantly superficial.

One resolution of this dilemma is to write longer works, and many of the best doctoral dissertations of the decade are of this sort. (See for example: Bennett (1972), Hennessey (1973), Hirsch (1973), Rosenblum (1973), Kealy (1974), Martorella (1974), Zolberg (1974), Kaimin (1975), Lyon (1975), Walker (1975), Brenneise (1976), Walters (1977), Simpson (1978), Powell (1978), Turow (1978), DiMaggio (1979), Donow (1979), Goodykoontz (1979), Griswold (1980), Rumble (1980), Ryan (1982) and Townsend (1982). But scholars today are under great pressure to publish quickly, and at the same time it is very difficult to find a publisher for an extended technical research monograph.

In consequence, only a few long technical monographs are being published. The popular cultural form which has been most completely explored in production of culture terms through a series of monographs is print and television news-making. See for example Epstein (1973), Tuchman (1978), Gans (1979), Gitlin (1980) and Scudson (1978). But even here, the periodical literature has been at least as important as monographs.

Another resolution of the dilemma of considering all the constraints on the production of culture is to publish brief focused articles that fit into a larger corpus of works which, taken together, consider all the influences on the production of culture. The explicit articulation of the production of culture perspective provides a framework in which specific detailed studies can gain greater meaning by relating to and building on each other.

Popular Music: An Example

Research on popular music provides an example of the benefits of building an increasingly complete picture by placing numerous specific research articles into the framework provided by the production of culture perspective. Focusing on the five constraints provides a way of thinking about the various factors which need to be taken into account. This can be illustrated by sampling from the set of studies which have analyzed the development of rock and roll.

LAW: Rumble (1980) and Ryan (1982) show how the formation of the song-writer royalty collection agency BMI in 1939 broke the hold that ASCAP had on popular music publishing and writing. While it was not formed for this purpose, the advent of BMI ended the control that Broadway musical song publishers had on the popular music market, making it possible for rock, soul and country music publishers to be profitable and greatly expanding the opportunities for songwriters in these genres.

TECHNOLOGY: A cluster of new technologies that became important in the 1950s, including television, 45 and L.P. records, transistor radios and tape recording equipment resulted in the transformation of radio programming. The old radio network programs and the major national advertisers went to television, and radio had to experiment with new formats and a cheaper way of programming radio air-time. The solution was to play records on the radio throughout the day. This created a vastly increased demand for new music (Peterson and Berger 1975).

MARKET: In the 1940s the four radio networks had competed with one another to gain as big a slice as possible of the total American listening market. With the advent of numerous independent radio stations in each market, stations began to play records aimed specifically at one or another segment of the market. Thus, top 40, soul, classical, country and western, jazz, easy listening, beautiful music, and other formats began to proliferate, creating opportunities for marketing music tailored to the aesthetic interest of one or another specific market segment (Hirsch 1972; Peterson and Davis 1975).

ORGANIZATIONAL STRUCTURE: Until the mid 1950s, the record industry had been dominated by four large firms, but the conditions just described made it possible for a number of small independent companies such as Motown, Atlantic and Sun Records to enter and successfully compete in at least one segment of the market or another. Thus, the range of aesthetic choices was greatly expanded (Peterson and Berger 1975). The large firms used a number of organizational strategies including a style of entrepreneurship in an effort to accommodate to the changing aesthetics of rock music (Peterson and Berger 1971). (See also Bennett [1980] and the Kealy article in this volume.)

OCCUPATIONAL CAREERS: These changes had profound effects on the job lives of all those in the popular music business from songwriters and session musicians to record producers and disc jockeys. Perhaps the most aesthetically influential change has been the emergence of the singer-songwriter in the 1960s. In the older Tin Pan Alley system of music production there was a clear division of labor between the composer, lyricist, publisher, recording artist, producer, session musician and recording engineer. Such a system of organization necessitated the standardization of production and the formation of strict conventions of production, as Sanders and Kealy note. Beginning with Chuck Berry, and especially following Bob Dylan and the Beatles, singers began to write their own songs and gain increasing control over the other aspects of the production process, transforming the popular music aesthetic in the process (Ryan and Peterson 1982).

The preceding paragraphs illustrate the utility of the production of culture perspective by showing the influence of five constraints, including law, technology, market, organizational structure, and occupational career both alone and in combination. This brief review is hardly complete, but it does suggest that rock music was not simply the creative response of a few musicians to the aesthetically stagnant popular music of the early 1950s, and that rock was not just the response to a new audience demand, although both these factors would have to be taken into account in a complete analysis of the development of popular music in this period. The five constraints do not exhaust the influences that shape the production of culture, but they do suggest the range of factors that should be taken into account.

Keeping Culture in Popular Culture

Give a kid a hammer and suddenly everything seems to need pounding. Much the same is true for converts to an intellectual orientation.

While this essay constitutes an apology for a particular point of view, the production of culture perspective, it is not intended as a critique of the other orientations that focus more attention on such elements as textual analysis, biographies of creative individuals, or audience studies. The purpose here has been to illustrate the utility of the production of culture perspective. Properly applied, it is a tool to be used to compliment and buttress these other approaches to understanding the dynamics of popular culture.

As with any tool, however, it is easy for researchers to concentrate on the technique of its use rather than on its application, thus making a fetish out of methodology. During the 1970s many who embraced the structuralist techniques of Levi-Strauss, Gremas and others seemed to have become absorbed in the method for its own sake. In the present instance, it is possible to become so involved in tracing the development of conventions or detailing the production process as to completely ignore the impact these have on the elements of culture being studied. As the articles in this volume generally illustrate, each application of the production perspective should begin and end by showing explicitly how the production process described influences the development and transmission of culture.

References
Adler, Judith. "Innovative art and obsolescent artists." *Social Research* 42 (1975):360-78.

Altheide, David L. and John M. Johnson. *Bureaucratic Propaganda.* Boston: Allyn and Bacon, (1980).

Barnouw, Erik. The Golden Web: A History of Broadcasting in the United States, Vol. II, 1933 to 1953. New York: Oxford University Press, (1968).

Becker, George. *The Mad Genius Controversy: A Study in the Sociology of Deviance.* Beverly Hills: Sage, (1978).

Becker, Howard S. *Art Worlds.* Berkeley: Univ. of Calif. Press, (1982).

Bennett, H. Stith. "Other people's music." Ph. D. Diss. Northwestern Univ.; (1972).

———. *On Becoming a Rock Musician.* Amherst: Univ. of Mass. Press, (1980).

Brenneise, Harvey R. "Art or entertainment?" "The development of the Metropolitan Opera, 1883-1900." M.A. thesis, Andrews Univ., (1976).

Cawelti, John. "The concept of formula in the study of popular literature." *Journal of Popular Culture* 3 (1969):381-403.

Crane, Diana. "Reward systems in art, science, and religion." Pp. 57-72 in Richard A. Peterson (ed), *The Production of Culture.* Beverly Hills: Ca.: Sage, (1976).

DiMaggio, Paul. "Market structure, the creative process, and popular culture." *Journal of Popular Culture* 11 (1977):436-52.

———. "Cultural capital and school success." Ph.D Diss. Harvard Univ., (1979).

———. and Paul Hirsch. "Production Organizations in the Arts." pp. 73-90 in Richard A. Peterson (Eo.), *The Production of Culture.* Beverly Hills, Co.: Sage Publications, (1976).

Donow, Kenneth. "The structure of art: a sociological analysis." Ph.D. Diss., Univ. of Calif., San Diego, (1979).

Epstein, E.J. *News from Nowhere.* New York: Random House, (1973).

Gans, Herbert J. "The creator-audience relationship in the mass media: an analysis of movie making." Pp. 315-24 in Bernard Rosenberg and David Manning White (eds.), *Mass Culture.* New York: Free Press, (1957).

———. *Deciding What's News.* New York: Pantheon, (1979).

Gitlin, Todd. *The Whole World is Watching: Mass Media in the Making and Unmaking of the New Left.* Berkeley: Univ. of Calif. Press, (1980).

Goodykoontz, William M. "Becoming a star: an interactionist perspective on the presentation of onstage identity." Ph.D. Diss., Univ. of Calif., Riverside, (1979).

Griswold, Wendy. "Revivals of Renaissance revenge tragedies and city comedies since 1966." Ph.D. Diss., Harvard Univ., (1980).

———. "The cultural diamond: alternative problems for research in the sociology of art." A paper presented at the annual meetings of the Eastern Sociological Society, New York, (1981a).

———. "American character and the American novel." *American Journal of Sociology,* 86 (1981b):740-65.

Habermas, Jurgen. *Legitimation Crisis.* Boston: Beacon, (1975).

Hennessey, Thomas. "From jazz to swing: black jazz musicians and their music, 1917-1935." Ph.D. Diss., Northwestern Univ., (1973).

Hirsch, Paul M. "Processing fads and fashions: an organization set analysis of the cultural industry system." *American Journal of Sociology* 77 (1972): 639-59.

———. "The Organization of consumption: a comparison of organizational effectiveness and product innovation in the pharmaceutical and recording industries." Ph.D. Diss., Univ. of Michigan, (1973).

Kamin, Jonathan L. "Rhythm and blues in white America: rock and roll as acculturation and perceptual learning." Ph.D. Diss., Princeton Univ., (1975).

Kealy, Edward R. "The real rock revolution: sound mixers, social inequality, and the aesthetics of popular music production." Ph.D. Diss., Northwestern Univ., (1974).

Kris, Ernest and Otto Kurz. "Legend, Myth, and Magic in the Image of the Artist." New Haven: Yale Univ. Press, (1979).

Lyon, Eleanor. "Behind the scenes: the organization of theatrical production." Ph.D. Diss., Northwestern Univ., (1975).

Martorella, Rosanne. "The performing artist as a member of an organization: a sociological study of opera." Ph.D. Diss., New School for Social Research, New York, (1974).

Mattelart, Armand. "Multinational Corporations and the Control of Culture: The Ideological Apparatus of Imperialism." New York: Humanities Press, (1979).

Mukerji, Chandra. "Mass culture and the modern world-system: the rise of the graphic arts." *Theory and Society* 8 (1979):245-68.

Peterson, Richard A. "The production of culture: a prolegomenon." *The Production of Culture*. Richard A. Peterson (ed.). Beverly Hills, Ca.: Sage, (1976). Pp. 7-22.

_____ "Revitalizing the culture concept." *Annual Review of Sociology* 5 (1979):137-66.

Peterson, Richard A and David G. Berger. "Entrepreneurship in organizations: evidence Peterson, Richard A and David G. Berger 1971 "Entrepreneurship in organizations: evidence from the popular music industry." *Administrative Science Quarterly* 16 (1971):97-107.

_____ "Cycles in symbol production: the case of popular music." *American Sociological Review* 40 (1975):158-73.

Peterson, Richard A. and Russell Davis, Jr. "The contemporary American radio audience." *Journal of Popular Music and Society.* 3 (1975):299-313.

Peterson, Richard A. and John Ryan. "Success, failure and anomie in art and craft work: breaking in to commercial country music songwriting." *Research in the Sociology of Work* 2 (1982):in press

Peterson, Richard A. and Howard G. White. "The simplex located in art worlds." Urban Life 7 (1979):411-39.

Plowman, Edward W. and L. Clark Hamilton. "Copyright: Intellectual Property in the Information Age". Boston: Routledge and Kegan Paul, (1980).

Powell, Walter. "Getting into print: the social organization of scholarly publishing." Ph.D. Diss., SUNY, Stony Brook, (1978).

Randall, Richard S. "Censorship of the Movies." Madison, Wisconsin. Univ. of Wisconsin Press, (1968).

Rosenblum, Barbara. "Photographers and their photographs." Ph.D. Diss., Northwestern Univ., (1973).

Rumble, John. "Fred Rose and the development of publishing in Nashville." Ph.D. Diss., Vanderbilt Univ., (1980).

Ryan, John. "Organization, environment, and cultural change: the ASCAP—BMI controversy." Ph.D. Diss., Vanderbilt Univ., (1982).

Ryan, John and Richard A. Peterson. " 'Product image' solving the problems of collaborative creativity in the media arts: the case of country music songwriters." *Current Research on Mass Communication* 10 (1982):in press.

Sanders, Clinton R. "Psyching out the crowd: folk performers and their audience." *Urban Life* 3(1974):264-81.

Schudson, Michael. "Discovering the News: A Social History of American Newspapers." New York: Basic Books, (1978).

Simpson, Charles R. "Soho: a residential-occupational community in lower Manhattan." Ph.D. Diss., New School for Social Research, (1978).

Smith, Anthony. "The Geopolitics of Information." New York: Oxford Univ. Press, (1980).

Smith, Philip. "The American anti-comic book movement: 1948-1954." Unpublished Ms., Nashville, Tenn., (1974).

Townsend, Helen. (Forthcoming) "Government and the arts: the case of the Federal Art Project." Ph.D. Diss., Vanderbilt Univ.

Tuchman, Gaye. Making News. New York: Free Press, (1978).

Turow, Joseph. "Getting books to children: an exploration of publisher-market relations." Ph.D. Diss. University of Pennsylvania, (1978).

Walker, A.W. "The empirical delineation of two musical taste cultures." Ph.D. Diss., New School for Social Research, New York, (1975).

Walters, Barbara R. "The politics of esthetic judgment: the impressionist movement and the Dreyfusist cause, France 1870-1912." Ph.D. Diss., SUNY Stony Brook, (1977).

White, Harrison C. and Cynthia A. White. "Canvases and Careers." New York: Wiley, (1965).

Zolberg, Vira L. "The Art Institute of Chicago: The sociology of a cultural organization." Ph.D. Diss., Univ. of Chicago, (1974).*

Acknowledgements

This work has benefited greatly from the numerous, promptly offered, and helpful comments of each of the following: George Becker, Daniel Cornfield, Paul DiMaggio, Claire L. Peterson, John Ryan, Clinton Sanders, Helen Townsend and Vera Zolberg. Thanks much to each of you.

Rock:
Youth and Its Music

Deena Weinstein

Since it burst upon the American cultural scene in the early 1950s rock music has been a center of controversy, a phenomenon that, it seems, cannot be treated neutrally. On the level of everyday public discourse rock has been alternately reviled as an agent of moral and civil corruption, and hailed as a stimulant to social reconstruction. The more general public polemics about rock have been reproduced, though in more subtle and sophisticated forms of expression, on the plane of academic discourse, where scholars and critics have debated whether rock music is an authentic artistic endeavor or a mere fabricated commodity, whether it represents genuine social forces seeking to contest established institutions or is but a cunning sort of mystification serving to lull its listeners into acquiescence while appearing to stimulate them. Missing from both the everyday and academic discourses has been any sustained attempt to consider rock music in light of its relation to the general practical problematic of the social group that uses it, that is, youth. Rock has been treated by its commentators globally, as part of a total cultural or social fact. Such a global viewpoint is not only legitimate but ultimately is the most significant one. But it is, perhaps, premature to jump to consider the most general significance of a cultural and social phenomenon before inquiring into the sense and meaning that it has for the specific group that uses it in the constitution of its daily life. Only through a consideration of what rock music means for youth as a social group faced with specific problems in contemporary social structure can its more global import be precisely defined.

The approach to be taken in analyzing rock music as a function of the problems of the youth group in contemporary industrial societies of the West is based on the broad theoretical view defined by such thinkers as Jean-Paul Sartre, Karl Mannheim and Jose Ortega y Gasset, each of whom coordinated cultural phenomena and social dynamics in terms of the specific situations of social actors within the total social structure. Sartre's "being-in-situation," Mannheim's sociology of knowledge and Ortega's idea of the reciprocity between self and concrete circumstances frame a sort of inquiry in which significations

Reprinted with permission from *Popular Music and Society*, Volume 9:3, (1983), pp. 2-16.

are anchored in the practical problems faced by the members of a social group relative to the larger social structure in which they must act. That is, the isolated cultural object and the global social dynamic (for example, Weberian "rationalization") are mediated by the specific groups' aspirations, dilemmas and life-chances. As Mannheim puts it: "Only when we know what are the interests and imperatives involved are we in a position to inquire into the possibilities of the present situation, and thus to gain our first insight into history. Here, finally, we see why no interpretation of history can exist except in so far as it is guided by interest and purposeful striving."[1] How the "interests and imperatives," what is called here aspirations, dilemmas and life-chances are determined is, in the present discussion, circular, in the sense that the rock music that is taken to respond to those aspirations will be used to identify them. Such circularity is not vicious, but is, rather, a consequence of the general being of social facts to refer to one another in dialectical patterns of reciprocity and opposition. The starting point here, which could be made in another sort of study the conclusion of an analysis of data on record sales and radio listenership, is that rock music is youth music and should be understood as such for sociological investigation.

Prevailing Approaches

Rock music has been traditionally understood globally within either a cultural or a societal framework. The cultural debate focuses on the *intent* of rock as a cultural object: is it produced as art or as commodity? The societal argument involves the *effect* of rock music: does it create social progress or does it function to maintain the *status quo*? Both of these two perspectives form the context within which rock is discussed by most of those in the rock press, scholarly analysts of popular music, rock fans and also rock artists.

Neither the cultural nor the societal debate about rock music remains static, because the music itself changes thematically and stylistically, as will be shown in a later section on the historical diversification of rock. For example, when rock music becomes tied to movements for "Progressive change" critics on the left tend to praise it both as culturally authentic and as an agent of change, whereas when rock loses a narrowly political dimension such critics tend to brand it as a commodity that bolsters the *status quo*. That the same occurs on the right, though in reverse, is evidenced by the conservative reaction to James Watt's attempt to ban the Beach Boys from performing at the Washington Monument. As reviewed here the global debates over rock music are presented in their clearest forms, but even when they appear to be muted the underlying issues brought out below are always present and, indeed, often form the themes of rock music itself.

The cultural debate centers on whether or not rock music is intended as art, that is, as the authentic expression of creative individuals. As art, rock might be viewed as "high culture" (seemingly aspired to by groups such as Pink Floyd and Emerson, Lake and Palmer) or as an urban derivative of a more rural "folk culture" (as the early works of Little Richard and Chuck Berry, or Bob Dylan's sixties' output, were understood). As appreciators of art, audiences are active, informed and critical. Record reviewers who lament the lack of greater achievement in the later album of an artist, for example, than in an earlier release, or who denounce the record because it is hook-laden, commercial-sounding or formulaic, hold the standard of rock as artistic expression, as do fans who complain that a group has sold out. If, in contrast, rock is not intended as art for self-conscious appreciators it is culturally interpreted as a commodity produced for the purpose of profit. Thus, the other side of the cultural debate over rock holds that the music is a tool of capitalism. In works unambiguously entitled "Rock for Sale" (Michael Lyndon) and *Rock 'n' Roll is Here to Pay* (Chapple and Garofolo) the creation of rock is interpreted as being shaped not by authentic expression but according to commercial standards to enable it to appeal in the marketplace to the mass audience. The standards for a successful commodity sharply contrast with those of art: a commodity is packaged with an audience in mind that is passive and unreflective, and that wants no challenges or surprises. Since rock as commodity is aimed at the largest possible number of consumers it must be geared to the lowest common denominator. Celebrity and image (hence the crucial importance of public-relations-marketing-advertising specialists) rather than artistic profundity and proficiency are the requirements of successful audience appeal. According to Simon Frith, rock critics work within this cultural debate: "...records and songs are valued for their artistic intensity, for their truth to experience; yet they are condemned for commercialism, the belief in a continuing struggle between music and commerce is the core of rock ideology."[2]

In contrast to the terms of the cultural debate, rock has also been embedded in a societal framework which focuses not on the intentions of its producers but on the effects of the music/lyrics on the general society. The antipodal positions in this societal debate are that rock is a force for change and that it is a force to maintain the *status quo*. Yet both positions share the assumption that some of the possibilities for social change are dependent upon the youth of the society—adults function at best to train or restrain the young, but youth is the locomotive factor in altering patterns of human relations.

Those who believe that rock is a factor that promotes social change come from both ends of the ideological spectrum. From the inception of rock those on the right have been hostile to it. Reacting against either the beat of the music ("jungle music" arousing the young to frenzy) or the lyrics (especially those advocating sexual promiscuity and drug use, and those involving satanic themes) rural and small-town fundamentalist preachers, former Vice President Spiro Agnew, and members of the John Birch Society, among others, have warned against the music. Periodically a minister will organize a mass rally to burn or, if environmental protection laws disallow burning, smash rock records. An article in the John Birch Society's *American Opinion*, for example, claims: "Rock music, universally in high regard among a whole generation of adolescents, has somehow evolved as one of the major influences on our children—and, through them, on our nation's future."[3] The author claims that the industry has been captured by a Communist plot: "Music is now the primary weapon used to make the perverse seem glamorous, exciting, and appealing.

Music is used to ridicule religion, morality, patriotism, and productivity—while glorifying drugs, destruction, revolution, and sexual promiscuity."[4]

Those in favor of change, whether it is called progressive or revolutionary, also interpret rock music as capable of effecting, or at least initiating, the movement toward securing the desired ends. The author of *The Age of Rock;* for example, claims: "Rock music was born of a revolt against the sham of Western culture; it was direct and gutsy and spoke to the senses. As such, it was profoundly subversive. It still is."[5] Leftists of various stripes, rock musicians, fans, or mere onlookers believed that the music of the mid and late sixties contained radical criticism of the existing society and calls to arms for change. Songs such as Barry McGuire's "Eve of Destruction," much of Bob Dylan's work such as "Highway 61" and "Maggie's Farm," and John Lennon's "Imagine" are among the host of those that are widely cited as examples of criticism of the dehumanizing, unjust and militaristic aspects of contemporary society. Irwin Kantor cites those on the "progressive" side of the debate over the social consequences of rock: "...several writers, such as Ralph Gleason, Paul Wolfe, and Susan Huck, agree that rock music has been central to the emergence of what Theodore Roszak calls a youth-oriented counter culture which radically diverges from the values and assumptions that have been in the mainstream of our society since the Scientific Revolution of the Seventeenth Century."[6]

As the optimism of the sixties' leftists faded in the wake of the world-wide repression of 1968; the shootings at Kent State two years later, which were seen as an explicit attack on progressive youth; and the horrors of Altamont, which indicated that love wasn't all you need or that youth did not have enough love to make a difference, the tide of opinion about the societal function of rock changed.

Rock was seen more and more to be a force that maintained the *status quo* than something that would help to combat it. The ambivalence in this shift is recognized by Levine and Harig's review of the rock literature: "On the one hand it is seen as stimulating change, while on the other it (rock) is portrayed as serving to reinforce the structure and ideology of the capitalists system."[7] The argument that rock reinforces established institution as appeals to the cathartic function of the music, which channels the energies, including the anger and frustration caused by an oppressive and unjust society, into harmless release. Herbert Marcuse's analysis of mass culture's repressive desublimation, which was argued most clearly in his 1964 *One—Dimensional Man,* is often cited. Others carry the argument further, using the understanding that rock is produced by the capitalist system to claim that it therefore must serve its ends. Capitalism's products are assumed to function for capitalist ends, creating profits as well as maintaining the *status quo* within which that economic system thrives. Michael Lyndon, for example, argues: "In fact, rock, rather than being an example of how freedom can be achieved within the capitalist structure, is an example of how capitalism can, almost without a conscious effort, deceive those whom it oppresses. Rather than being liberated heroes, rock and roll stars are captives on a leash, and their plight is but a metaphor for that of all young people and black people in America."

The Youth Group and Its Music

The debates in the rock literature over whether rock music is an authentic expression of creative impulse or a commercial commodity, and whether the music has progressive or reactionary social consequences can be enlightened by considering the group that uses it in the constitution of its life. As the music of youth in the period following World War II, rock has been a response to the general and historically and socio-culturally specific problems that the youth or adolescent group has encountered in the contemporary societies of the West. A sociological understanding of rock, then, is premised on a description of the structural situation of the contemporary youth group, structural here not being understood in a static sense, as a fixed position relative to others, but dynamically, as a set, in Mannheim's sense, of interests and imperatives, an array, as Max Weber had it, of "life-chances."

Youth, in the sense that is meant here, is not primarily a biological or even a psychological category, but a sociological one. As forming a distinctive social group adolescents are the product of an industrial society that has reached the stage at which, firstly, extended training (education) is necessary to fit individuals to be competent contributors to ongoing institutional projects, and, secondly, young people, in the chronological sense, are not generally needed in and might even be disruptive of the labor market. The adolescent as a social type is betwixt and between childhood dependency and adult responsibility, in the sense of Mary Douglas, an anomaly who does not fit into any fixed category and is, therefore, impure from the society's standpoint, that is, a "danger." The special tension between dependency and responsibility that structures adolescent life is, from the viewpoint of youth, both a blessing and a curse. To be beyond dependency, but still dependent, and moving towards responsibility, but not responsible yet, releases the adolescent into a suspended state of social freedom that ends to become an end-in-itself, particularly in light of the possibilities of the young body to enjoy intense pleasures and to recover relatively quickly from physical stress. This freedom, however, is circumscribed and, indeed, checked by the double pressure to acknowledge continued dependency and to undertake responsibilities and to prepare for future self-responsibility. Youth experiences its freedom and spontaneity as both intensely and intimately real, and as precarious and fleeting. The freedom and vitality that shoots forth in the space tilled by it tend to become, indeed, fetishes, icons of an evanescent distinction.

The freedom opened up by the transition from dependency to responsibility places the youth group in a particularly privileged position to problematize society as a whole, that is, to make of participation in society a problem to be faced prior to any dilemma about how to participate. Children are taught to have ideas of what they would like to "be" when they grow up. Adolescents have the privilege and torment of raising the question of whether they want to be anything that the society holds out as a possibility for them. In the sense of George Simmel, the very "form" of the youth group is to question the category of "form" itself and, in strictly Simmelian terms, to oppose to it the solipsism of unlimited or at least overflowing "life."[9] Not all adolescents, of course, carry their freedom to a questioning of form itself, but all of them in some way decide what they do in terms of that utmost possibility. Some adolescents seek to remain as children, whereas others seek to short-circuit freedom and become responsible immediately; but either of these strategies is undertaken against a prevailing possibility of escaping, albeit momentarily, from either pole. In circumstances of intense social conflict youth may even hypostatize its freedom into an image of an ideal society in which freedom is perpetual and social relations need not be formally mediated. The adolescent who is suspended in freedom yet is pulled backwards into dependency and pushed forwards into responsibility is a marginal in the Simmelian sense, someone who is similar to the stranger or the wanderer, but not the same.[10] The model for the stranger is the trader who is here today and stays tomorrow, but who is never one with the group to which he refers and yet is performing an often necessary function in its social life. The stranger, then, problematizes the absoluteness of particular forms, but not of social form itself. The wanderer does problematize form in itself but does so as a confirmed outsider, so in a sense, form is no longer a problem, but is merely an environing condition like an inert object that provides either advantages or disadvantages, or a mixture of both. Like the stranger the adolescent is relevant to a larger social group, but like the wanderer the adolescent escapes any fixed definition within that group. Thus, form itself is a problem that structures the adolescent's being-in-the-world: it is neither accepted as a demystified way, as in the case of the stranger, nor is it treated as a thing, as for the wanderer; form, for the adolescent can be opposed, played with, shunned or desperately grasped, but it cannot be fully subjectified or objectified.

The general structural predicament of the adolescent typically appears in the conscious form of a dualism between freedom and constraint. The latter is interpreted alternately as being treated as a child when one is capable of exerting one's own will, and as being forced into a system of obligations and responsibilities that must alienate one from one's new-found will. Freedom, in contrast, is interpreted as doing what one wants, the content of such vacant freedom being found primarily in direct bodily pleasures or in thinly-veiled sublimations of those pleasures, though a counterpoint of existential loneliness and of resentment against the constraint of form may arise and sometimes become the dominant theme. The dualistic consciousness of the adolescent may be described in Freudian terms as a dichotomous choice, without any mediating terms, between release of the id and subjection to the super-ego, and as a consequent failure to acknowledge the executive function and powers of the ego at the very moment that the ego is being most strongly affirmed in the form of a will to power and pleasure, and as a repository of treasured feelings. Rock music is, at its heart, a response to and an enhancement of this dualistic consciousness of youth, catering to the desires for freedom and the immediate goods that the independent and irresponsible life offers, or holding out a utopia in which the suspension of coercive routine is the normal state of affairs.

Caught between the moment of suspended freedom and the transition from dependency to responsibility, the typical dualistic consciousness of youth is modified by the counter-tendencies to sink back into childhood and to advance towards adulthood. The complex dialectic of adolescent mentality is the ground of the many ambivalences of youth, to which rock music appeals. Most of rock music is what Freud called a "compromise formation,"[11] in this case between the wish to remain in the stage of youth and the counter-wish to become a self-sustaining member of the wider society, or less frequently between the wishes to be free and to sink back into childishness. There is a kind of music that can be called "pure rock," which expresses clearly the typical dualistic consciousness that counterpoises spontaneity to regimentation, vitality to sociality, and the irreplaceably pleasurable event to the routine performance of social roles that are alien to the self. And there is also the conventional pop music that romanticizes and mystifies the everyday life of everyman, particularly in its sexual dimension. The bulk of rock music falls between the poles of pure rock and pop, reflecting and representing the fundamental ambivalence between the thirst for freedom, pleasure and momentary execution of will, and the imperative of transiting from dependency to responsibility. The general compromise formation is diversified historically according to the vicissitudes of youth's life chances in the economy and the demands made upon it by the polity, and socially, according to the different sub-groups that make up youth.

Historical Diversification

As a compromise formation appealing to the ambivalent aspirations of youth, the style and content of rock music changes in relation to the specific life chances (interests and imperatives) that the youth group encounters in successive historical periods. The periodization of rock music, which has become integral both to the merchandising of rock as nostalgia and to the critical and academic literature concerned with the music, may be grounded on broader historical transformations. Rock began in the mid-1950s and expressed the search of the first generation of suburban youth for a position from which to declare itself independent of parental standards and to rationalize and satisfy, simultaneously, its desires for the free play of immediate pleasure. In the first era of rock, white middle and working class youth used the music of poor Southern whites and urban blacks to context the norms of bureaucratic careerism and programmed suburban consumption. By the late 1950s, however, the raw origins of rock had been smoothed out by the process of commercialization. The youth group had become solidified as a separate category in society with substantial purchasing power in a generally expanding economy. Rock merged with pop and "youth culture" tended to spill over into the wider social life.

Economic conditions, reflected in suburbanization and the baby boom, were the environing determinants of the first era of rock. The next phase of the music's historical development was politically conditioned by the draft and more generally by the black's quest for social justice and the movements opposed to the Viet Nam War. In this period the youth group no longer sought support in other sub-cultures but generated its own musical expressions and went in some cases so far as to create utopian visions of a society that would incorporate the spontaneous exercise of will and the venting of primal emotions. The hedonism and protest of mid-to-late 1960s rock reflected the life chances of youth under the "guns and butter" policies of Lyndon Johnson's administration: employment opportunities were expanding but one might be called to arms. The combination of affluence and vulnerability led to the formation of a counter-culture in which intense sensualism enhanced by drugs was mixed with political utopianism in an uneasy blend that was ideologically reflected in the debate between "cultural" and "political" revolution. Rock music was an integral component of the counter-culture, expressing its hedonism and its moralism, its dependence upon the "affluent society" and its rejection of the "warfare state" and of organizational discipline and consumership.

The next era of rock music was conditioned by the economic decline that began with the inflation of the early 1970s and has run through the recession of the early 1980s. In the wake of the baby boom the relative proportion of youth in the society declined at the same time as employment opportunities contracted. The competition engendered by the struggle for places in the society was reflected in the separation of the youth group into fragmented sub-cultures, each of which was expressed by a particular style of music. Currently, in the mid-1980s, a momentarily expanding economy and an awakening fear of militarism seems to be supporting a "new wave" of rock music expressing multiple syntheses of the styles that were diversified in the 1970s.

Most generally the historical sequence of rock music follows a dialectical pattern in which periods of consolidation of the youth group alternate with periods of dispersion. An era of consolidation is most marked when adolescents have expanding economic opportunities ahead of them and experienced political threats to the realization of their hopes, as was the case in the 1960s. In contrast, dispersion is most pronounced when economic opportunities are contracting and the youth group is not jeopardized politically. Political quiescence and economic expansion, as occurred in the 1950s and are occurring, perhaps, at present, generate an individualistic cohesiveness, a shared style without a distinctive and militant "consciousness of kind." There has yet to be a period of economic decline and political threat. Such an era might be adverse to rock music because of the limitations it would place on freedom and enjoyment. The wavelike rhythm of consolidation and dispersion is not an imminent historical dynamic but a derivative of economic cycles and political conflicts which themselves do not have a fixed periodicity: it is an empirical generalization that has the use of being a diagnostic measure of the situation of youth.

Sub-Group Diversification

In addition to the dialectical changes in rock described above, there are synchronic variations that are manifest in different rock genres and life styles that make specific appeals to subsets of youth. As a category youth is not an undifferentiated mass. Adolescents behave more or less homogeneously: their significant differentiations come to the fore or are submerged on different occasions and in different contexts. Among the more important distinctions dividing the broader youth group are those of gender, race, age (best understood as junior high school, high school and college age groups), geographical location (for example, urban versus small town, coast versus heartland), and social class affiliation (roughly working class versus middle class).

Each of these synchronic distinctions is, of course relative to diachronic variations. In periods of consolidation the more static structural differences tend to become blurred, whereas in times of dispersion they tend to become sharpened. For example, in the 1960s specialized taste groups were often submerged in a thematic consensus on protest and pleasure, and a musical fusion of diverse style (instance Dylan, Hendrix and Joplin), whereas in the 1970s diverse themes and styles arose that were based on structurally and demographically grounded sub-groups. The following brief exploration of the division of youth on the basis of gender will draw primarily upon the music of the 1970s, which brings out the correspondence between variations in musical genre and differences of gender more clearly than does the music of other periods. Synchronic distinctions, however, are present in every period and are merely highlighted by the type-case.

The ambivalence felt about entering the society, its intensity and its particular expressions are in part a function of the socialization patterns to which individuals have been exposed. In American society and with little variation in all modern societies boys are allowed greater freedom than are girls. Boys are permitted from an earlier age to be less supervised by adults, to go further from home, to be away from home for longer periods of time, including at night, than are girls. Boys are encouraged to be active in their bodily movements and are dressed to permit such activity. Girls, in contrast, are urged to be quiet and still, and are clothed in ways that hinder movement (clothes that are binding, that expose underwear easily if one is active, and that are easily dirtied and torn by activity). Boys are allowed to be aggressive vocally (cursing) and physically (fighting); such opportunities are not extended to girls. Boys are expected to be "naughty" ("He's all boy!") and to have little ability to defer gratification, whereas girls are supposed to be patient and "good," conforming to stipulated rules and constantly planning for a future and deferring present happiness for some ideal storybook ending of happily-ever-after. As a result of these socialization patterns the male has more problems with the transition from youth to adulthood, since the adult role is closer to the female pattern of low aggression, strict conformity to the "rules" and supervision by adults (bosses and wives). The music that male youths (especially those in high school who are beginning clearly to see their adult options) enjoy reflects their ambivalence. They tend to admire the proficiency of artists who are committed to their careers. One often hears them complaining about how long it takes a certain artist or group to come out with a new album, implying that it is wrong for the artists not to be hard at work at their music. On the other hand, the music evokes themes of exuberant aggression through its ear-shattering amplification; its strutting, muscular and often black-leather-clad stars who have been applauded by their imitative fans for trashing their instruments onstage and their hotel rooms offstage; and its lyrics which express aggression in every possible dimension. The extreme rock genre that exemplifies the male youth is Heavy Metal. Ominously named groups such as Judas Priest, Black Sabbath, AC/DC, Iron Maiden and Scorpions attract almost all-male audiences with attire that make the Hell's Angels appear effeminate and with songs that exult THE BAD ("Bad Boy Boggie" AC/DC, "Breaking the Law" Judas Priest "Running Wild" Judas Priest "Sinner" Judas Priest "Hell Ain't a Bad Place to Be" AC/DC) and THE AGGRESSIVE ("You've Got Another Thing Coming" Judas Priest "Killing Machine" Judas Priest, "Murders in the Rue Morgue" Iron Maiden). The music admires the very qualities that the male youths must sacrifice in order to become members of society. For many of them Heavy Metal sublimates these qualities and therefore allows them both to have their cake (behave as an adult) and eat it too (feel naughty and aggressive through participation in the music).

Similarly to Heavy Metal, the strong rhythm section and the high amplification characteristic of hard rock appeal to males more than to females. Hard rock is redolent with themes of getting one's pleasure now and of misogyny. Pleasure is not of the world of the adult; at best society metes out small dollops of it in return for what Freud terms "unpleasure" *(unlust)*. The anti-female bias of hard rock is intelligible in terms of the preceding discussion since women represent a check on vitality and a social responsibility that sharply contrasts with the active hedonism of male youthfulness. A "macho" stance, not necessarily one that is cultivated within a lifestyle to which music is integral, is a compromise formation for men in general, who are in society but do not want to be of it.

Rock music serves as a compromise formation for females, too, although in a sharply contrasting way to that in which it caters to males. In accordance with the passive and obedient female socialization pattern, the music directed to female youth is soft, both in terms of its beat and its amplification. The lyrical themes are almost exclusively concerned with romance and the rock stars are soft-spoken, often blond (the manufactured teen idols such as Fabian), non-threatening, and somewhat androgynous in appearance. Rock music that appeals to female youth serves to ease tensions about sexual activity, which whether or not they are actively engaging in it, is threatening to female selfhood. For women, who are socialized to fit into society, it is this relatively wild act, in which one is a raw and pleasure-seeking being for a moment, that is in some sense their destiny and their major vulnerability. The fears of rape, of being used (of being seen not as a person but only as a sexual object), and of becoming pregnant are never far from a teenage girl's concerns. Romance is a way of taming these fears as well as preparing one to partake in sexual relations, engage in courtship and ultimately find a husband.

The extreme rock genre that exemplifies the female youth is "soft rock," which like Heavy Metal came to prominence after the period of consolidation of the 1960s ended. Whereas Heavy Metal heightened and disciplined the hard aspects of acid rock, customizing it for a male taste group, soft rock muted and tamed folk rock, adapting it to a predominantly female audience. Such performers as Cat Stevens, James Taylor, Jackson Browne and Carole King transformed the protest themes of the 1960s into sentimental commentaries on manners and mores, often keying in on the vicissitudes of romance and the illusions of youth. The soft rock performers cultivated a normal, if "laid back" appearance and often strove for acoustical effects and an intimate atmosphere even in their large-scale performances, evincing the comfort and security ultimately sought by females. More recently there has been an upsurge of harder female rock by female performers such as Joan Jett, Chrissie Hyne and Pat Benatar stressing the themes of independence, sexual expression and love of pleasure.

This new development responds to the aspirations of a generation of women who seek a compromise between the two tendencies of the 1970s and a return to traditional femininity and institutional openings towards equal opportunity, and indicates the beginnings of consolidation.

Although the preceding discussions of the gender differences among youth and the types of music that respond to the particular problems highlighted by them oversimplify gender roles, the arguments hold for each male and female to greater and lesser degrees, and in addition the relevant cultural object, in this case music, tends to emphasize the differences and, indeed to reinforce them.

Conclusion

The foregoing analysis of rock music in terms of its relations to the opportunities and imperatives encountered by youth in the contemporary industrial societies of the West can be used to inform the debates over the global cultural and societal import of rock that dominate the current and recent literature on this form of music. The cultural debate over whether rock is an authentic creative expression or merely a commodity for sale can be enlightened by referring to the distinction made in the discussion of rock as a compromise formation between pure rock and pop. Pure rock, which expresses directly the dualistic consciousness of freedom in opposition to societal constraint tends to be authentic, whereas pop music, which romanticizes the adult world tend to be merely a commodity. In between the two poles, where most of rock music falls, there is often a mix of genuine creative intent and programmed and formulaic commodity production. Indeed, some of the most sensitive and authentic rock is a commentary on the tensions within the mixed mode from the creator's viewpoint, and on the ambivalence of youth itself. One should not make the mistake of confusing high sales figures with the intent to produce a commodity. Those listeners who follow a particular group or artist are aware of when the performer has "sold out" and when the music is "real," and they are, perhaps, the best judges in the cultural debate, at least as it pertains to specific cases.

Similarly, the social debate over whether rock music supports the *status quo* or favors progressive change can be illuminated by reference to the remarks above on the historical process of rock. In periods of expanding economic horizons for and political threats to youth, rock music will tend to become politically confrontational, whereas in periods of contracting economic horizons and political quiescence, rock will tend, if only by neglect, to support prevailing institutions. Of course, the deeper social debate is not merely over the content of rock music but over the question of whether rock's appeal to the adolescent idea of freedom constitutes liberation or repressive desublimation. If one views liberation as the creation of a solidary community that is now only potential rock music will appear, for the most part, to be reactionary, whereas if one intuits liberation as a release of vitality that is damned by repressive social roles, then at least pure rock will be interpreted as a genuine social expression of revolt, the quintessence, one might argue, of modernism, created for and often by the social group whose members have the temporary privilege of problematizing society as a whole, of affirming, if only momentarily, life against form.

Whether or not "rock 'n' roll is here to stay" has been a concern of both friends and foes of the music. The latter believed that it was a fad that, like the hula hoop and gold fish swallowing, would soon fade into oblivion or be relegated to the warehouse of nostalgia. Adherents of rock, in contrast, were treated every so often to thematic songs proclaiming the immortality of the music ("Rock and Roll Ain't Noise Pollution—Rock and Roll will Never Die," AC/DC) or rallying the faithful with chants of "Long Live Rock and Roll," (Rainbow). From the perspective taken in the foregoing discussion the continued existence of rock music is understood as a function of the continued existence of youth as a social category, as a social group with distinctive structural problems in contemporary society. And despite a demographic shrinkage in the number of people and the proportion of the population in the age group from 13 to 19, the social category of youth can be seen as expanding. On one end the category of childhood is shrinking. For various reasons, people as young as 8 or 9 years old are sharing in the youth life-style in terms of consumption of products such as clothing and accessories; leisure activities from video games and television programs to record purchases; and knowledge of the "real world"—sexual, political, ecological, etc. On the other side of the demographic distribution the expansion of youth may be witnessed in people in their twenties and many in their thirties and forties who have not become adults. As a result of prolonged involvement in school, high unemployment rates and psychological factors there are a host of people in their twenties and thirties who are "still" living at "home" with their parents. Also, there has been a great increase in the number of those adults who remain single and those who marry but choose to remain childless. These situations encourage the prolongation of youthful life-styles. And rock stars are not switching to adult music; at forty years of age members of the Rolling Stones and The Who are still rocking out their music with the fervor and passion that they had two decades earlier. Grey-haired rockers, fans and musicians, have increased the size of the youth category. And as long as youth as a social category survives, so will the musical expression of youth, rock, endure.

Notes

[1]Karl Mannheim, *Ideology and Utopia* (New York: Harcourt, Brace and World, 1936), pp. 260-261.

[2]Simon Frith *Sound Effects: Youth, Leisure and the Politics of Rock 'n' Roll* (New York: Pantheon, 1981), pp. 40-41.

[3]Gary Allen, "More Subversion than Meets the Eye," in *The Sounds of Social Change*, ed Serge Denisoff and Richard A. Peterson (Chicago: Rand McNally, 1972), p. 151.

[4] *Ibid* p. 165.

[5]Jonathon Eisen, *The Age of Rock* (New York: Vintage, 1969), p. xv.

[6]Irwin Kanton, "This Thing Called Rock: An Interpretation," *Popular Music and Society*, 3 (1974), pp. 204-205.

[7]Mark H. Levine and Thomas J. Harig, "The Role of Rock: A Review and *Critique of Alternative* Perspectives on the Impact of Rock Music," *Popular Music and Society*, 4 (1975), p. 200.

[8]Michael Lyndon, "Rock for Sale," in *Side-Saddle on the Golden Calf*, ed. by G.H. Lewis (Pacific Palisades: Goodyear, 1972), p. 316.

[9]Georg Simmel, "The Conflict in Modern Culture, in *Georg Simmel: On Individuality and Social Forms*, ed. by Donald N. Levin (Chicago: University of Chicago Press, 1971), pp. 375-393.

[10]Georg Simmel, "The Stranger" and "The Adventurer," in Levine, *op. cit.*, pp. 143-149, 187-198.

[11]Sigmund Freud, *The Interpretation of Dreams* (New York: Basic Books, 1955).

The Nineteenth Century

Introduction

On May 25, 1852 Stephen Foster wrote a letter to Edwin P. Christy:

Dear Sir:
As I once intimated to you, I had the intention of omitting my name on my Ethiopian songs, owing to the prejudice against them by some which might injure my reputation as a writer of another style of music, but I find that by my efforts I have done a great deal to build up a taste for the Ethiopian songs among refined people by making the words suitable to their taste, instead of the trashy and really offensive words which belong to some songs of that order.

Herein we are given a glimpse into the musical world of the nineteenth-century American. Foster, embarrassed by tunes like "Old Folks at Home" because they would be associated with the vogue of Ethiopian songs written for minstrel shows, literally sold authorship rights to Christy. Later, as the letter demonstrates, Foster wanted his right to authorship back. But more importantly there is a line in the letter that reveals popular music's role and position in nineteenth century society. He states that he doesn't want his "reputation as a writer of another style of music" ruined; in short, songwriters did not want to be associated with the most popular form of song. This would continue until the late teens of the twentieth century when composers such as Kern, Gershwin, Rodgers, and Porter, trained and talented musicians, opted clearly for the world of musical theatre and popular song. In the 1850's, however, composers saw a great contradiction between writing in the classical tradition and writing in the popular tradition.

The reasons for this are quite clear. Music in the nineteenth century was dominated by European styles. The practice of publishing popular songs did not really begin, as Charles Hamm notes, until the end of the 1780s[1]; that, coupled with a natural cultural inferiority complex, kept songwriters working in the style of their European forebears. Bellini and Donizetti were preferable to the works of *any* native born composer. As Wilfrid Mellers writes, "Most nineteenth century American music was 'Bracebridge Hall music'. Like that of Edwardian England, it manifested a passive veneration of the Teutonic, which represented Art; and was usually well written, cheerful and agreeable: a pretense that the wilderness did not exist, that the heart was not a 'lonely hunter' ".[2] Looking over the "hits" of the first seventy years of the nineteenth century one sees a predominance of Irish songs (Thomas Moore), Scottish songs, Italian songs (especially the operas of Bellini and Donizetti), and German melodies (lieder and opera). Charles Hamm notes as well that there was little stylistic distinction between popular and classical music in the first half of the nineteenth century.[3]

The nineteenth century, however, was the era in which America came into its own, in which it carved out an artistic niche and identity for itself. The period saw the efflorescence of the American Renaissance and the works of Melville, Hawthorne, Poe, Cooper, Thoreau and Emerson, and Whitman. In the visual arts Albert Bierstadt, Winslow Homer and Thomas Eakins celebrated the mythology, contradictions, preoccupations, and realities of the American landscape and the American experience. In music we also encounter our first distinctive voices, and those first distinctive voices work largely in the domain of popular song; Stephen Foster, Henry Clay Work, James A. Bland, and John Philip Sousa are but four of our early popular music pioneers. Far better known and more distinguished as "American" composers than their classical contemporaries Horatio Parker and Lowell Mason, these men played important roles in shaping the sound and style of American popular song.

The nineteenth century is important to the development of popular music in other ways as well. First, during this time period the crucial symbiotic relationship between the music and the stage was clearly established, first in the minstrel show and eventually in musical comedies (i.e., *The Black Crook*, the plays of Harrigan and Hart, and indigenous operetta later in the century). Orrin Clayton Suthern's essay in the minstrel show tradition deals with the impact and importance of this most popular and influential form of theatre.

Second, toward the middle of the century popular music gained more importance in addressing social concerns. The Hutchinson family, as Caroline Moseley shows, used their music to support issues ranging from abolition, to pacifism, to women's rights. The civil war occasioned a wide variety of tunes and even temperance received a boost from Henry Clay Work's "Come Home, Father" (1864) inspired by the then popular novel *Ten Nights in a Barroom*. Popular music in this era responded quickly to contemporary concerns and showed its ability as literature did, to quote James Hart, to express "the people's minds and paraphrase what they consider[ed] their private feelings."[4]

A third way in which nineteenth century popular music was important to the development of later music related to commerce. Although the fine-tuned wheels of business would not turn under the songwriter's treadmill until the emergence of Tin Pan Alley later in the century, the capitalist system would slowly become an essential component of this popular art and would begin to make itself felt. During this great age of expansion and individualism, composers came to the realization that music, in this country, was but another form of work. Consequently, like other forms of work, it need not be supported by wealthy patrons, but instead, like other services, it had to please the consumer to reap its reward. Foster never had the benefit of the institution of Tin Pan Alley—he probably would not have fared much better if he had—but he did blaze a path by demonstrating that one could be a songwriter and live off one's earnings. His tragic life, however, brought to the forefront the corresponding dilemma of trying to retain one's artistic integrity and surviving in the culture largely dominated by business. Foster's tragic legacy, moreover, can be observed throughout the history of popular music in the careers of people like Charlie Parker, Janis Joplin, and Jimi Hendrix, and, to a lesser extent, in the critical denunciation of the rock band who "sold out."

Finally, popular song in the nineteenth century contributed some of our most durable themes, themes which have become staples in our mythology, and which continue to shape our values and attitudes. As we shall see, our contemporary notions about women and love (the central concern of Nicholas Tawa's essay), home, inventions, heroes and sports, and America ("America" and "America the Beautiful" are not folk tunes but popular songs) itself are still influenced by nineteenth century songs. Stereotypes of minorities and women were, moreover, given form and substance in nineteenth century popular song, and there are vestiges of those stereotypes operating in our music in the 1980's.

The essays in this chapter illustrate the general goals of our volumes. Nicholas Tawa's essay on "The Ways of Love in the Mid-nineteenth Century American Song" deals with one of the most enduring theme of all of popular music, and provides us with a good insight into the values of that time period. It will also provide a point of reference for future discussions of this theme in subsequent essays. Caroline Moseley's essay shows us music's role as a powerful social force in nineteenth century life. Her essay will also deal with the important relationship of performance and the creation of music itself. Finally, Orrin Clayton's essay on minstrels introduces us to an early form of musical theatre that also played a major role in the stereotyping of blacks.

Although the nineteenth century clearly marks the infancy of American popular music, it is an important era. As popular music grew up and became a major business and seedbed for entrepreneurial adventure in the 1880's, it also gained a musical *savior faire* and a sort of mechanistic sophistication unknown in the early and mid-nineteenth century. Nonetheless, the same fantasies, dreams, and myths that preoccupied nineteenth century Americans carried over into the new century. Composers, moreover, faced the same struggles, and there would be social issues to which popular music would lend its voice. Thus we can hear the echoes of Foster, Work, and dozens of other nineteenth century songwriters well into the twentieth century and even into our own times.

Notes

[1]Hamm, *Yesterdays*, p. 2.

[2]Mellers, *Music In a New Found Land: Themes and Developments in the History of American Music* (New York: Hillstone, 1964, 1975), p. 25.

[3]Hamm, p. 76.

[4]Hart, *The Popular Book: A History of America's Literary Taste* (Berkeley: Univ. of California Press, 1950), p. 285.

References

Austin, William W. *Susanna, Jeanie, and The Old Folks at Home: The Songs of Stephen C. Foster from His Time to Ours.* New York: MacMillan, 1975.

Howard, John Tasker, *Stephen Foster, America's Troubador.* Thomas Y. Crowell, 1934.

Mates, Julian. *America's Musical Stage: Two Hundred Years of Musical Theatre.* Westport, CT: Greenwood Press, 1985.

Moseley, Caroline. " 'The Old Arm Chair': A Study in Popular Musical Taste." *Journal of American Culture* 4 (1081), 177-82.

Tawa, Nicholas. *A Sound of Strangers: Musical Culture, Acculturation, and the Post-Civil War American.* Metuchen, NJ: Scarecrow Press, 1982.

_____ *Sweet Songs for Gentle Americans: The Parlor Song in America, 1790-1860.* Bowling Green, OH: The Popular Press, 1980.

Toll, Robert. *Blacking Up: The Minstrel Show in Nineteenth Century America.* New York: Oxford Univ. Press, 1974.

The Ways Of Love In The Mid-Nineteenth Century American Song

Nicholas E. Tawa

Songs of affection have often figured importantly in man's cultural history, and particularly in periods that put a high valuation on emotional expression. One such period occurred in the United States during the nineteenth century, especially in the years after 1840.[1] In the 1840s love songs became popular vehicles for expressing personal feeling, many of these compositions stressing sentiment to an excessive degree. A typical instance of the sentimentality prevalent in these decades is seen in the last stanza of Luther Emerson's song *Cora Bell*, lyrics by Dr. J. Haynes (Boston, 1857):

> With bitter smart, and broken heart,
> I'll weep in Primrose Dell,
> My hopes are fled, my darling's dead,
> Then farewell Cora Bell.
> Loving, gentle, Cora Bell.
> Sleeping in the Primrose Dell,
> Would my bleeding heart could tell,
> Half the love of Cora Bell.

The theme of sentimental love is treated four ways in the American songs of the mid-century. First, love may be expressed as devotion to a family member, as in John Ordway's *Mother Dear, I'm Thinking of You* (Boston, 1857). Second, love may appear as a warm regard for friends, as in John R. Thomas's *Old Friends and Old Times* (Boston, 1856). Third, love may take the form of a fond attachment for an inanimate object associated with a loved one, as in the Hutchinson Family's *My Mother's Bible* (New York, 1848). It is, however, the fourth type of song, whose theme is a lover's devotion to someone of the opposite sex, with which this study is concerned.

Reprinted with permission from the *Journal of Popular Culture*, Volume 10:2 (Fall 1976), pp. 337-51.

This last category of song reflected the attitude held by most mid-nineteenth-century Americans toward the role of love in the relationship between a man and a woman. These Americans thought of love as the bond of affection which created enduring personal, family, and societal relationships. In addition, the respected contemporary observer Alexis de Tocqueville writes that nineteenth-century Americans considered it important to practice restraint and observe order in private lives, in the home, and in the intimacies of marriage. He states further that the American woman was thought of as the protector of morals. By loving her and winning her as his bride, the American man hoped to insure for himself a happy and tranquil home live. "There is certainly no country in the world," he concludes, "where the tie of marriage is more respected than in America or where conjugal happiness is more highly or worthily appreciated."[2]

It is, therefore, to be expected that the song enjoyed by these Americans, as the nineteenth-century New York musician Thomas Hastings writes, "should be such as to inspire us with sentiments of refinement, and of virtuous sensibility. In this way, it blends innocent amusement with useful thoughts and contemplations.[3]

Most love songs do employ lyrics that exemplify the values of American society, while at the same time affording "innocent amusement." For instance, R.G. Shrival's *Oh! Share My Cottage Gentle Maid* (Baltimore, 1843) depicts a lover whose object is an honorable marriage; his plea to his beloved is genteel, with no hint of indelicacy:

> Oh! share my cottage gentle maid,
>   It only waits for thee
> To give a sweetness to its shade,
>   And happiness to me,
> Here from the splendid gay parade,
>   Of noise and folly free,
> No sorrows can my peace invade
>   If only bless'd with thee.

The melody to these words is simple and pleasant to sing.

It should be pointed out that in the years before 1840 love songs intended for polite society had appeared, though at no time were they ever numerous, which exhibited some vulgarity or touched on the physical aspects of love. One instance that can be cited is the verbal exchange between the lovers in Alexander Reinagle's *Says I to Dear Laura* (Philadelphia, ca. 1803). After a young man has proposed marriage the following conversation takes place:

> Says she if we've children, pray what shall we do,
>   The merrier the more, says I with a leer.

Such coarseness is found in very few of the love songs published after 1840.

Another early song, Charles Gilfert's *Return, O My Love* (New York, 1827), is exceptional because of the reference to physical contact between lovers and because a woman describes and even endorses the contact:

> Return, O my Love and we'll never part
> While the moon her soft light shall shed,
> I'll hold thee fast to my throbbing heart
> And my bosom shall pillow thy head.
>
> The breath of the woodbine is on my lip
> Empearl'd in the dew of May;
> And none but thou of its sweetness shall sip,
> Or steal its honey away.

In contrast, lovers are hardly ever described as touching each other in the songs published after 1840.

A final early example, Alexander Ball's *Thou Can'st Not Forget Me*, the lyric by "Amelia of Louisville, Ky." (Baltimore, 1838), again represents a woman's point-of-view. Moreover, it contains an evocation of sensuality that is extraordinary in the American song of the time:

> Thou canst not forget me, too long thou hast flung,
> Thy spirit's soft pinion o'er mine.
> Too deep was the promise, that round my lips clung,
> As they softly responded to thine.
> In the hush of the twilight, beneath the blue skies,
> My presence will mantle thy soul,
> And a feeling of softness will rush in thine eyes,
> Too deep for thy manhood's control.

Though songs like those of Reinagle, Gilfert, and Ball were in the minority in the earlier years of the century, they are rare indeed after 1840. Indelicate allusions are almost completely banished. Extreme circumspection surrounds any mention of physical contact between lovers. It is perhaps proper in some songs to contain a line such as "I kiss'd her lip and left her side"[4] or "I shall clasp thy gentle form."[5] However, in most compositions lovers neither kiss nor clasp one another.

Indeed, there is sufficient evidence to conclude that during most of the first sixty years of the nineteenth century and especially in the 1840s and 1850s, those few popular songs which treated love as a physical passion were unpopular. Contemporary writers on music seldom mention them as performed in public; musical amateurs scarcely ever purchased them for singing in their homes.[6]

An important reason for the unpopularity was that to mid-century Americans physical love, like the serpent in the Garden of Eden, had the power to destroy the soul, to dominate reason, and to make a shambles of duty and moral obligations.[7] They seem to have felt of love songs as Edgar Allan Poe did of poetry, that passion should be excluded from them and, if introduced, treated as having "the general effect as do discords in music."[8]

Without question the most admired songs of the mid-century, written by composers like H.S. Thompson, John Baker, Stephen Foster, and George Root, never mention strong desire. For example, George Root's *The Hazel Dell* (New York, 1853), which had a widespread popularity in the fifties, is highly discreet in tone. It begins:

> In the Hazel Dell my Nelly's sleeping
> Nelly loved so long;
> And my lonely, lonely watch I'm keeping,
> Nelly lost and gone.
> Here in moonlight often we have wandered
> Thro' the silent shade,
> Now where leafy branches drooping downward
> Little Nelly's laid.

Root writes that in 1853 *"Hazel Dell* began the run which was not to end until the boys whistled it and the hand organs played it from Maine to Georgia, and no ambition for a songwriter could go higher than that."[9]

Sentimental songs like *Hazel Dell* were available in sheet-music form for purchase by the middle and upper classes. For the most part, these compositions could be easily performed by amateurs with a modicum of musical training. The melodies are appealing, the demands on singer and accompanist modest, and the verbal messages easily assimilated.

The less affluent and the musically illiterate, a New Yorker writes, learned the tunes aurally and sang the texts from the "cheap and humble sheets...sold for a penny" on the streets. Of a dozen ballads purchased from a hawker, this New Yorker observes, he "found but one which might not be sung by a modest woman. A recapitulation of the titles will at once recall to the reader the character of these productions. We have 'Annie Laurie,' 'Ellen Bayne,' [and]...'Jeannie with the Light-brown Hair.'..." Compositions such as these songs, he concludes, are "productions of widely differing poetical merit, but all of them honest and true in their sentiment and decorous in their expression."[10]

Several important characteristics are shared by a majority of the love songs. In almost all of them the "I", usually a male, speaks and reveals his inmost feelings. The lovers are commonplace persons drawn from the middle or non-urban lower class. Rarely do they represent the rich or well-born.[11] Usually they dwell in "cots" or "cottages" on mountains, in valleys, or by the sea. If a wealthy or noble suitor woos a maid with promises of mansions and riches, as he does in *Mary of the Glen*, words by Charles G. Eastman, music by *George Root* (New York, 1852), the maid is expected to spurn him for someone more humble. In the song by Root, Mary replies that her heart is given to honest "Willie, who labors with the men" and "has neither lands nor leases."

Also characteristic of the love songs is the portrayal of the idealized woman as a native American, who is pious, gentle, pure, sweet, and graceful. Her hair, eyes, and skin are light; her figure is slender. While a girl, she is carefree and smiles easily. But regrettably, her health is often poor. She may die young, leaving a loyal lover to lament nostalgically over her passing. If she is widowed, or the man she loves dies before he marries her, or if he casts her aside for another, she is expected to either endure severe and lasting agony or lose her life.[12]

The idealized woman just described can be discovered in most of the songs from the mid-century. Typical descriptions of her occur in Stephen Foster's *Sweetly She Sleeps, My Alice Fair* (Baltimore, 1851) and *Gentle Lena Claire* (New York, 1862), and in J.R. Thomas's *Blue-Eyed Jeannie* (Boston, 1856) and *Annie Law* (New York, 1857). The first three songs have lyrics written by the composer; the last one has one by W.W. Fosdick.

In contrast to the idealized woman, now and again, the love songs may refer to a foreign lady, with darker hair, eyes, and skin, who hypnotizes men with her innate seductiveness. However, this dark lady is seldom described as marrying anyone.[13]

In *Oh! Must We Part to Meet No More?*, words and music by Laura A. Hewitt (Baltimore, 1851), a foreign lady is introduced, at least in the imagination of a woman who is bidding farewell to the man she loves, knowing they will "meet no more...cruel fate decreed it so." She first tells him she is a "drooping plant whose feeble tendrels cling to thee." Then, in the last stanza, she cries out:

> Yes, thou wilt roam through foreign climes
> And smiling seek the dazzling throng,
> List fondly to some dark-eyed maid,
> The while she breathes her syren-song.

A further characteristic of the love songs is the rather stereotyped manipulation of natural phenomena in order to project the dominant emotional tone of the text. For instance when the beloved is described, the setting is often one of cheerful sunlight, singing birds, glittering brooks, verdant meadows, and blooming flowers. The weather turns mild; the season is spring or summer. Melodious sound and gay activity prevail. This is the setting for Stephen Foster's dream of the past, in the first stanza of *Jeanie with the Light Brown Hair* (New York, 1854):

> I dream of Jeanie with the light brown hair,
> Borne like a vapor, on the summer air'
> I see her tripping where the bright streams play,
> Happy as the daisies that dance on her way.
> Many were the blithe birds that warbled them o'er.
> Oh! I dream of Jeanie with the light brown hair,
> Floating like a vapor on the soft summer air.

Nature may also be invoked in order to contrast past happiness with present sorrow brought on by love thwarted and lovers parted. In this kind of song, the present, as compared to the summery past, is autumnal or wintry. Now the reference may be to the chill of night, rain falling in a bleak countryside, and natural sounds suggestive of grief. In the second and third stanzas of the

Foster song, the speaker puts aside his dream of past happiness and instead becomes aware of his yearning for the departed Jeanie. He hears her melodies "Sighing like the night wind and sobbing like the rain," and adds that "Now the nodding wild flowers may wither on the shore."

If the song portrays the nocturnal tryst of young lovers, then nature turns benign, as in John P. Ordway' *Witching Love by Moonlight* (Boston, 1857)

> Lovely flowers by moonlight,
>   Sleep when daylight's gone,
> Placid shades of twilight,
>   Beckon love to come
> Come to rural happy bowers,
>   Queenly moon invites;
> She will strew thy path with flowers,
>   Tipt with golden light.
> Witching love by moonlight,
>   Ever bright and fair;
> Shining with the starlight,
>   Cupids watching there.

On the other hand, the sight and sounds of nature create a mood of disquiet when lovers remain eternally separated by distance or death. In H.S. Thompson's *Marion Lee* (Boston, 1858), the woman awaiting the return of her loved one is unaware that he has drowned at sea. But nature is made to signal the hopelessness of her wait and the defeat of her expectations:

> Come to me love for here I am waiting,
>   Sadly and lone by the dark rolling sea;
> Cold winds are blowing and strange voices moaning
>   And fast flow the tears of thy Marion Lee.

> Long have I watched thro' the night's gloomy shadows,
>   Gazing far out o'er the dark troubled sea;
> Striving in vain, thro' mists that are hov'ring,
>   To catch but one glance of the proud bark and thee.

The lyrics to the American love songs from the 1840s and 1850s differ from those of earlier songs and similar compositions of British origin, which had had and continued to have a large American following, in the smaller variety of motifs employed, the more greatly conventionalized presentation of these motifs, and the high incidence of a very limited number of subjects that were peculiarly mid-century American in their emotionally charged delineation of lovers' situations. Amongst the subjects that distinguish the several types of love songs, about nine are prominent. The first subject is one of leave-taking, of lovers saying farewell, perhaps forever.

This type of song was already well established in America before 1840, early examples being Dr. George K. Jackson's *One Kind Kiss* (Boston, ca. 1809), and *No More*, by a "Young Lady of Georgia" (Philadelphia, 1836). However, after 1840, this type of song is made to bear a heavier emotional burden, as in *Come Love and Sit Awhile By Me,* by H.S. Wheaton (Boston, 1847). As often happens, in this song a man is about to depart, apparently never to return, and with no explanation given as to why he is leaving or where he is going. He begins:

> Come, love, and sit awhile by me,
>   That, once more, ere we say farewell,
> My soul may give itself to thee
> And all its grief and sadness tell.

The first stanza ends with him warning his beloved that their "cherished hopes... now must die."

Next, in the second stanza, he senses her torment:

> Thy gentle heart throbs wearily
>   Beneath the grief that's brooding there,
> Thy soul's deep joys, pressed heavily,
>   Shrink crushed in all thy love's despair.

and suggests, although without much conviction, that "passing time shall soothe thy pain."

The song concludes, as is typical of most such songs, with his prophecy of eternal and hopeless love and constant sorrow for himself:

> I still shall see thee—but in dreams—
> I still shall love thee—but in vain—
> No hope from out the future gleams!
> No joy shall thrill my soul again!

To give a second example, the parting in Mrs. C.E. Habicht's *The Sun Is In The West* (Boston, 1848) is depicted in slightly dissimilar fashion. Now the speaker concentrates on his own, to the exclusion of his beloved's, feelings. As in the song just quoted, he vows to love her forever. In a world that will be joyless, her memory will be "A lamp within a tomb/To burn tho' all unseen/ ...To light—tho' but a gloom."

Now and again, this type of song depicts the narrator as simulating gaiety while suffering inwardly. This is the message of John C. Andrew's *Come I've Something Sweet to Sing You* (New York, 1848):

> Come I've something sweet to sing you
>   And a parting word to say,
> Nay gaze not thus upon me.
>   That tonight I seem so gay,
>   For though my lips look mirthful
>   And my cheek is glowing too,
> Ah, my heart is very joyless
>   For its thoughts are all on you.

The second type of song describes a person, usually a young woman, still awaiting and expecting the return of her loved one after a long separation.[14] In most such songs the woman watches at the seashore for one who is a sailor or absent overseas.[15] Like the subject of leave taking, that of the waiting woman is old, an early example being Francis Hopkinson's *My Love is Gone to Sea*.[16] After 1840, most of the waiting women are described as lonely and distressed and perched on a promontory overlooking the water. The scene described in Charlie C. Converse' *The Rock Beside the Sea* (Philadelphia, 1857) contains most of the conventions of this song type:[17]

> The wild waves' thunder on the shore,
>   The curlew's restless cries,
> Unto my watching heart are more
>   Than all earth's melodies.
> Come back; my ocean rover, come!
>   There's but one place for me.
> Till I can greet thy swift sail home,
>   My lone rock by the sea!

One variation on this subject shows the watcher to be unaware that the man she awaits is dead. In Stephen Fosters *Willie, My Brave* (New York, 1851), no one has the courage to "tell her of the fragile bark that sank beneath the ocean." At the song's end she gives up hope and dies.

In the third type of love song, lovers remain separated with no expectation of ever meeting again. Although eternal separation and its attendant miseries were dealt with in earlier works,[18] it became one of the most ubiquitous of all mid-century subjects. The viewpoint is almost always a male's.[19] As in the other song types, the emotions are all; the why, where, and what of the situation are rarely given. Running through most of these songs is the sentiment in *Jenny Grey*, words by Benjamin Jones, music by George R. Poulton (Bowton, 1855), that the beloved's "image clingeth to memory yet/And this bosom still beats for thee sweet Jenny Grey." The speaker adds that he will forever "remember [her] in sorrow, in joy and in pain/ One heart shall be faithful unchangeable still."

Stephen Foster often wrote words and music for this kind of love song. Invariably he has a male speaker describe an idealized woman, then ask again and again, why and where has she gone. The speaker provides no answers and never truly expects a reunion. Two examples are Foster's *Laura Lee* (Baltimore, 1851) and *Where has Lula Gone* (New York, 1858).

An occasional minstrel song has as its subject the permanent separation of slaves who are lovers. However, unlike non-dialect compositions, the reasons for the separation are stated. Either one of the two slaves has been sold and sent to a distant owner, as in James P. Carter's *Cynthia Sue* (Boston, 1844), or the man has thrown over his enslavement and escaped to the North, leaving behind his beloved, as in *Young Clem Brown*, words by Marshall S. Pike, music by L.V.H. Crosby (Boston, 1846).

The fourth type of love song is the elegy on the beloved, uttered by a disconsolate lover, and usually over her grave. For years this subject has been favored in poetry and song, many examples having been written in the eighteenth century, in the British Isles.[20] As early as the 1790s, American music publishers were reprinting British songs of this type, two examples being James Hook's *Lucy Gray of Allendale* (Philadelphia, ca. 1794), and Charles Dignum's *Fair Rosale* (New York, ca. 1797). But the lyrics of most of these songs tended to be highly artificial. They were told mostly in the third person and concerned themselves mainly with unreal people, like the classically-inspired shepherds and shepherdesses who inhabited a world distant from the concerns of everyday people. In these songs gracefulness took precedence over feeling.[21]

A tremendous increase in the popularity of the elegiac song of affection was initiated in America with the New York publication in 1837 of *Near the Lake Where Droop'd the Willow*, words by George P. Morris, music adapted from the minstrel melody *Long Time Ago* by Charles E. Horn. This song quickly attracted a vast following amongst Americans. In it are contained most of the conventions that reappear with such regularity in the mid-century songs of this type: the beautiful and idealized "maid, belov'd and cherished" by high and low, now buried "near the lake where droop'd the willow," and a bereaved lover, who can never forget her, weeping over her grave.

Most often a weeping willow, sometimes a yew of cypress, overhangs the grave. In a special study of the symbolic use of the willow, John W. Draper states that this tree was at one time the symbol of distressed lovers, and that it was not until after the weeping variety of the tree had been imported from China, a little before the middle of the eighteenth century, and begun to replace the yew and cypress in cemeteries, that it became the symbol of death.[22]

The willow still symbolizes distressed lovers in Francis Hopkinson's song of 1788, *Beneath a Weeping Willow's Shade*.[23] Nevertheless, according to Draper, by the end of the eighteenth century the weeping willow became widely accepted in America as the symbol of death. It was planted in burial grounds and appeared with some frequency on gravestones.[24]

During the 1820s, American songs were picturing the tree as drooping over graves situated near a body of water:

> By the side of yon streamlet,
>   There grows a green willow,
> Which bends to its surface, and kisses each wave;
> Under whose dark shades,
>   With the sod for his pillow,
> In peace rests the spirit of William the Brave.[25]

Then, in the 1840s, almost invariably, a young woman is mentioned as buried beneath the tree.[26]

The mid-nineteenth-century creators of the elegiac songs of affection seem to be in agreement with Edgar Allan Poe when, in his essay "The Philosophy of Composition," he explains his own approach to writing poetry:

I asked myself—"Of all melancholy topics what, according to the *Universal* understanding of mankind is the most melancholy?" Death, was the obvious reply. "And when," I said, "is this most melancholy of topics most poetical?"...The answer here also is obvious—"When it most closely allies itself to *Beauty*." The death then of a beautiful woman is unquestionably the most poetical topic in the world and equally is it beyond doubt that the lips best suited for such a topic are those of a bereaved lover.[27]

Two elegiac songs conforming to the Poe dictum have already been cited in this study, Emerson's *Cora Bell* and Root's *The Hazel Dell*. Among the many examples of this song type that Foster wrote,[28] *Eulalie* (New York, 1851) may possibly have been the one most directly influenced by Poe's poetry. The change of the death symbol from a willow to a yew was made, at least in part, for the sake of the assonance "yee-tree, Eulalie." The last stanza reads as follows:

> Streamlet chanting at her feet
>   Mournful music sad and sweet,
> Wake her not, she dreams of me
>   'Neath the yew-tree, Eulalie!
> Eulalie, but yesternight,
>   Came a spirit veiled in white,
> I knew it could be none but thee,
>   Bride of Death, lost Eulalie.

The fifth type of song explores the feelings of a rejected lover, a subject with a long history in poetry and song. Two early examples of the song of rejection are James Hewitt's *How Happy Was My Humble Lot* (New York, ca. 1800) and *When First Maria Won My Heart* (New York, ca. 1807). The text of the song of rejection began to take on more and more of the characteristics associated with mid-century song during the thirties, as can be seen in *The Broken Heart*, words by R.N.H., music by Edwin Merriott (New York, ca. 1830), and *There Was a Time*, "Words from the Lady's Book," music by Tau Delta (Philadelphia, 1833). The lyric of *There Was a Time*, however, still is somewhat reticent in its depiction of feeling. It begins:

> There was a bright and sunny time
>   When ev're hope was gay
> But the vision's gone, and each fairy dream
>   has floated far away!
> There was a time when I believed,
>   She whom I lov'd was true:
> I twin'd her roses flowers she gave,
>   But ah! her flowers were rue.

After 1840, personal emotion is more naked. Note, for example, the ending of *Hopeless Love*, words and music by J.T.S. Sullivan (Philadelphia, 1849):

> Tho' in this world I ne'er may possess thee,

Tho' those charms I may never embrace,
Tho' these lips love may never caress thee,
I still worship thy beauty and grace;
Oh would that I never had met thee
Thou bright vision of all that is fair,
Or that power were mine to forget thee,
I had vanquished this aching despair.

The usual reason given as to why the speaker may never again possess the one he loves and must succumb to despair is that the one loved has married another. Her turning-away is explained as owing to her fickleness or the insistence of her parents. Since the marriage state was as immutable as death itself, neither a divorce nor an illicit relationship being conceivable, all that is left the speaker is the never-ending ache of unsatisfied love. As the "Lady" who wrote *Thou Hast Wounded the Spirit that Loved Thee* (Baltimore, 1846) explains it in the last stanza: "Thus we're taught in this cold world to smother/ Each feeling that once was so dear."

Another "Lady" ends her song of rejection, *My Hopes Have Departed Forever* (New York, 1851), with a reference to willows and death. The speaker here is a woman:

He came, but another had rifled
His heart of the love once my own,
I grieved, but my anguish was stifled,
And shrunk from his cold formal tone.
The sun is now sinking in billows,
That roll in the far distant west,
But morning will shine through the willows,
And find me forever at rest.

Fortunately for the mental health of mid-century singers, happier compositions also existed. One type of happy song that was available to them was the idyllic song in praise of the still living and presumably approachable beloved, as in J.R. Thomas's *Annie Law*, words by W.W. Fosdick (New York, 1857), and Stephen Foster's *Fairy-Belle* (New York, 1859). Another type of song that the musical public enjoyed has a suitor beg his beloved to come with him, away from the grimness and sorrow of the world that surrounds her and, through marriage, escape with him to a happier existence elsewhere. The elsewhere may be an isolated mountain side, as in Francis H. Brown's *Will You Come to My Mountain Home?*, words by Alfred Wheeler (New York, 1845), or an island paradise, as in Henry Williams's *Bermuda's Fairy Isle*, words by T.M.Y. (Boston, 1854), or to a distant and exotic land, as in John Baker's *The Burman Lover* (Boston, 1849).

Still another type of love song from this period is the serenade. Two examples are *The Lone Starry Hours*, words by Marshall S. Pike, music by James Power and arranged by John P. Ordway (Boston, 1849), and *Twinkling*

Stars Are Laughing, Love, words and music by John P. Ordway (Boston, 1855). The suitor in *The Lone Starry Hours* twice sings the refrain:

> When no winds through the low woods sweep, love,
> And I gaze on some bright rising star,
> When the world is in dream and sleep, love,
> Oh! wake while I touch my guitar.

In some songs of this type, the speaker is not depicted as singing to his sleeping beloved, but simply as thinking of her as she sleeps and wishing her all the joys and none of the unhappinesses of life, as in *Oh, Were I a Bird,* words and music by J.T.S. Sullivan (Philadelphia, 1846), and *Sweetly She Sleeps, My Alice Fair,* words and music by Stephen Foster (New York, 1851).

The last type of love song to be described is one of good-humor, which frequently makes sport of the sentimentality pervading the other types. An amusing example is *Joe Hardy,* words and melody by James Pierpont, arranged by Edward Leroy (Boston, 1853). The first two stanzas are as follows:

> Yes, I know that you were my lover,
> But that sort of thing has an end,
> Tho' love and its transports are over,
> You know you can still be my friend,
> Don't kneel at my feet I implore you,
> Don't write on the drawings you bring,
> Don't ask me to say I adore you,
> For indeed it is *now* no such thing.
> I confess when at Bangor we parted,
> I swore that I worshipped you then,
> That I was a maid broken hearted,
> And you the most charming of men;
> I confess when I read your first letter,
> I blotted your name with a tear,
> I was young then, but now I know better,
> Could I tell that I'd meet Hardy here?

More biting are the following verses of Nathaniel Parker Willis, a versifier who also wrote his own fair share of sentimental lyrics:[29]

> Your love in a cottage is hungry
> Your vine is a nest of flies--
> Your milkmaid shocks the Graces,
> And simplicity talks of pies!
> You lie down to your shady slumber
> And wake with a bug in your ear.
> And your damsel that walks in the morning
> Is shod like a mountaineer.

> True love is at home on a carpet,

And nightly likes his ease—
And true love has an eye for a dinner,
And starves beneath shady trees.
His wing is the fan of a lady,
His foot's an invisible thing
And his arrow is tipped with a jewel,
And shot from a silver string.[30]

The nineteenth-century Americans, who enjoyed the love song and wept or smiled at its message, were quite aware of the problems troubling their society.[31] Certainly, they had first-hand knowledge of friends and family members who had left loved ones behind and travelled great distances, sometimes never to return. The American West, and the oceans had swallowed up many of these travellers. Moreover, a large number of the women they knew did die young, especially during childbirth.[22] Love, under these circumstances, took a buffeting and was so depicted in song.

In the restless, constantly changing nineteenth-century social environment, where mobility and competition allowed little room for the development of warmth and intimacy between people, the relationship of suitor and beloved, of husband and wife, became of great consequence,[33] The importance of love in cementing personal relationships, therefore, was stressed in song.

It is clear that these Americans lived constantly with life's harsh truths.[34] However, it is also clear that when they turned to song for entertainment, they preferred that these truths be softened with sentimentality. For them, to relive the actualities of the American experience in song that held nothing back would have been incomprehensible. Instead, they wished some relief from stark reality.[35] In order for love songs to take on a recreative and therapeutic function, realistic details were suppressed, situations generalized, and the violent emotions muted.

As for the composers and versifiers of the songs, their attitude is well expressed by George Root when he states that in his time few people knew, required, or understood artistic songs such as those of Schubert. His choice was to write in artistic isolation or attempt to meet the needs of the American people. He chose the latter and "was thankful when... [he] could write something that all the people would sing."[36] What he wrote had to be simple and sentimental, since it was this kind of musical composition alone that would "be received and live in the hearts of the people."[37]

Given the democratic temper of the time, and the felt need to articulate what was a "people's music,"[38] the creators of the American love song behaved like representatives of the people and did give shape to a musical form with meaning for their own age.

Notes

[1]For a general history of the rise of sentimental expression in the eighteenth and

nineteenth centuries, see "Rococo, Classicism and Romanticism," in volume II of Arnold Hauser's *Social History of Art*, trans. Stanley Goodman (New York: Knopf, 1951), For studies concerned primarily with mid-nineteenth-century America, see Carl Bode, *The Anatomy of American Popular Culture, 1840-1861* (Berkeley: Univ. of Cal., 1959); *American Life in the 1840s*, ed. Carl Bode (New York: Doubleday, 1967); and *Romanticism in America*, ed. George Boas (New York: Russell and Russell, 1961).

²Alexis de Tocquerville, *Democracy in America*, trans. Henry Reeve, ed. Francis-Bowen (New York: Knopf, 1945), I, 315-16. Much the same thing has been written by recent historians, such as Carl Bode; see *American Life*, pp. XIII-XIV, 55.

³*The Musical World and the New York Musical Times*, II December, 1852, p. 227.

⁴*Agnes May*, words by Anson C. Chester, music by Henry Tucker (New York: Firth, Pond, 1853).

⁵*At Eve I Miss Thee When Alone*, music by L.V.H. Crosby (Boston: Ditson, 1847).

⁶The author of this study has examined several hundred song collections that belonged to Americans who lived in the first sixty years of the nineteenth century. Among the thousands of compositions examined, only a small handful makes any reference to physical passion.

⁷William Charvat, *The Origins of American Critical Thought, 1810-1835* (New York: Russell and Russell, 1968), pp. 13-16.

⁸Edgar Allan Poe, "The Philosophy of Composition," *The Complete Poems and Stories of Edgar Allar Poe*, ed. Arthur Hobson Quinn and Edward H. O'Mell (New York: Knopf, 1970), II, 981.

⁹George F. Root, *The Story of a Musical Life* (Cincinnati: Church, 1891), p. 89.

¹⁰New York *Musical Review and Gazette*, 29 May 1858, p. 166.

¹¹Some pre-1840 songs had knights and their ladies as subjects: for example, John Hewitt's *The Minstrel's Return from the War* (New York: Hewitt, 1827) and *The Knight of the Raven-Black Plume* (New York: Hewitt, ca. 1833). Hewitt, however, reflected the views of the American South, which was considerably taken with the ideas of chivalry. After 1840, as the settlements in the Mid-West, populated mainly by ordinary people from New England, grew, the music publishers increasingly issued songs that centered on everyday people and their experiences in order to accommodate the tastes of the populous North-East and North-West. At the same time they felt it less and less necessary to cultivate the preferences of the largely rural South, with its limited market for music, and hardly any songs were issued on chivalric themes; see Charvat, pp. 300-01; and John Bayley, *The Characters of Love* (New York: Basic Books, 1960), pp. 282-83.

¹²This picture of the idealized woman is found not only in the love songs, but in most of the American literature of the period; see Charvat, p. 22; Leslie A. Fiedler, *Love and Death in the American Novel*, rev. ed. (New York: Stein and Day, 1966), pp. 80, 296; Eleanor M. Sickels, *The Gloomy Egoist* (New York: Columbia Univ., 1932), p. 228; Ralph Boas, "The Romantic Lady," in *Romanticism in America*, p. 63.

¹³This type of woman also appears in contemporary American literature; see Fiedler, p. 296; Charvat, p. 23.

¹⁴One composition, the minstrel song *The Yellow Rose of Texas*, by J.K. (New York: Firth, Pond, 1858), is unusual in that a man speaks and says that he is returning to the woman he loves after a prolonged separation from her. Another song told from the viewpoint of the absent man is Stephen Foster's *Gentle Lena Clare* (New York: Gordon, 1862).

¹⁵In one or two songs, the watcher is a rustic maiden living in a "del" or "glen",

as in *The Absent Soldier*, words by William Lewers, music by S.O. Dyer (New York: Holt, 1847).

[16]*Seven Songs for the Harpsichord or Forte Piano* (Philadelphia: Dobson, 1788), p. 2.

[17]For another example of this song type, see the lyric to Thompson's *Marion Lee*, quoted earlier in this study. The same subject, from a man's viewpoint, is found in Charlie C. Converse's *Aileen Aroon* (Boston: Ditson, 1853).

[18]See the British song *The Beautiful Maid*, words by Thomas Dibdin, music by John Braham (New York: Geib, ca. 1802); also *The Link is not Broken*, words by a Gentleman of Boston, music by E.T. Coolidge (Boston: Bradlee, 1835).

[19]One of the few songs with a woman's point-of-view is *Come Back*, words by Letty Linwood (Brooklyn: Braun, 1856).

[20]See Sickels, p. 186.

[21]Sickels, p. 188, states that the artificialness was true also of the eighteenth-century poetry.

[22]John W. Draper, "Notes on the Symbolic Use of the Willow," *The Funeral Elegy* (New York: New York Univ., 1929), pp. 335-37.

[23] *Seven Songs*, pp. 3-4. The willow continues to be used in some British songs as the symbol of distressed lovers into the first decade of the nineteenth century; for example in Sir John Stevenson's *The Willow*, first issued in Philadelphia by Benjamin Carr, around 1801; and in John Braham's *The Willow Tree*, words by Thomas Dibdin, also first issued by Carr, around 1808.

[24]Draper, p. 337.

[25]*William the Brave*, words by a "Young Lady of Kentucky," music by Charles Gilfert (New York: Riley, 1823). The well-known psychiatrist Carl G. Jung, in *Analytical Psychology* (New York: Random House, 1968), pp. 130-32, 138, 177, speaks of water as an archetypal symbol of death, especially when connected with a tomb.

[26]Some examples of elegiac songs of affection employing the willow as the symbol of a beautiful woman's death are *Bessie Gray*, words by W.R. Lawrence, music by George Poulton (Boston: Ditson, 1854); *Alice Clair*, words by J.M. Fletcher, music by Lyman Heath (New York: Waters, 1853); andI *Annie Lisle*,R words and music by H.S. Thompson (Boston: Ditson, 1860). Examples of minstrel songs in dialect that are of this type are *Nelly Was a Lady*, words and music by Stephen Foster (New York: Firth, Pond, 1849), and *Jenny Lane*, words and music by R. Bishop Buckley (Boston: Wade, 1850).

[27]*The Complete Poems*, II, 982. Two of Poe's poems that illustrate his ideas and employ similar conventions as those in the elegiac songs are *Ulalume* and *Annabel Lee*. Since many songs portray the lover as watching over the grave, it is of interest that Norman Brown, a Freudian, states, in *Life Against Death* (Middletown, Conn.: Wesleyan Univ., 1959), p. 100, that man, unlike all other animals, instinctively guards his dead.

[28]See *Lila Ray* (New York: Firth, Pond, 1850), *Gentle Annie* (New York: Firth, Pond, 1856), and *Virginia Belle* (New York: Firth, Pond, 1860).

[29]Examples of Willis's poetry may be found in Rufus W. Griswald, *The Poets and Poetry of America* (Philadelphia: Carey and Hart, 1842), pp. 278-86.

[30]James L. Onderdonk, *History of American Verse (1610-1897)* (Chicago: McClurg, 1901), pp. 145-46.

[31]For an examination of these problems, see Fred Lewis Pattee, *The Feminine Fifties* (Port Washington: Kennikat Press, 1966), pp. 4-16; also Charvat, pp. 49-50.

[32]Pattee, p. 308; Wilma Clark, "Wilma Clark, "Four Popular Poets," *New Dimensions*

in Popular Culture, ed. Russel B. Nye (Bowling Green: Bowling Green Univ., 1972), p. 193; and Ann Douglas Wood, "Mrs. Sigourney and the Sensibility of Inner Space," *New England Quarterly,* XLV (1972), 177.

[33]This kind of relationship is discussed in Robim M. Williams, Jr., *American Society,* *rev. ed.* (New York: Knopf, 1960), p. 81.

[34]See Tocqueville, II, 208; Onderdonk, pp. 157-58.

[35]A conclusion also reached by Pattee, pp. 53-54, and Tocqueville, II, 210-11.

[36]Root, p. 83. For a report on the failure of German songs to gain a following in America, see the New York *Musical Review,* 17 April 1858, p. 117.

[37]Root, p. 97.

[38]Root, pp. 19-20, 95-96; also, the New York *Musical Review,* 16 February 1854, pp. 57-58.

The Hutchinson Family:
The Function of Their Song in
Ante-Bellum America

Caroline Moseley

The Hutchinson Family was a travelling band of singers which enjoyed considerable popularity, and some notoriety, in ante-bellum America. This essay explores the reasons for their celebrity: it suggests that, in a period of increasing social disorganization, the Hutchinsons provided an image of America in which contemporary audiences wanted and needed to believe. The Hutchinsons were indigenous American artists: they hymned reassuringly traditional values of home, family, and farm: and, they sang of the past and the future, thereby lessening the threat of the present. The Hutchinson Family sang of America, not as it was, but as they and their contemporaries wished it to be.

The original Hutchinson Family troupe was composed of John, Asa, Judson and Abigail (Abby) Hutchinson, with brother Jesse as manager. A New York journalist styled them "a nest of brothers with a sister in it."[1] The Hutchinsons came from farming country in Milford, New Hampshire. Even when the quartet travelled in service of their muse, the farm was attended by a Yankee litany of siblings: David, Noah, Polly, Andrew, Zephaniah, Caleb, Joshua, Benjamin, Rhoda and Elizabeth; and, of course, the parents, Jesse and Polly Hutchinson.

The quartet, known as the "Tribe of Jesse," was reduced to a trio when Abby married. It eventually disintegrated completely and produced several competing groups of singers. John Hutchinson continued to sing in public until almost 1900, and so, occasionally, did Abby. Thomas Wentworth Higginson could write, as late as 1892, of "some stray member of the 'Hutchinson Family' who still comes before the public with now whitening locks...and continues to sing with unchanged sweetness the plaintive melodies that hushed the stormiest meeting when he and his four or five long-haired brothers stood grouped round their one rose-bud of a sister like a band of Puritan Bohemians."[2] The Hutchinson Family name was applied to various musicians who performed over a period of fifty years and an area of six thousand miles: the quartet in England; John, Asa, and Judson in the western territory (where they founded the town of Hutchinson, Minnesota); and Jesse in Gold Rush California. The

Reprinted with permission from the *Journal of American Culture*, Volume 1:4 (Winter 1978), pp. 713-23.

"Hutchinson Family" of this essay is the original quartet, or the trio of brothers, best known in the eighteen-forties and fifties. The songs mentioned are those in their repertoire—a repertoire which changed little over the years and the miles.

The Hutchinsons were formed in imitation of a highly successful Swiss troupe, the Rainers. John Hutchinson reported: "I was the only one of the family that ever heard the Rainers sing...I was overwhelmed." He taught his brothers "to sing...as the Rainers did."[3] For many years the Hutchinsons were known as the "New Hampshire Rainers," in much the same way that James Fenimore Cooper was the "American Sir Walter Scott." Emerson's clarion call to native-born American artists had just been issued, there were nationalist stirrings, but Americans still hearkened to "the courtly muses of Europe."[4] Blackface minstrelsy, to be sure, was strongly nativist, and derided all foreign influences.[5] On the popular concert stage, however, foreign musicians, such as the Rainers, Henry Russell and Jenny Lind, were much in vogue; an American troupe had to struggle for attention.

As American artists of the period, the Hutchinsons presented themselves somewhat ambiguously. On the one hand, they unashamedly imitated the Rainers and tailored their image to that of the foreigners. Abby's early appearances were in a Tyrolean costume. The Hutchinsons drove through country villages singing "The Alpine Hunter's Song"; and many of their songs were those popularized by the Rainers. They tried to appear as Alpine as possible by emphasizing the mountains of their native state. They altered the lithograph cover of their first published songs to depict more and higher mountains. They sang "The Mountaineer," "The Tyrolese War Song," "The Vulture of the Alps," and "We've Left Again Our Mountain Home"—their "mountain home," Milford, New Hampshire, being characterized by farmland and rolling hills.

On the other hand, Judson Hutchinson pleaded:

> When foreigners approach your shores
> You welcome them with open doors.
> Now we have come, to seek our lot,
> Shall native talent be forgot?"[6]

The Hutchinsons' rhetoric emphasized their Americanism. Asa says they are "descendants of some of those who, flying from oppression in their native land, sought and found shelter on the shores of the New World." He tells us of "the progress of a band of brothers, who are the architects of their own fortunes"—good Jacksonian men. He reassures us that, despite their love of music, "the useful was never sacrificed for the merely agreeable"; they "neglected no duty." Asa asserts that the Hutchinsons "stand at the head of American Vocalists, as they deserve to do, for they were the first company who ever started in the United States."[7]

John Hutchinson certainly voiced his version of the contemporary American Dream: "All through my boyhood, while engaged in labors on the farm, I had prophetic dreams...which in after years proved real. I saw our company

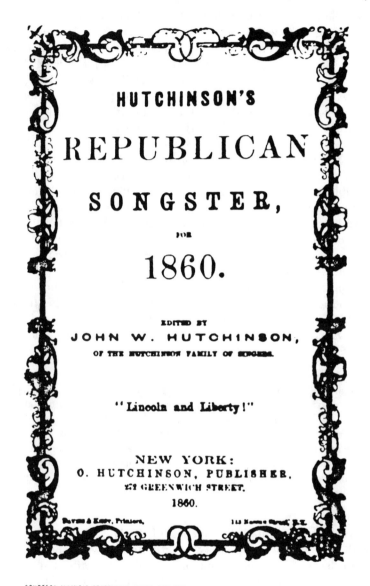

"HUTCHINSON'S REPUBLICAN SONGSTER"
This campaign songster, edited by John W. Hutchinson, helped to elect Lincoln in 1860.

standing and singing to numerous audiences, heard the plaudits and compliments as they dispersed, and witnessed the gathering-in of piles of money...gold, silver and quantities of paper."[8]

The Hutchinsons' Tyrolean ditties catered to the popular taste for exoticism, but otherwise their repertoire accorded with Emerson's assertions in "The American Scholar": "Events, actions arise, that must be sung, that will sing themselves." "The literature of the poor, the feelings of the child, the philosophy of the street, the meaning of household life, are the topics of the time."[9] The Hutchinsons sang sentimental songs ("The Blind Orphan's Lament"), comic songs ("Anti-Calomel"), dramatic songs ("The Maniac"), musical homilies ("Kind Words Can Never Die"), patriotic and nationalistic pieces which bespoke their belief in manifest destiny ("Uncle Sam's Farm," "Westward Ho!"). Many of their songs rang a reformist note. James Russell Lowell later noted that in the eighteen-forties "Everybody had a mission (with a capital M) to attend to everybody else's business,"[10] and the Hutchinsons were no exception. They espoused many of the nineteenth century's causes, great and small: Grahamism, Thompsonian medicine, phrenology, spiritualism,[11] temperance, and, most important, abolitionism. The Hutchinsons' temperance songs ("King Alcohol") were acceptable in a perfectionist era. Their abolitionist songs ("Get Off the Track") were not acceptable, except among a small band of evangelical reformers. A New York journalist observed: "As far as 'a man of the world' could judge, seven-eights of this family are now engaged in procuring flannel shirts and moral tracts for every new born nigger baby." An Easton, Pennsylvania paper condemned their "abolitionist trash."[12]

Abolitionism, in the eighteen-forties and fifties was certainly not a popular cause, even in the North. It was the Hutchinsons' reformism, rather than their gentility, which kept them from appealing to the mass audiences of, say the minstrel shows. Gilbert Chase situates the Hutchinsons vis a vis "the classes" and "the masses":

My view is that they allied themselves with the genteel tradition as far as repertoire is concerned and in their desire to obtain the approval of fashionable urban audiences. Compared with the repertoire of Italian opera, that appealed only to the initiated or the snobbish, their programs were popular and designed for mass appeal. They therefore represented what might be called the "left wing" of the genteel tradition, approaching the popular tradition while retaining the prestige of elegance and refinement associated with such names as Morris and Longfellow and with the accolade of urban culture acquired in Boston and New York.[13]

Chase provides a qualitative evaluation of the Hutchinsons' popularity. It is difficult to assess their popularity quantitatively, as we have no concert receipts, no ledgers of income and outgo, few reliable records of sheet music sales or copyright deposits. It is possible to say that they were widely known, and widely, if not universally, admired. They sang throughout the East, Northeast, and West, in innumerable villages and towns, and in cities too: Schenectady, Detroit, Philadelphia, Cleveland, Boston, Minneapolis, New York. They did not perform in the South, as one visit to Baltimore convinced them that abolitionists, even musical ones, were unwelcome. The quartet visited England, where they met Charles Dickens and Harriet Martineau. They sang in the White House. A contemporary music reviewer referred to "a kind of Hutchinson-family arrangement, that being the sort of music then most enjoyed by the public."[14] Many of their songs were still included in an 1870 catalogue of sheet music.[15] They were sufficiently celebrated to be parodied on the minstrel

THE HUTCHINSON FAMILY

THE HUTCHINSON SINGERS
Henry, John, and Viola Hutchinson. (John was a member of the original group.)

stage. Their theme song, "The Old Granite State," was metamorphosed at the hands of the Georgia Champions:

> We're a band of brothers,
> And we live among the hills

became:

> We're a family of niggers,
> And our story we'll relate.

and

> We have eight other Brothers,
> And of Sisters, just another,
> Besides our Father, and our Mother,
> In the "Old Granite State."

became:

> We hab Twenty leben broders,
> And Lebenteen sisters,
> And dere all as black as niggers
> In ole Virginny State[16]

One reason for such popularity as the Hutchinsons enjoyed must have been the quality of their singing. Nothing is so evanescent as song; although we do have many of their four-part arrangements, we cannot hear their voices. John Hutchinson, admittedly biased, said: "The leading characteristic in the 'Hutchinson family's' singing was the exact balance of parts in their harmonies, each one striving to merge himself in the interest of the whole, forming a perfect quartet, which was rare in those early days...neither's voice could be distinguished until he arose and sang a solo."[17] This description could apply to a democracy as well as to a quartet. The Hutchinsons' popularity may have been enhanced by a musical display of equilibrium between individual and group which accorded with the ideals of their democratic society.

A New Haven admirer rhapsodized:

> If earthly voices our ears may greet
> With strains so heavenly clear and sweet,
> So full of the spirit of harmony,
> What must the songs of the angels be?[18]

America, in the years of the Hutchinson Family's greatest popularity, was in social and economic turmoil. Industrialization, urbanization, westward expansion, immigration, sectional strife, all combined to destroy the stable social order which had existed through the early National period. It was the era of the Mexican War, the Gold Rush, manifest destiny, the common man, the self-made man, the millionaire. There seemed no limit to the miracles which could be wrought by what Edward Everett apotheosed as "practical science and wisely applied capital."[19] Popular rhetoric was determinedly optimistic. The Scientific American, 1849, stated: "so far as we can judge...opinion is favorable to the *now* being the *golden age*."[20]

Still, many Americans must have shared the panic of Ishmael at the helm of the *Pequod:* "Uppermost was the impression, that whatever swift rushing thing I stood on was not so much bound to any haven ahead as rushing from all havens astern."[21] As Alexis de Tocqueville commented: "In America I saw the freest and most enlightened men placed in the happiest circumstances the world affords; it seemed to me as if a cloud habitually hung upon their brow..."[22] There was a pervasive malaise which suggested that the beautiful republican promise had not been fulfilled, that somehow things had gone terribly wrong.

This ambiguity between the love of technologic progress and the yearning for old republican simplicity has been characterized by Leo Marx as "the national preference for having it both ways,"[23] and the Hutchinson Family expressed it in their songs. Their material ranged from perfectionist propaganda to the most nostalgic of sentimental effusions. A glance at the Table of Contents of any Hutchinson Family songster shows this Janus-faced world view. Looking toward the (perfect) future, we see "The Millenium" "Coming Right Along, or Right Over Wrong," "Ho, For California," or "There's a Good Time Coming." Looking toward the (perfect) past, we see "The Good Old Days of Yore," "Recollections of Home," "The Cot Where We Were Born," or "Forty Years Ago." The Hutchinsons, singing in the (imperfect) present, combined avant garde enthusiasms with tearful nostalgia, to address and allay the deepest concerns of their contemporaries.

Robert Frost has said that poetry provides us with "a momentary stay against confusion"[24]...an artistic organization of otherwise inchoate experience. This is what all art forms provide...cultivated, folk and popular arts. Folk and popular music have the added aspect of shared experience and group identification. Alan Lomax points out that "from the point of view of its social function, the primary effect of music is to give the listener a feeling of security, for it symbolizes...all of [his] personality-shaping experiences. As soon as the familiar sound pattern is established...[his] heart is opened."[25] Asa Hutchinson said much the same thing of his family's music: "It comes to us with its quaintness and its melody, and soothes us as a mother her tired child....It washes away from the soul the dirt of everyday life."[26]

The stated message of the Hutchinson's songs is not enough to account for this pacific effect. Music must be seen, along with all expressive forms, as behavior; as "a dynamic element of culture and a focus for human interaction."[27] It is essential to comprehend the cultural context of a song before attempting to interpret it, and to know what it does not say as well as what it does say. The Hutchinsons' songs do not reflect culture; rather, they interact with culture, and mediate between fact and fantasy. Let us examine a few items from the repertoire of the Hutchinson family.

My Mother's Bible

This book is all that's left me now;
　　Tears will unbidden start.
With faltering lip and throbbing brow,
　　I press it to my heart
For many generations past
　　Here is our Family tree;
My mother's hands this Bible clasp'd,
　　She dying gave it me.[28]

　　Much has been written about the status of women in the early nineteenth century, their exile from productive labor and their relegation to the suburban home. We are familiar with the constellation of behaviors which Barbara Welter has called "The Cult of True Womanhood:"[29] purity, piety, submissiveness, domesticity. Such a woman would produce children "to whom no word ever sounds half so sweet as *mother* and for whom no place possesses one half the charms of *home.*"[30] These concepts represent institutionalized values and have never corresponded to reality; the institutionalization of the idea that "a woman's place is in the home," coincided with women leaving the home to enter the labor force.[31]

　　I do not believe that this apotheosis of motherhood represented a conscious politicization or exploitation of women, but rather, answered to very real psychic needs of a troubled society. At the time that the stereotype of the True Woman emerged, it may have been conservative in the most positive sense: conservative not as "reactionary" but as "saving." In the America of 1843, "My Mother's Bible" provided an ideal of nurturance and familial security which was supportive, even necessary, in an increasingly disorganized society. The sentimental effulgence of so much of the Hutchinson Family's repertoire was, I think, a response to the national malaise observed by de Tocqueville, and represented a longing for security: for home, family, "the good old days of yore," when life was (it seemed) less complicated and threatening. It is curious that this is the very period which we, today, seem to regard as our "good old days of yore."

　　"My Mother's Bible" must have been a favorite selection. John Hutchinson notes that the group sang it at Sing Sing for the female convicts, and "every one was in tears."[32] They also sang it for President Tyler; as Mrs. Tyler had just died, it caused the Tyler children to weep. Such programming might seem thoughtless to us, but not so, perhaps to President Tyler. A contemporary encyclopedia of music states that simple songs which encourage affective display are valuable as a "means of informing and enlarging the mighty hearts of a free people."[33]

Not only did the Hutchinsons sing nostalgic songs of home and the idealized past; they brought the image alive with their presence. The Hutchinsons themselves, as a "Family," were an emblem of home wherever they travelled. The closeness of their musical harmonies authenticated the closeness of their family relationship. They emphasized familial ties, even when spurious. Indeed, Asa Hutchinson continued to bill himself as the "Hutchinson Family" even when his quartet consisted of himself and three black singers.

The Hutchinsons' theme song, "The Old Granite State," presented them as Jeffersonian yeoman farmers, although, as time went on, they added more reformist stanzas.

The Old Granite State

We have come from the mountains,
We have come from the mountains,
We have come from the mountains,
    Of the Old Granite State.

We're a band of brothers, &c
    And we live among the hills.

We have left our aged parents, &c.
    In the Old Granite State.

We obtained their blessings, &c.
    And we bless then in return.

Party threats are not alarming,
For when music ceases charming,
We can earn our bread by farming,
    In the Old Granite State.

We're a band of farmers, &c.
    And we love to till the soil...[34]

Industrialism might threaten family, social structure and the agrarian order, but the Hutchinsons were singing proof of the enduring value of family and land. The Hutchinsons certainly had an eye to the market value of any image they projected, but they seem to have been sincere in their presentation of self. John Hutchinson says that friends advised them to wear gloves in the concert room, but "Gloves did not seem to be correct adornments to horny-handed sons of toil like ourselves, and we simply vetoed them. Then our friends tried to compromise by having Abby wear them, any way. We sternly refused."[35] Nathaniel P. Rogers was inspired to describe the Hutchinsons in the Agricultural Sublime: "Those hands that can so 'handle the harp and the organ,' can play skillfully on the great and glorious plough handle, the majestic hoe, and the mighty ax helve."[36]

Those of the Hutchinson Family's songs which were forward-looking must also be listened to with an ear for what is rhetoric and what is reality.

Coming Right Along

Behold the Day of Promise comes
-full of inspiration
The blessed day by prophets sung,
-for the healing of nations

Old midnight errors flee away:
they soon will be goon
While Heavenly angels seem to say,
the "god time" 's coming on.

Coming right along,
Coming right along,
The blessed day of promise is coming right along.[37]

John Hutchinson recalled that, when they performed this song at Brook Farm, "We felt that we had struck the chord re-echoing down the centuries from the day of Pentecost and sung by the angels."[38] The Hutchinsons' millenial optimism was well-received by audiences, so long as the millenium did not include freedom for slaves. If we recall that 1846 was the year of the Mexican War, 1850 the Compromise and Fugitive Slave Law, 1854 the Kansas-Nebraska Act, 1857 the Dred Scott decision, and 1859 Harper's Ferry, it is easy to see that even as the Hutchinsons sang such songs, America was "a house dividing." Increased sectional strife must have made it difficult to see the day of promise at hand. We were faced with the encroaching specter of Civil War and social cataclysm, America's expulsion from the Garden; but those who sang and heard "Coming Right Along" could temporarily deny these threats. Institutionalized values may not correspond to reality, but neither are they externally imposed. Perfectionism began as a naive reaction to technological advance. Even as social conditions belied perfectionist ideals, the optimistic rhetoric remained; partly from habit, but also because rhetorical optimism became more necessary as it became more spurious. A hopeful song could provide increasingly vital escape from hopelessness.

Daniel Webster of Massachusetts proclaimed: "It is an extraordinary era in which we live. It is altogether new...The progress of our age has outstripped human belief."[39] Henry Thoreau, also of Massachusetts, disdained the same era as "this restless, nervous, bustling, trivial Nineteenth Century."[40] The Hutchinson Family's songs mediated between these poles of popular opinion. In the disintegrating America of the eighteen forties and fifties, the Hutchinsons offered "a momentary stay against confusion" to those who shared their music.

Notes

[1] John W. Hutchinson, *Story of the Hutchinsons* (Boston: Lee and Shepard, 1896), I, 46.

[2] Thomas W. Higginson, *Margaret Fuller Ossoli* (Boston: Houghton Mifflin, 1892), pp. 176-77.

[3] John Hutchinson, II, 296.

[4] Ralph Waldo Emerson, "The American Scholar," in *The Selected Writings of Ralph Waldo Emerson*, ed. Brooks Atkinson (New York: Modern Library, 1950), p.62.

[5] Including the Rainers. One minstrel troupe presented "We Come from the Hills, burlesque a la Rainer family," H. Wiley Hitchcock, *Music in the United States: A Historical Introduction* (Englewood Cliffs, N.J.: Prentice-Hall, 1974), p. 108.

[6] John Hutchinson, I, 46.

[7] Asa B. Hutchinson, *Book of Words of the Hutchinson Family, to which is added The Book of Brothers* (Boston: J.S. Potter, 1855), pp. 5, 7.

[8] John Hutchinson, I. 35.

[9] Emerson, pp. 45, 61.

[10] James Russell Lowell, "Thoreau," in *Literary Criticism of James Russell Lowell*, ed. Herbert F. Smith (Lincoln, Neb.: Univ. of Nebraska Press, 1969), p. 218.

[11] Jesse Hutchinson's last appearance was one year post mortem, at a seance where his spirit was reportedly evoked (Philip D. Jordan, *Singin' Yankee* [Minneapolis: Univ. of Minn. Press. 1946], p. 189).

[12] Jordan, pp. 167, 237.

[13] Gilbert Chase, *America's Music* (New York: McGraw-Hill, 1966), p. 175.

[14] Nicholas E. Tawa, "The Performance of Parlor Songs in America, 1790-1860," *Yearbook for Inter-American Musical Research, II* (1975), 73.

[15] *Complete Catalogue of Sheet Music and Musical Works Published by the Board of Music Trade of the United States, 1870* (Rpt. DaCapo, New York, 1973, ed. Dena J. Epstein).

[16] Hans Nathan, "The Career of a Revival Hymn," *Southern Folklore Quarterly*, 7 (1943), 98-99.

[17] John Hutchinson, I, 63-64. Judson sang melody, John tenor, Abby contralto, and Asa bass.

[18] Asa B. Hutchinson, *The Granite Songster* (Boston: Hutchinson, 1847), p. 64.

[19] Edward Everett, "Fourth of July at Lowell," in *The Nature of Jacksonian America*, ed. Douglas T. Miller (New York: Wiley, 1972), p. 30.

[20] Leo Marx, *The Machine in the Garden: Technology and the Pastoral Ideal* (New York: Oxford, 1976), p. 226.

[21] Herman Melville, *Moby Dick* (New York: Norton, 1970), p. 354.

[22] Alexis De Tocquerville, *Democracy in America* (New York: Vintage, 1945), II, 145.

[23] Marx, p. 226.

[24] Robert Frost, "The Figure a Poem Makes," *Collected Poems of Robert Frost* (Garden City, N.Y.: Garden City, 1942), n.p.

[25] Alan Lomax, "Folk Song Style," *American Anthropologist*, 61. (1959), p. 929.

[26] Jordan, pp. 251-2.

[27] Roger Elbourne, "A Mirror of Man? Traditional Music as a Reflection of Society," *Journal of American Folklore*, 89 (1976), 464.

[28] New York, Firth & Hall, 1843.

[29] Barbara Welter, "The Cult of the True Womanhood," *The American Family in*

Social-Historical Perspectives, ed. Michael Gordon (New York: St. Martin's Press, 1973), pp. 224-250.

[30]Ann Firor Scott, The Southern Lady: From Pedestal to Politics 1830-1930 (Chicago: Univ. of Chicago Press, 1970), n.p.

[31]Gerda Lerner, "The Lady and the Mill Girl: Changes in the Status of Women in the Age of Jackson," Mid-Continent American Studies (Spring 1969), pp. 5-15.

[32]John Hutchinson, I, 139.

[33]Tawa, p. 70.

[34]New York, Firth & Hall, 1843.

[35]John Hutchinson, II, 305.

[36]Jordan, p. 116.

[37]Book of Words of the Hutchinson Family (Boston: J.S. Potter, 1855), pp. 19-20.

[38]John Hutchinson, I, 84.

[39]Marx, p. 214.

[40]Henry D. Thoreau, Walden and Other Writings, ed. Brooks Atkinson (New York: Modern Library, 1950), p. 293.

Minstrelsy And Popular Culture

Orrin Clayton Suthern, II

The transplanted African, during the course of his search for survival in the new world, produced the Spiritual, Blues, Gospel Song, Ragtime, and Jazz. Frequently overlooked is the contribution which the Negro made during the extent of slavery and after Emancipation in spite of the attempt of white show people to rob the Negro of the new spawned art form. American lyric theater begins with minstrelsy which was black in its inception.

The original minstrel was a plantation clown, with music as one of his tricks. "Every plantation had its talented band that could crack Negro jokes and sing and dance to the accompaniment of the banjo and the 'bones', these being the actual ribs of a sheep or other small animal cut the proper length, scraped clean and bleached in the sun," writes Weldon Johnson. "When the planter wished to entertain his guests, he needed only to call his troupe of black minstrels." These bands became semi-professional traveling around a circuit, but chattel slavery set definite bonds to that.

White showmen, sensing entertainment value and economic gain, took over this inherently Negro form of fun-making, and its popularity spread. Rudi Blesh and Hariet Janis in *They All Played Ragtime*, observe: "The black-face minstrelsy, although a travesty, was still a sort of tribute to the real thing. From the 1840's it prepared the way for the acceptance of Negro music, though it defined in advance much of the nature and extent of the acceptance, very much as the obnoxious poll tax at the end of the last century began to define the political boundaries of poor Southern citizens of both races."

The minstrels, from start to finish, were compact with irony. The good natured imitation by whites became, in time, cruel ridicule which fostered vicious prejudice. The canny Negro, on the other hand, turned *his* version of the burnt cork divertissement into a subtle but devastating caricature of the white *ubermensch*, employing the black face like an African ceremonial mask, and through the whole thing, insinuated his way onto the white stage.

The white monopoly did not last long, even though Negro companies had to be managed and booked by white impresarios. The minstrel stage provided the stage training and theatrical experience which, at the time, could not have been provided from any other source. From this experience came the idea for

Reprinted with permission from the *Journal of Popular Culture*, Volume 4:3 (Winter 1971), pp. 658-73.

the flood of musical shows which gave prominence to many Negro song writers and performers.

Two shows which were very popular were Lew Johnson's "Plantation Minstrel Company" and the "Georgia Minstrels" which was founded in 1865 by George Hicks, a native Georgian. This group underwent several reorganizations until 1882 when Charles Frohman, of the noted theatrical family, began to manage the group as "Callenders Consolidated Minstrels." Under this name was assembled a group which included such famous names as W. C. Handy, the father of the blues; James Bland, song writer; and Sam Lucas whose full name was Sam Lucas Milady.

Lucas, born in Washington, Ohio, August 7, 1848, was actually the first writer of popular ballads, one of which, "Grandfather's Clock", enjoyed enormous popularity. Although words and music are credited to Henry Clay Work, Lucas sold the song to Work who published it as his own. As actor-comedian-composer for these minstrel shows, Lucas originated several hit tunes.

James Bland, who had joined Callender's Minstrels after having left his unfinished studies at Howard University, was born at Flushing, Long Island, in 1854. Bland's musical life parallels song writer Stephen Foster. Bland's life was as tragic as Foster's. Both were reckless and irresponsible troubadours. Neither was a Southerner. The music of both was pirated by others. Foster and Bland were the sweet minstrels responsible for the romantic southern legend and the sentimental ballad which for two generations dominated American song.

Callender's Minstrels enjoyed a tremendous vogue in the United States and abroad. James Bland was one of its brightest stars. Three songs placed Bland in the front rank of American song writers: "Oh Dem Golden Slippers", "In the Evening By The Moonlight", and "Carry Me Back to Ol' Virginny", the now-acknowledged state song of Virginia. (How many Virginians know that their beloved song was composed by a black?)

As a stage tradition, minstrelsy was, and remained, a caricature of Negro life and ways, so that when Negroes themselves came into stage minstrelsy, the mold was too set to be changed radically. However, they did bring expert ease on many instruments, besides the banjo, to add to the appeal and attraction of orthodox minstrelsy.

When, in 1843, a white quartet appeared in New York City as the "Virginia Minstrels," their tenor was a Dan Emmett who composed "Dixie" (the WASP national anthem.) *But...* "Dixie" was a Negro song before it was a Confederate song, since its first official title was "Dixie Land, and Ethiopean Walk Around", the "Walk Around" being a type of dance, Negro style.

Negroes did not appreciate either the texts or the sentiments contained in these songs. Indicative of this sense of opposition is this verse by a contemporary poet.

> "Carry me back to ol' Virginny
> Magnolia blossoms fill the air
> Carry me back to ol' Virginny

the *only way* you'll get me there."

Bland died in 1911 and is buried in an honored plot in Philadelphia. Thus while the infant lyric theater was abornin' and providing a spawning place for future Thespians, performers, and composers for the lyric stage, the free men of color were at it again. As far back as 1821 there were semi-professional groups engaged in dramatic activity. One such company was "The African Company."

James Weldon Johnson in his book "Black Manhattan" relates that, "the African company gave performances of 'Othello,' 'Richard the III' and other classic plays, interspersed with comic acts, at the African Grove, corner of Bleecker and Mercer Streets, in the rear of the One Mile Stone." The "One Mile Stone" refers to a stone which once stood at the corner of Broadway and Prince Street to mark the distance of one mile from City Hall. Later, the company becoming more prosperous, or more ambitious, hired the hotel next door to the Grove for their performances. The New York *Advocate* of October 27, 1821, had this to say: "The gentlemen of color announce another play at their Pantheon, on Monday evening. They have graciously made a partition at the back of the house for the accommodation of whites."

The same paper also discloses that because of the attendance of the whites, so much disorder resulted that the theater had to be closed.

Later Simon Snipe in a booklet entitled "Sports of New York," portrays a scene which could be found there. The theater was evidently open air; breezes were able to come through the crevices of the boards. Be that as it may, he found an orchestra composed of three players...a violin, a clarinet and a bass fiddle; that the audience was composed of white, black, copper-colored and light-brown, and that the play was *Othello*. A play bill cited by George C.D. Odell in "Annals of the New York Stage" gives evidence that the African Company was flourishing as late as 1823.

The prices of admission charged by the African Company were high considering the times and the clientele. Boxes were seventy-five cents ($.75) pit, fifty cents ($.50) and the gallery thirty-five and a half cents ($.35 1/2). At this later period there was *"Nota Bene"* attached to the advertisement to the effect that "Proper officers will attend to keep order."

One of the more noted players in the African Company was James Hewlett whose favorite roles were "Othello' and "Richard III."

Not far from this New York area, which was the center of Negro activity for the city, was established in 1787 the African Free School, later aided by grants from the Corporation of the City of New York.

Out of this school and its environment came one of the world's great tragedians—Ira Aldridge. His birthplace is given to at least three areas—Bel Air, Maryland; Senegal, Africa; and New York City. By now we have eliminated African site in favor of either Maryland, or New York City. The Encyclopedia Americana lists Baltimore, Md., as his birth place, while admitting a possible discrepancy; the date given is July 24, 1807. From his childhood the stage produced a tremendous attraction for him and he obtained a job at the Chatham theater where, behind scenes, he could watch the actors and observe delivery of their lines.

His first appearance on stage took place in the character of "Rolla"— the hero of Sheridan's "Pizarro," with an all-Negro cast at a private theater. However, his father interrupted this embryonic career and sent him to Scotland to further his education. After having matriculated at the University of Glasgow, he made several records for scholarship, won several prizes and a medal for Latin composition. But, the call of the boards was too much for him and away to London he went, where, not immediately, to be sure, he played the part of "Othello" at the Royalty theater in London. His rise to fame and stardom began. From the Royalty he went to the Coburg, where in addition to playing several roles he met a girl fan of his, and shortly married her. April 10, 1833, was an event of great import to Aldridge, for on this date he played "Othello" for the first time in the celebrated theater, Covent Garden. It was while playing the part of the Moor in Dublin (and this after some delay since the manager just couldn't quite see hiring a Negro for the role) that Aldridge came to the attention of Edmund Kean. Kean engaged him at once to play "Othello" to his "Iago" and the two men became great friends, touring both England and the continent together.

As his fame spread over the Continent he met and became friendly with Alexander Dumas the great French novelist, also a Negro.

It may be of interest to note that in the correspondence between Richard Wagner and Mathilde Wesendonck there appears a memorandum, "For Your Attention, Wednesday, 'Othello' with Ira Aldridge—Tickets should be booked well in advance—the top of the morning to you, signed R.W."

Finally in 1865 Aldridge returned to London—after France had bestowed upon him the order of Chevalier (remember the Chevalier de St. George)— to play again Shakespeare's "Moor." His "Desdemona" at the elite Haymarket Theatre was Madge Robertson later Mrs. Kendall. This was at the beginning of her great career and of this engagement, she wrote, "During the time I was there, Mr. Ira Aldridge was engaged to act. Mr. Aldridge was a man, who being black, always picked out the fairest woman he could, to play Desdemona with him—not because she was capable of acting the part, but because she had a fair head. One of the great bits of business that he used to do was where in one of the scenes he had to say, "Your hand, Desdemona." He made a very great point of opening his hand and making you place yours in it, and the audience used to see the contrast.

"He always made a point of it, and got a round of applause; how, I do not know. It always struck me that he had some species of—well, I will not say genius—because I dislike that word as used nowadays—but gleams of great intelligence. Although a genuine black, he was quite a preax chevalier in his manners to women."

But for all his fame, and glory America—the land of his birth never saw him in his greatness. He died in Lodz, Poland, in 1867 and was given a civic funeral.

Regretfully it must be said that Aldridge was not a product of the American theater because it was *minstrelsy* which paved the way for subsequent Negro actors and composers. And Negro minstrelsy was a much more varied form of entertainment than its white counterpart which, by the end of the century, had degenerated into a vicious garble of hatred and diatribe.

In 1890 the first successful departure from original Minstrelsy was launched by Sam T. Jack, who managed a burlesque circuit. He conceived the idea of putting on an All-Negro show, immediately different. It would glorify the Colored girl. Among the men whom Jack contacted was Sam Lucas (the Composer) and sixteen of the prettiest girls he could find who could sing and dance. It had none of the features of the plantation shows although, with the exception of the element of the girls, it kept the format of the minstrel show. The production entitled "Creole Show," opened in Boston in 1891, played in Chicago at Sam Jack's Opera House during the whole season of the World's Fair of that year. It played in one form or another for five years. In New York they played on Broadway's edge at the Atandard theater in Greely Square.

Meanwhile—during the success of the Creole Show, two white managers brought up from Louisville, Ky., a show called "South Before the War," which was popular in burlesque houses and played for a number of years.

Then John Isham of the staff of the "Creole Show" produced a show called the "Octoroons" very much on the order of "Creole Show." This (and this certainly has been true of every important Negro show since) was organized in New York. Although following the minstrel pattern, it was billed as a musical farce. It was separated into three parts with no connecting link. The first part had an opening chorus and a medley of songs by soloists with assistance from the girls; the second part was a specialty section with a very tenous line of connection, and the third part closed with a *cake-walk*, a military drill, and chorus-marching finale. All the scenes were reputedly laid in New York City. The "Octoroons" differed from the "Creole Show" in that the girls were not only chorus members, but some served as principals, it also played the burlesque houses.

In 1886 Isham changed his format in the production of "Oriental America." In this show, in addition to the specialties and the pretty girls, the final after-piece was a medley of *operatic* selections for which the finest singing talent available was obtained. It consisted of solos and choruses from "Faust," "Martha," "Rigoletto," "Carmen" and "Il Trovatore," and among its singers were James Rosemund Johnson (brother of James Weldon Johnson, whose quotations we have been using, and who was a young man studying singing in New York at the time), Sidney Woodward, the tenor from Boston and Inez Clough, by now well known on the legitimate stage. "Oriental America" differed from its predecessor in still another manner. It was the first show, all-Negro, to play Broadway proper. Debuting at Palmer's theater, later named Wallack's, this was the first show to break away from the burlesque houses.

It will be necessary to pass over many of the shows which enjoyed popularity in this period, but we can mention some of the contributors. Among the earliest of earliest of the comedians was Ernest Hogan; composer, singer and actor, who, with Black Patti's Troubadours, alone among the Negro shows was able to tour successfully in the South. Bob Cole collaborated with J. Rosamund Johnson to write *Red Moon* and the *Shoo Fly Regiment*—which were the first true Negro operettas.

In the summer of 1898, another great step forward. From the text of Paul Laurence Dunbar and the music of Will Marion Cook came *Clorindy—The Origin of the Cake Walk.* Cook, European trained under the famed Joachim, demonstrated to the musical world the possibilities of the new syncopated music, called "Rag-time." George Lederer produced the play at the Casino Roof Garden, where it ran all summer. Once again Ernest Hogan was the featured comedian in this play.

Appearing for an audition for the lead role in "Clorindy" was Abbie Mitchell, then a young girl from Baltimore. At fourteen she took over the lead and later married the composer. For Abbie Mitchell this was the beginning of a career which included vocal study with Jean de Reske, two command performances for two kings of England, sang the title roles in "Carmen" and "La Traviata" (in Europe, of course-since she was born too early for that possibility in these United States). Returning home she appeared in concerts and Negro shows such as "Porgy and Bess," and "In Abraham's Bosom," and still later as "Abbie" in "The Little Foxes" in the production which starred Tallulah Bankhead. On Broadway she cheerfully accepted parts as a maid, for "she was." she said, "not built for anything else." She felt that a colored actor should accept any part that he could do well, so long as it called for creative talent, and argued that doctrinaire opposition to unflattering stereotypes would only exclude the Negro from the theater altogether. Succeeding years brought her radio network engagements, but the widening opportunities for colored actors on the stage and later on television, passed her by, because she was too fair to be plausible as a Negro.

At this point I will digress from the pure lyric theater discussion to say a word about a kind of music which the musical theater was using to great advantage and popularity.

As we have mentioned already the sketch "Clorindy" was subtitled—*The Origin of the Cake Walk.* The Cake Walk was one of the first Negro dances to sweep the country. Most of the popular minstrel shows featured the Cake Walk at some part of the program. Nor was the craze confined to this country. One of the first Edition Films—vintage 1903—featured the Cake Walk in the production of "Uncle Tom's Cabin." The music of the Cake Walk was "Rag-time." And what was Ragtime? It was a different kind of music for a different kind of time.

As Blesh and Janis put it in their very fine volume, *They All Played Ragtime,* "the land was galled and restless with riots, hunger marches, and threats of revolution; the people over ready to smile again and to dance the Cake Walk. It was all like a fresh start; no past associations, good or bad, clung to the new music; there was not a tear in ragtime, and no irony, no malice, bitterness or regret hid in its laughter. It was a song that came from the people—and then got lost." Today we are just beginning to evaluate this tremendous pile of rejected music. Ragtime as devised by the classic masters Scott Joplin, Tom Turpin, James Scott, and Joseph Lamb is more than just syncopation music—for syncopation has been with us since the early days of counterpoint and polyphony. The really unique thing about ragtime when it appeared, was the way the pianist opposed syncopations, or accents on the weak and normally unaccented second and third beats of the measure in his right hand, against a precise and regularly accented bass. This leads to a tremendous drive and infectious excitement which is a common-place in the music of Negro Africa and the Americas, and is used by the Afro-American to transform all other music. It is, at its best, an improvised art.

Opera Magazine in 1916 observed, "Ragtime has carried the complexity of the rhythmic subdivision of the measure to a point never before reached in the history of music." And Blesh and Janis comment with my blessing, "The treatment of folk music—both white and Negro—according to the African rhythm principles (for in the African drum corps one or more drums play in an off-beat rhythm over the regular meter of another drum) produced a completely new sort of music. It also produced a music truly American."

Ragtime rhythm characterizes all Negro singing, but classical ragtime is instrumental music for the piano and generally when one refers to ragtime one refers to music composed for this instrument.

Negro theatrical history was made again in 1902 with the arrival on Broadway of Bert Williams and George Walker, who came out of the West singing one of the catchiest tunes of the day, "Dora Deen." Walker was the dancer and stooge, and Williams the straight man and singer. Edith Isaac in her book, "The Negro in the American Theater" records that, "every trick of voice, inflection and gesture that Williams used in the theatre was learned by careful study and observation." He was, by nature, a tall straight handsome man with no trace in *his* English of the vernacular of his homeland. Yet, in the theatre, playing in the blackface, Williams was the slouching, lazy, careless, unlucky Negro for whom everything went wrong. His dialect was so perfect that it became the archetype for lowgrade Negro speech much as Amos and Andy used it a few years ago. Walker was the dandy, the sporting Negro, dressed a little too high, spending generously whatever he was able to borrow or filch from the "Jonah Man's" hard money.

The play was *In Dahomey* and opened in the very heart of the theater district at the New York Theatre in Times Square. Although arriving on Broadway was a triumph, it is its later history which makes it remarkable. In 1903 the show as taken to London where it ran for 7 months at the Shaftes Theater, afterwards touring the provinces. At the close of the first month of performance a royal command for performance at Buckingham Palace on the occasion of the 9th birthday of the Prince of Wales sealed approval. The Cake Walk became a social fad in England and France.

Two more plays were "In Abbysinia"—played at the Majestic Theater in Columbus Circle New York in 1906, and *Bandana Land* in 1907. Then George Walker died and Williams turned from the Negro stage to a new career in the Ziegfield Follies where he was an instantaneous hit. Some say he deserted his race but Charles Anderson and Booker Washington summed up his contribution.

Said Anderson, "His services to the race were great and multiple. He blazed a pathway from the minstrel house to the legitimate theatre. He unlocked the door, which had, for centuries, shut out colored performers from white shows. He lessened discrimination by conquering the prejudice of managers and producers. He overcame much of the hostility of the press against mixed casts and he reformed and refined the art, so called, of the white-black face comedians, by teaching them to substitute drollery and repose for roughness."

And Booker Washington understood, "Bert Williams has done more for the race than I have. He has smiled his way into people's hearts. I have been obliged to fight my way..."

That Negro singers were attempting to make inroads into the field of opera was proved by the final after-piece of the 1896 Isham production of "Oriental America" mentioned earlier. Twenty-four years earlier, the Colored Opera Co. of Washington, D.C., had presented Eichberg's "The Doctor of Alcantara" on Feb. 3rd and 4th, 1872, at Lincoln Hall. The company was composed of the musical director, Mr. John Esputo; Mrs. Agnes Gray Smallwood, soprano; Lena Miller, contralto; Henry Grant and Richard Tempkins, tenors; William T. Benjamin and George Jackson, baritones and Thomas Williams, basso profundo. The Washington Daily Chronicle reported as follows: "The full opera dresses scattered liberally throughout the audience reminded one not a little of the scene at a concert by Carlotta Patti or the Theodore Thomas orchestra. Quite a third of the audience was composed of white ladies and gentlemen, largely attracted, perhaps, by the novelty of the affair; and among them were many representatives of the musical circles of the city... The choruses were effective. In dramatic ability there was little lacking and the singers were quite as natural as many who appear in German and French operas."

"The Doctor" was repeated at Agricultural (Horticultural) Hall in Philadelphia the following February and had two succeeding performances at the Ford Theater in Washington, D.C.

In the spring of 1876 Mrs. Nellie Brown Mitchell of Haverhill, Mass., produced through the Juvenile Operetta Co., an all-girl "Laila" in Boston which was repeated in the winter at the Haverhill City Hall.

Among American musicians of Afro-American descent, H. Lawrence Freeman, (Cleveland, Ohio, 1875) composer, had his opera "The Martyr" sung at the Deutches Theater in Denver, Color., in September of 1893. "The Martyr" was given in concert form at Carnegie Hall on September 21, 1947. Other operas by Freeman were: "The Tryst" sung in the Crescent Theater, N.Y.C., in May, 1909; "Valdo" produced in Weisgerbeer's Hall, Cleveland, Ohio, May 1906; The "Vendetta"—Lafayette Theater, Harlem, N.Y., November 2, 1923; "Voodoo" sung over station WGBS, N.Y.C., May 20, 1928, and produced in the Fifty-Second Street Theater, September 10, 1928.

Other operas not yet produced from the pen of H. Lawrence Freemanare "The Prophecy," "The Plantation," and "The Octoroon," which is not to be confused with "The Octoroons," a musical farce.

While H. Lawrence Freeman was the sole *American* Negro operatic composer, other non-American Negroes were producing operas in European and South American music circles.

In the same period prior to 1900 that sword wielding, swash-buckling Frenchman, the Chevalier de St. George had written five operas of varying lengths which were produced at the Comedie Italienne in Paris. "Ernestine" a three act comedy had its debut in 1777, followed by "Le Chase" in 1778. A single opera was completed in 1780—"L'Amour Anonyme." After a lapse of seven years the Chevalier returned to opera in 1787 with "La Fille Garcon" which was succeeded in 1788 by "Le Marchand de Marrons."

Meantime in America, one of the early New Orleans composers, Edmund Dede, who died in 1903, had written an opera entitled "Sultan D' Ispahn," but there is no record that this opera was ever performed.

The brilliant Brazilian composer, Antonio Carlos Gomez, devoted most of his genius to opera. On March 19, 1870, his "Il Guarany" was heard at La Covent Garden in London. This opera was produced in the United States by the Italian Opera company in November of 1884 at the Star Theater in New York City. "Il Guarany" was also sung in Moscow in 1879 on February 17th. Other operas from this talented pen were "Fosca" at La Scala, Milan, February 16, 1873; "Salvator Rosa" at the Carlo Felice Teatro, Genoa, Italy. This was repeated in the Fall of what year at La Scala. In addition "La Schiavo" was heard in Rio de Janeiro on the 29th of September in 1889, and "Condor" played Milan in 1891.

Meanwhile Luranah, the talented daughter of Ira Aldridge, the distinguished actor, made her debut as a leading contralto at the Bayreuth Festival in 1896. Her success here was continued at Convent Garden in London. She, thus, was the first Negro opera singer to win acclaim in Europe.

Although "Clorindy-the Origin of the Cake Walk" would not be in operatic caliber, its production in 1898 with music by Will Marion Cook was a great step forward for the Negro theater, and the Negro *in* theater. Cook was the first competent Negro composer to recognize the potential of the Negro idiomsyncopated music. He was the first to use the potential lyrics that were provided by Paul Laurence Dunbar, the noted Negro poet.

May 11, 1903 marked the first of all-Negro performances of non-Negro operas. Verdi's "Aida" was sung by an all-Negro cast which included such competent artists as Mme. Estelle Pinckney Clough as "Aida"; George Ruffin as "Amonasro" and Theodore Drury as "Rhadames." The latter, according to James Weldon Johnson's account of the first decade of the 1900's, had formed the Theodore Drury Opera Company and annually performed grand operas such as "Carmen," "Faust," and "Aida" at the Lexington Avenue Opera House in New York City.

In England and the British Empire Negroes were making a contribution. The distinguished composer, Samuel Coleridge-Taylor had composed four works in the operatic vein. "Endymion's Dream" was presented at the Brighton Music Festival on April 2, 1910. But on both sides of the Atlantic it was obviously true that the elite black performer was not so well received as the popular one. The undaunted fled to Europe, while popular black culture flourished in America.

A glance at some of the most talented expatriates might be in order here. Florence Cole Talbert sang "Aida" in Milan (1928), and Lillian Evanti was successful throughout Europe. When she returned to America she sang at the White House for President and Mrs. Franklin Roosevelt. Katerina Yarboro was acclaimed in Italy, after which her reputation spread back to the United States. Thus with Jules Bledsoe, now an experienced baritone in his own right, on July 22, 1933, together they sang the title roles of "Aida" at the Chicago Civic Opera House. Again a success. Alfredo Salmaggi signed her for appearances with his company and later in 1933 at the Hippodrome Theater in New York City she appeared as "Aida"—the first Negro singer to be singed with an American Opera company. Tolbert, Evanti and Yarboro accomplished for the Negro opera singer what Marian Anderson, Roland Hayes and Paul Robeson had done for the Negro concert singer. They paved the road in Europe and pushed the door open in the United States, if only a crack, for the youngsters who were treading closely on their heels.

Amidst the adulation being accorded Negro operatic performers one Negro composer created an opera in the early days of the thirties. The opera "Tom-Tom" was presented by the Summer Grand Opera of Cleveland, Ohio, in 1932. Its composer was Shirley Graham, the first female composer of Opera. The leading role was assigned to Jules Bledsoe, who by now had made quite a reputation for himself in singing roles on Broadway and radio. He was, for years, identified with the song "Ol' Man River".

One year later in 1934 Edward Matthews, baritone, who had been concertizing widely, was given the part of "St. Ignatius" in Virgil Thomson's unique opera "Four Saints in Three Acts" when it premiered in New York City.

It remained for George Gershwin to complete the music for the folk-opera "Porgy and Bess" which proved the highpoint in Negro artistic participation for the decade. The original cast was really "Star-Studded" employing such singers as Todd Duncan, who had retired to teaching at Howard University; Anne Wiggins Brown, soprano of Baltimore; Ruby Elzy, soprano, who had already made a name for herself concertizing and on Broadway; Abbie Mitchell, soprano, who held a European reputation in both music and the drama; Eddie Matthews, baritone; and James Rosamund Johnson already well regarded the lyric theater. "Porgy and Bess" was produced under the aegis of the Theater Guild and ran for 124 performances. In 1942 it was revived and ran for 286 performances. It was again produced in 1953, after a European tour under the auspices of the State Department, for a long run.

In the forties, two All-Negro companies were active in opera production. They were the National Negro Opera Company formed by Marty Cardwell Dawson, then of Pittsburg, Pa., and the Dra-Mu Opera company assembled by Raymond Smith of Philadelphia. Pennsylvania.

At the annual meeting of the National Association of Negro Musicians in August of 1941, the Dawson National Negro Opera Company sang Aida at the Syria Mosque in Pittsburg, Pa. and the following August of 1942 presented Lillian Evanti as "Violetta" in their production of "Traviata", at the Watergate in Washington, D.C.

Clarence Cameron White, the distinguished violinist and composer, in 1930 won a $3,000.00 fellowship from the Rosenwald Fund of Chicago for creative work. White chose to use the grant to enable him to write an opera based on the life of the Haitian hero Dessalines. John Matheus, then Professor of Romance languages at West Virginia State University wrote the Libretto. In November of 1932 the opera "Ouanga" was given a concert performance in Chicago, Illinois and the American Opera Society awarded White the David Bispham Medal. After a second concert performance at the New School of Social Research in New York City, the Dra-Mu Opera Company of Philadelphia, Pa. produced "Ouanga" in the fall of 1950 at the Academy of Music with Henry Elkan conducting.

The tradition of the Black man's contribution to popular culture, rich in the past, gets richer and richer in the present. The story presented here is not complete in the contemporary scene. But the trend is clear. And no story which is every day growing can ever be finished.

The Tin Pan Alley Years
(1890-1950)

Introduction
The Tin Pan Alley Years
(1890-1950)

Tin Pan Alley. Along with Hollywood it is one of the most monolithic institutions in all of American culture. It symbolizes not only a type of music produced between 1880 and 1950, but also a style of promotion and production of popular music. It produced in the works of people such as George Gershwin, Jerome Kern, Cole Porter, Richard Rodgers (with Lorenz Hart and Oscar Hammerstein II), Arthur Schwartz and Howard Dietz, Harold Arlen, and Irving Berlin some of the country's finest music—music which serves even to this day as a benchmark for popular songwriting throughout the world. It dictated America's musical diet for nearly 70 years, and its influence can still be felt in advertising, movies, radio and any other place where music is produced or used.

Before there was Tin Pan Alley, however, there was Union Square, a section of New York to which music publishers steadily flocked in the 1880's from locations as far-flung as Boston and Detroit. Publishers such as M. Witmark and Sons, Charles K. Harris, Shapiro-Bernstein, Leo Feist, T.B. Harms, and Jerome Remick all set up shop near the vaudeville and burlesque houses and other prime locations for live musical entertainment. There, in the best monopolistic fashion, they hired composers to write songs with titles ripped from the daily news and which tugged at the heart. They then printed those songs, and plugged them (the practice of getting a performer or someone else of influence in the entertainment industry to hear and then perform the song), distributed them to stores where someone would plug them for the average consumer. In the process, according to Charles Hamm,"...[they] did not draw on traditional music—[they] created traditional music."[1]

By 1900 the publishers, following the inexorable move of theatres and live entertainment uptown, found themselves located securely on a single block on 28th Street between Broadway and 5th Avenue, an area which would come to be called Tin Pan Alley. A newspaperman and sometime lyricist Monroe Rosenfeld gave the street its name, and little did he know when he coined it that it would be fraught with so much meaning in our culture. Ironically, the Alleymen did not see themselves as designing works for posterity; like much everything else in the burgeoning and rapidly changing culture of the turn-of-the century, the product served an immediate need and was sure to be replaced by something else in a couple of months time. Consequently, the Alleymen

87

were expected to respond on a second's notice and in musical terms to the prevailing trend, the catastrophe, the joke, the romantic fad, the historical moment. Their response, furthermore, had to engage the fancy and emotions of millions of people.

Sales of sheet music was the bottom line. People had to buy sheet music to make a song a success. This may seem like an impossibility today, but one must remember that instead of boom boxes and stereos, the turn-of-the-century American had the parlor piano, and, moreover, someone in the household more than likely could play. Consequently, during the height of its popularity "After the Ball" (1892) was earning Charles K. Harris $25,000 a week. (This with a mere $500 dollar "investment"—i.e., he paid singer J. Aldrich Libby to first perform the song in a show. Yes, today we call it payola!) With so much money at stake, the competition was fierce. Pluggers performed the songs in theatres, bars, in dime-stores and departments stores; pluggers called boomers stood outside publishing houses and theatres or rode around the city (especially the theatre district) in horse drawn wagons or flatbed trucks singing the current hits and distributing flyers. Audience desires, in turn, shaped creativity. Irving Berlin, in many ways the archetypal Tin Pan Alley songsmith, best epitomizes the Alleyman's attitude. When told by Max Wilk that one songwriter said a song he writes must please him first, Mr. Berlin responded: "All right, I'll tell you what I think about that. I write a song to please the public—and if the public doesn't like it in New Haven, I change it!"[2] Upon that simple philosophy an industry was founded and continues to this day—proof of which could be seen in a recent *Rolling Stone* article on Bon Jovi where the group quite unapologetically stated they gave the kids what they wanted.

In spite of the fact that Tin Pan Alley was so "market driven," it fostered a growing sophistication in popular songwriting. Between 1915 and 1945 names like Jerome Kern, George Gershwin, Cole Porter, Harold Arlen, Howard Dietz and Arthur Schwartz, Hoagy Carmichael, Irving Berlin, Richard Rodgers and Hart/Hammerstein, Vincent Youmans, and Duke Ellington became household words. They produced a body of music known for its melodic, harmonic, rhythmic and lyric sophistication. Where a Stephen Foster song from the 19th century or even an Irving Berlin song from c. 1911 might feature a simple harmonic progression of G-C-Em-D7, the opening progression of a Gerswhin song might look like this, from "Embraceable You" (1930): G-C#dim-D7-D[add9]-Fm6-D7. One sees in that movement from a G major chord to the more distant C# diminished chord as well as those 7th and 9th chords, the influence of late nineteenth century classical harmony and theory. This is not to say that the Foster and Berlin songs are inferior, they are just built upon a simpler harmonic foundation. The Gershwin tune shows the influence of classical training on the songwriters of the later Tin Pan Alley years. And with the explosions of first ragtime and then jazz, the rhythmic language of the music also became more sophisticated. In the hands of these composers popular music reached a point that could occasion comments like that of Virgil Thomson's about Irving Berlin: "I don't know of five American 'art composers,' who can be compared as songwriters, for either technical skill or artistic responsibility, with Irving Berlin."[3] This is high praise from a tough, highly respected, "serious" composer; that Berlin was just one of a number of such endowed songwriters is testimony not only to the Alley's ability to launch talent but to the public's ability to recognize quality when they heard it. The music of the great composers clearly gives the lie to the idea that the "Mairzy Doats" type song was the standard product of the Tin Pan Alley years.

During the same time period (1890-1950) there was a corresponding information/entertainment explosion. More new media came into existence within a thirty year time period than had come into existence during the whole of the 19th century. In 1900 popular composers had at their disposal the media of Broadway and other live entertainment; by 1930 they had, in addition to the stage, the phonograph (remember the practice of recording popular song did not really start until around 1909), the radio, and movies (with special emphasis on the talkies—the first Academy Award winner for best picture in the sound era was *The Broadway Melody*). All these media, moreover, relied heavily upon the Alley for their product and, in turn, they also played important roles in shaping the music of Tin Pan Alley. For instance, both George Gershwin and Richard Rodgers committed themselves to careers as songwriters because when they heard Jerome Kern's "They Didn't Believe Me" in a 1914 show they became convinced one could write "good" music for the theatre. Another example of this is Fred Astaire's influence on the songwriters who wrote for his film musicals. Alec Wilder writes, "Every writer, in my opinion, was vitalized by Astaire and wrote in a manner they had never quite written in before: he brought out in them something a little better than their best....."[4] Consequently, in time, sheet music sales would be but a part of a larger complex of money making enterprises for the composers.

The essays in this section, befitting the time period, deal with a wide range of topics. We begin with Eugene Levy's essay on ragtime and the work of composer/performer James Weldon Johnson; in his essay Levy tackles not only the music itself but also the issue of ethnicity in the production of popular music. The essay, "Thou Witty," on the evolution of lyric writing between 1890 and 1940, attempts first, to deal with some of the major themes and myths of popular song during that period, and, second, with how styles of lyric writing changed in the 20's and 30's and what that meant for the future of popular song. John S. Otto and Augustus M. Burns' essay, " 'Welfare Store Blues'— Blues Recordings and the Great Depression," on the other hand, is a reminder that "musical subcultures" were making significant contributions to popular music during this era and in media besides publishing (which was the dominant force in the music industry until the advent of rock in the 1950's).

Russel Nye's essay on Paul Whiteman will deal with that famous and most popular of all 1920's band leader's place in American popular song. Whiteman, in a sense is symbolic of the whole shift in popular music from the early days of Tin Pan Alley. Drawing on jazz and classical musical styles, he produced a type of music and encouraged talent (i.e., George Gershwin, Ferde Grofe) who drew together those worlds and, in the process, helped redefine our notions of popular music. J. Fred McDonald deals with that rebellious child of the Whiteman generation: Swing. His essay perceptively concentrates on the relationship of the music to dance and the larger cultural issue of youthful rebellion. Tin Pan Alley surprisingly handled the nascent rebellious potential of ragtime, jazz, and swing quite handily; McDonald's essay will help us understand how that happened.

Timothy Donovan's essay on the landmark Rodgers and Hammerstein musical *Oklahoma!* (1943) relates that musical's enormous popularity to the currents and events of the war years. In a sense, *Oklahoma!* also signals Tin Pan Alley's final hurrah. *Oklahoma!*, you see, not only forever altered (and probably eliminated) a type of musical play which had been around since the earliest composers invaded Union Square, but it also produced a creative attitude among songwriters distinct from the early Alleymen's. The music of the "integrated" musical followed a different set of rules than those Charles K. Harris laid down at the turn-of-the-century; the song had to first fit the dramatic situation, and if it could not be played on *The Hit Parade* or crooned by Crosby or Sinatra, so be it. What mattered was the integrity of the play. Finally, Paul Hirsch's overview of the changing popular song will provide us with a transition into the Age of Rock.

Did the Alley finally lose touch with its audience and is that why rock was able to find one so readily? In 1945, with Broadway once again reasserting its hold on popular music, it probably did not appear so. Tin Pan Alley, however, was different in 1945 than it was in 1905. It was no longer just a street in New York where publishers set up shop. It was now something more, something bigger—it really wasn't even that strongly centered in New York on 28th street— it was an institution, a type of music and, more importantly, an attitude about the kind of music the average American wanted and should get. No longer did composers walk the street picking up fragments of conversations or appropriating headlines for song lines that spoke to the immediate needs of their audience. And never mind about those rhythmic hillbilly rumblings from the south and that raucous noise with the "backbeat" emanating from the inner cities. The term rock 'n' roll wasn't even known in 1945.

Oh what a difference a war and ten years would make.

Notes

[1]*Yesterdays*, p. 325.

[2]Max Wilk, *They're Playing Our Song* (New York: Atheneum, 1973), pp. 262-63.

[3]David Ewen, *Great Men of American Popular Song*, rev. and enlarged (Englewood Cliffs, NJ: Prentice-Hall, 1972, p. 113.

[4]*American Popular Song: The Great Innovators, 1900-1950* (New York: Oxford Univ. Press, 1972). p. 109.

References

Blesh, Rudi and Harriet Janis. *They All Played Ragtime.* 4th ed. New York: Oak Publications, 1971.

Burton, Jack. *The Blue Book of Tin Pan Alley.* Rev. ed. Watkins Glen: Century House, 1965. Mr. Burton has also compiled a *Blue Book of Hollywood Musicals* and a *Blue Book of Broadway Musicals.*

Engel, Lehman. *Their Words Are Music: The Great Theatre Lyricists and Their Lyrics.* New York: Crown Publishers, 1975.

Ewen, David. *The Life and Death of Tin Pan Alley: The Golden Age of American Popular Music.* New York: Funk and Wagnalls, 1964.

Gilbert, Douglas. *American Vaudeville: Its Life and Times.* New York: Dover Publications, 1940.

Goldberg, Isaac. *Tin Pan Alley: A Chronicle of American Popular Music.* New York: Frederick Ungar, 1930, 1961 rprt.

Green, Stanley. *The World of Musical Comedy.* 4th ed. rev. and enl. New York: DaCapo, 1980.

Kinkle, Roger D. *The Complete Encyclopedia of Popular Music and Jazz, 1900-1950.* 4 vols. New Rochelle, NY: Arlington House, 1974.

Pleasants, Henry. *The Great American Popular Singers.* New York: Simon and Schuster, 1974.

Schuller, Gunther. *Early Jazz: Its Roots and Development.* New York: Oxford Univ. Press, 1968.

Stearns, Marshall. *The Story of Jazz.* New York: Oxford Univ. Press, 1956, 1970.

Tirro, Frank. *Jazz: A History.* New York: W.W. Norton, 1977.

Wilder, Alex. *American Popular Song: The Great Innovators, 1900-1950.* New York: Oxford Univ. Press, 1972.

Wilk, Max. *They're Playing Our Song.* New York: Atheneum, 1973.

There are also numerous biographies of composers of the Tin Pan Alley years which might provide useful information and insights. David Ewen, for instance, has written biographies of Gershwin, Kern, Richard Rodgers, and Irving Berlin. Charles Schwartz has written probing biographies of Gershwin and Cole Porter, and Gerald Bordman has written about Kern and Vincent Youmans. Edward Jablonski has written superb books about Harold Arlen, the Gershwins and their times as well as a new biography of George Gershwin.

Ragtime and Race Pride: The Career of James Weldon Johnson

Eugene Levy

FEW AMERICAN INTELLECTUALS, Negro or "other," were as active in as wide a variety of fields as James Weldon Johnson (1871-1938). Broadway songwriter, Foreign Service Officer, poet, novelist, essayist, newspaper editor, a leader of the National Association for the Advancement of Colored People from 1916 to 1931, Johnson ended his career as Professor of Creative Literature at Fisk University. Though he was not as well known among white Americans as his co-workers in the N.A.A.C.P., W.E.B. DuBois, Johnson nevertheless made a considerable impact in the fields in which he was active, and at all times he reflected both the problems and opportunities which faced his generation of Negro-Americans.

In his writings, Johnson repeatedly urged his fellow Negroes to take pride in their racial identity. In his poem "Fifty Years," for example, Johnson wrote of how "A few black bondmen strewn along/the borders of our eastern coast,/ Now grown a race, ten million strong,/ An upward, onward, marching host."[1] Since he considered himself above all a man of letters, Johnson frequently pointed out that the American Negro's artistic contributions to American culture, particularly in music, provided ample justification for pride in being Negro.[2] Johnson was not unique in urging race pride. As August Meier recently noted, the concept of race pride has been a key theme in American Negro thought since the late nineteenth century.[3] Whatever else they might think of him, most Negro intellectuals would agree with Booker T. Washington's succinct injunction: "It is with a race as it is with an individual: it must respect itself if it would win the respect of others."[4]

Yet the reason for race pride was not always clear. Was it simply a *means* to unify the race so as eventually to achieve full assimilation into American life? Or was the group identity generated by race pride an *end* in itself—the goal toward which all Negroes ought to strive? Though intellectuals of Johnson's generation usually emphasized group solidarity and race pride as means, the possibility that these two concepts might be ends in themselves was sometimes explicit and frequently implicit in their writings. Few raised the question as

Reprinted with permission from the *Journal of Popular Culture*, Volume 1:4 (Spring 1968), pp. 357-70.

directly as James Baldwin did a few years ago when he asked, "Do I really *want* to be integrated into a burning house?"[5] Many of the earlier generation, however, showed the marks on their thought and action produced by an ambivalent attitude over the goal of the race once it had achieved group solidarity through race pride.

Johnson shared the ethnic ambivalence of his peers. Because of his background, his flexibility, and his creativity, however, he reflected this ambivalence in a unique manner, a manner which sheds considerable light on the entire question. His racial beliefs came out in a number of his poems, such as "Fifty Years" (1913), or the poems in *God's Trombones* (1919-1927), in his novel, *The Autobiography of an Ex-Colored Man* (1912), in many of his essays, and in his work in the N.A.A.C.P. But for the purposes of this paper I would like to explore this ambivalence as seen in a relatively little-known period of Johnson's life, but an important phase in the history of the American Negro—the period between 1900 and 1906, when he lived in New York and wrote lyrics for the ragtime songs composed by his brother Rosamond and a third partner, Bob Cole.

In terms of the average Southern Negro, Johnson was extremely well-off in the late 1890's. He had been brought up in Jacksonville, Florida, by educated parents, neither of whom had been slaves. They provided their sons a secure home and instilled in them respect for personal character, ethical behavior, and economic success, characteristics which formed the core of the American middle-class way of life. Johnson graduated from Atlanta University in 1894 and returned to his hometown as principal of Stanton Grammar School (colored). An ambitious young man, he started a daily newspaper aimed at the town's Negro community, but lack of support forced him to close down within six months. He studied law, passed the bar, but soon lost interest in the dull grind of legal practice. In fact there was little more a talented Negro could do in Jacksonville in 1900. As a school principal he was already on the top of the social ladder and pushing against the restraints a segregated society put on the ambitions of members of the "inferior" caste.[6]

In 1902, disgusted with the situation in Jacksonville, Johnson joined his brother Rosamond, a trained musician, in New York City. There he became a member of the songwriting team of Cole and Johnson Brothers.[7]

Johnson soon took on the role of an urbane New Yorker, a role to which he was well suited. A reporter for the *New York Age*, a Negro weekly, described him as a "suave and graceful" gentleman whose organizational ability was a key element in the team's success.[8] Johnson, however, never completely committed himself to show business, especially its seamier side. He was always a careful observer, but the values imbibed in his youth would not let him settle for what most Americans considered the morally questionable high life generated by Broadway's lights.

His lack of commitment to his new life, however, was a subtle affair. He was far from a recluse. James, Rosamond, and Bob Cole lived at the Hotel Marshall, then newly established in a large brownstone on West 53rd Street, a few blocks from the present-day Museum of Modern Art. After the turn of the century many of the upper-strata of the Negro theatrical group left the old Tenderloin District in the West 30's and moved to the 53rd Street neighborhood off Broadway. The Marshall soon became the principal meeting place for this increasingly successful group, and a popular spot for whites who wanted to see the latest in colored entertainment. The Marshall offered one of the first cabaret shows in the city and in this sense anticipated the Harlem cabarets so popular in the 1920's.[9]

The Broadway that Johnson worked on at the turn of the century was making a place for the Negro in person to match the place it had already made for the race in its musical idiom. With very few exceptions, the first Negroes to appear on the professional stage did so in minstrel shows and occasionally in performances of *Uncle Tom's Cabin*.[10] After the Civil War, all-Negro minstrel shows were formed, but such groups followed the accepted minstrel pattern even to the extent of donning the mask of burnt cork to become the state "darkies."[11] The 1890's were the era of the so-called "coon song" and its companion, the cakewalk. Ragtime, a musical style widely identified as Negro in origin, was well on its way to becoming an integral part of the nation's popular musical tradition.[12]

By the late nineties, there were four variety shows with Negro performers playing in New York and on the road: two groups known as the 'Octoroons,' the 'Oriental America' show, and the 'Black Patti Troubadours.' These groups usually played to white audiences and none of them broke completely with the Negro stereotypes they acquired from the contemporary American stage. Bob Cole, later Johnson's partner, wrote and acted in much of the Troubadours' show, generally considered the most finished of the groups. In the show's central skit, "At Jolly Cooney Island," Cole and the chorus sang such songs as "I'll Make dat Black Gal Mine," and "Black Four Hundred Ball."[13]

Whatever later generations, or even Johnson's generation, thought of these songs, they served a function at the time. Negroes could break into the musical world only by working within the white stereotypes of their race, much as they had to put on the traditional burnt cork to play in minstrel shows. In the sense that they gave Negroes a foothold on other than the lowest level of popular entertainment, these shows marked a step upward in terms of conventional American culture. The "refined woman," one reviewer wrote of the 'Octoroons' would find "nothing from first to last to shock her modesty."[14]

The last years of the century saw Negroes move into first-class vaudeville as well as Broadway musical comedy. Ernest Hogan, originally a minstrel, became a successful vaudeville comedian and songwriter; he wrote one of the most popular coon songs of the period, "All Coons Look Alike to Me." In 1897 the comedy team of Bert Williams and George Walker made an extremely successful New York appearance at Koster and Bial's, a first-class vaudeville house. Williams, as the shuffling, slow-witted, but extremely funny darky, and Walker, as the flashy-dressed colored sport, soon became one of the most popular comedy teams in show business.[15]

In 1898, a year before the Johnson brothers arrived in New York, Negroes finally made Broadway proper in other than a vaudeville act. The first to do it was Will Marion Cook, who was born in Washington, D.C., of middle-class, college-educated parents. When he showed musical ability, his parents saw that he received the best training available and when he was eighteen, he went to Berlin to continue his studies. When he returned to his native country, however, Cook turned to popular music. He saw considerable artistic value in ragtime and he soon realized that a Negro's chance of success in classical music was exceedingly slim.[16]

In 1897 Cook urged his friend, Paul Laurance Dunbar, to collaborate with him on a musical skit which emerged as *Clorindy, the Origin of the Cakewalk*. Cook rewrote Dunbar's lyrics extensively, but they were still thoroughly in the coon song tradition. The opening "strut song," for example, was "Hottes' Coon":

> Behold the hottes' coon
> Your eyes have lit on!
> Velvet ain't good enough
> For him to sit on
> When he walks down the street,
> Folks yell like sixty,
> Behold the hottes' coon in Dixie![17]

The combination of words and ragtime music made Cook's mother, an Oberlin graduate, exclaim, "Oh, Will! Will! I sent you all over the world to study and become a great musician, and you return such a nigger!"[18] Cook, however, did not think he was degrading himself for this was his only chance for success given the place of the Negro in American society. When Ernest Hogan, the Negro vaudeville star, strutted onto the roof garden stage of Broadway's Casino Theatre, his rendition of "Hottes' Coon" not only pleased Cook, but the crowd as well.[19]

The Johnson brothers arrived in New York just as coon songs and ragtime were becoming popular. Yet the lyrics James wrote for "Tolosa," the light opera they brought with them in hopes of finding a producer, clearly revealed his lack of contact with the latest musical trends. Unlike Cook's *Clorindy*, "Tolosa" had nothing to do with Negroes. Set on an imaginary Pacific isle, James concocted a stylized plot and lyrics involving a patent-medicine salesman, a native princess, and the crew of an American man-of-war.[20]

James' lyrics, like the plot, had strong overtones of W.S. Gilbert's conventional approach. The crew of the warship, for example, burst forth with:

> A man-of-war is a great big ship,
> That carries a great big gun;
> Her crew is a jolly set of boys,
> Who are ready for fight or fun.[21]

The style of Johnson's book and lyrics harkened back to a model, English comic opera, which was rapidly becoming outdated on the American musical stage. By 1899 comic opera, burlesque, the minstrel show, and the variety show were merging into a new type of production—the musical comedy. The new musical comedy, like Cook's *Clorindy*, emphasized vernacular types of songs, dances, and subject matter, as well as some attempt at a plot with consistent characterization.[22] Johnson's lyrics for "Tolosa," which was never produced, seem a formal exercise in the writing of a comic opera rather than the sometimes crude, but always spirited, lyrics of Dunbar and Cook in *Clorindy*.

Johnson soon renounced his anachronistic approach. Before the summer of 1899 was over James, Rosamond, and Bob Cole worked over one of Cole's old tunes to produce a dialect love song, "Louisiana Lize" which they sold for fifty dollars to May Irwin, a well-known white singer, who promptly inserted it into her current musical comedy.[23] From that time on, Cole and Johnson concentrated largely, though by no means exclusively, on songs with Negro themes.

Johnson was also conscious of the artistic significance of the Negro's role in music. In the same summer of 1899, Johnson read and preserved what was probably the first attempt to appreciate critically the new ragtime music—an appraisal by a white intellectual, the future novelist, Rupert Hughes.[24] Neither the charge of crude innovation nor equally crude copying, Hughes maintained, would discredit ragtime, the new "negro music." Both James and Rosamond might have felt that Hughes was addressing them personally when he wrote, "the negroes themselves will rise to the emergency and develop the vast potential significance of their own school."[25]

Their big break came in the fall of 1902. Marie Cahill heard one of their new songs, "Under the Bamboo Tree," and immediately put it in her new musical comedy. Alone on the stage, but assisted by a hidden chorus and orchestra, she sang "this pretty coon ballad in a manner both charming and captivating."[26] Evidently it was not Miss Cahill's rendition alone which was captivating, for by mid-1903 "Under the Bamboo Tree" had sold over 400,000 copies.[27] By 1903, wrote one out-of-town paper with a little exaggeration, almost every Broadway musical featured one of the songs of Cole and Johnson Brothers.[28] "Those ebony Offenbachs," as a New York critic dubbed them, had finally arrived.[29]

The trio's contemporary success rested firmly on their songs with Negro themes. They wrote a number of songs having nothing to do with Negroes, but such hits as "Under the Bamboo Tree," "The Congo Love Song," and "Nobody's Lookin' but de Owl and de Moon" built their reputation.[30] Between 1899 and 1903 they managed to write and publish almost thirty songs.[31] Many of these were sung by such leading white performers as Marie Cahill, May Irwin and Virginia Earle in one or another of their musical productions.[32] Even though one critic damned *The Belle of Bridgeport* as a "stupid farce," he had nothing but praise for the trio's "I Ain't Gwine Ter Work No Mo'" and the way Miss Irwin inimitably rendered its "droll bad darky philosophy."[33]

James was largely responsible for the lyrics.[34] Many of his lyrics, especially in the first few years, employed common Negro stereotypes. The Negro's proverbial laziness came out, for example, in "I Ain't Gwine Ter Work No Mo'." In another early song, "My Castle on the Nile" (1901), Johnson used the colored sport's desire for the high life: "In my castle on the River Nile I am gwinter live in style. Inlaid diamonds on de flo', a baboon butler at my do'." The trio wrote "I've Got Troubles of My Own" (1900), again for Miss Irwin, and their publishers labeled it "A Bit of Coon Philosophy."

In these songs Johnson used common coon song rhetoric, but admirers of the group expected more than the common run of lyrics. Nor were Cole and Johnson Brothers entirely happy. R.C. Simmons, a close friend, was quick to point out they knew they had "written words for some of their music that are not in keeping with the spirit of such music."[35] Years later, Rosamond echoed Simmons' comment; Rosamond recalled that when he and Bob Cole sang the title phrase from the song "All Coons Look Alike to Me," they substituted "boys" for "coons." The latter word, Rosamond wrote, always had a choking effect on their voices.[36]

Despite the crudity of some of their lyrics, the trio did not cater to the lowest level of contemporary musical taste. In the hands of Cole and Johnson Brothers coon song lyrics became noticeably more genteel. They immediately allied themselves with the movement within the musical comedy world away from Bowery bawdiness and toward well-mannered exuberance.

In 1903 Marie Cahill sang the trio's "Congo Love Song," and one reviewer correctly saw the song as part of the trend separating Broadway musicals from Tenderloin vaudeville.[37] "There business is not simply to grind out coon songs," a Jacksonville paper noted in analyzing the success of the hometown boys. "They have elevated that species of popular music by ridding it of obscene and vulgar doggerel...."[38] If Cole and Johnson were the "Musical Moses to lead the coon song into the Promised Land,"[39] they led not in the sense of being original musical creators of ragtime, but rather as popularizes fitting the songs to the more refined demands of middle-class America.

Such a role flowed naturally from Johnson's upbringing and education. He used several approaches in bringing a more refined quality into his lyrics. At times he chose carefully among the available stereotypes and avoided all those which pictured the Negro as a razor-swinging rowdy or as a semi-human buffoon. Rather, probably influenced by Dunbar's dialect poems, Johnson emphasized the fun-loving aspect of the American Negro stereotype. For instance in "Sambo and Dinah" (1904), he wrote of naive love:

> Their love you hear them stammer
> Without respect to grammar,
> For this is how these dusky lovers
> bill and coo....

In a second and more significant approach, Johnson retained the coon song format but broke away from Negro stereotypes. The lyrics he wrote for the trio's most successful songs, "Nobody's Looking' but de Owl and de Moon," "Under the Bamboo Tree," and "Congo Love Song," sought an empathy with the listener by emphasizing experiences and emotions common to the human race and not those supposedly limited to the black man. Johnson's lyrics were not especially original, but it was original for him to imply that both Negroes and whites experience the same romantic emotions in the same way. In this sense it is significant that one of their first songs written in this manner, "Nobody's Lookin' but de Owl and de Moon" had emblazoned on the cover not "a darky croon," or "a bit of coon philosophy," but "A Stirring American Song."

The universality and simplicity of their lyrics account in part, at least, for the enormous popularity of Cole and Johnson Brothers' most enduring song, "Under the Bamboo Tree," a ragtime hit in both Europe and America.[40] "Under the Bamboo Tree" was not a complicated song either in its music or lyrics. Musically, its theme was a variation in ragtime of the spiritual, "Nobody Knows de Trouble I See"—a fact which largely accounted for Bob Cole's name alone appearing on the published sheet music. At the time, Rosamond later wrote, he felt such musical antics beneath the dignity of a graduate of the Boston Conservatory of Music![41]

James' lyrics concerned a "maid of royal blood though dusky shade" who attracted the attention of an ardent "Zulu." The Zulu offered his love in this famous proposal:

> If you lak-a-me, I lak-a-you;
> And we lak-a-both the same,
> I lak-a-say, this very day,
> I lak-a-change your name;
> 'Cause I love-a-you and love-a-you true,
> And if you a-love-a-me,
> One live as two, two live as one,
> Under the bamboo tree.

Though the boy and girl were "Zulus," and the refrain was in dialect, the simple sweetness of the lyrics bore little resemblance to the average coon song. Rather, the expression of love was universal enough to be sung everywhere by young people around parlor pianos.

Another of their hits, "Congo Love Song," like "Under the Bamboo Tree," spoke of love, and not "nigger love." Johnson made this explicit in the last verse when he told how the young maid

> May have been perhaps a trifle cruder,
> Than girls on the Hudson or the Seine;
> Yet, though she was a little Zulu,
> She did what other artful maids do.......

By refining and universalizing the lyrics, Johnson and his partners succeeded in altering the lusty coon song and making it palatable to white middle-class audiences.

By 1903 Cole and Johnson Brothers had achieved considerable fame in an area dominated by whites. Perhaps the advance in the musical world of Negroes like Cole and Johnson, wrote one critic, "will some day settle their status in the community."[42] No one had ever expected such social significance from any white man on Tin Pan Alley.

The Negro's success on Broadway, Johnson felt, demonstrated not only the race's artistic ability, but also his ability to compete in the profession with the white man. Johnson's commercial success drew the attention of the most influential Negro in America, Booker T. Washington. The Tuskegean had been acquainted with Johnson as a school principal in Jacksonville, but it was as a professional songwriter that Washington asked him to speak at the 1904 meeting of his National Negro Business League. Johnson's topic, "The Composition of Music as a Business," fitted perfectly the practical success ethic Washington ceaselessly preached.[43]

After their rise to fame, the trio was several times asked their ultimate musical goal. Each time they responded in racial terms. Bob Cole spoke for them when he told a reporter that they were trying to retain the racial traits of Negro music while avoiding the vulgarity of the coon song.[44] Rosamond said much the same thing when he told of the group's efforts to "evolve a type of music that will have all that is distinctive in the old Negro music and yet which shall be sophisticated enough to appeal to the cultured musician."[45] In 1903 the trio began to work in *The Evolution of Ragtime,* a series of songs designed to show the development of Negro music. The first in the series they patterned after the spirituals while the second tried to capture the spirit of the minstrel show. The third tune illustrated secular folk music while "Lindy: A Love Song," was a ragtime song typical of Cole and Johnson Brothers.[46]

Yet there was an uncertainty in the minds of Cole and Johnson Brothers about the development of a specifically American Negro music. At the same time Bob Cole spoke of retaining the racial quality of Negro music he also predicted that ragtime would be swallowed up by Spanish music. "The syncopation," he explained, "is the same."[47] Whatever the similarity between the flamenco and ragtime, Cole's statement seemed to de-emphasize the racial aspect of the tradition within which he was supposedly working.

Johnson's reaction to ragtime showed a similar ambiguity. In 1905 a national magazine asked him to write an article on Negroes in contemporary music.[48] In the article Johnson gave his highest praise to those colored composers and performers whose music was *least* identifiably Negro. At the top of his list were Samuel Coleridge-Taylor and Harry T. Turleigh—"Negro" composers who made their reputation in conventional classical music. Following them were writers and performers of popular music: Williams and Walker, Ernest Hogan, and Cole and Johnson. He nowhere mentioned those Negroes who were creatively developing the ragtime style popularized by Cole and Johnson.

Composers like Scott Joplin, James Lamb, and Tom Turpin were well known among ragtime musicians, but their piano compositions were too complex and too difficult to compete in the market place with "Under the Bamboo Tree."[49]

A conflict between class identity and racial identity lay at the root of Johnson's praise for the conventional music of Coleridge-Taylor over the unconventional work of Scott Joplin. This conflict was not necessarily destructive or even incapable of resolution. To a large measure it illustrates Ralph Ellison's insight that the "dynamism of American life is as much a part of the American Negro's personality as it is of the white American's."[50] Johnson believed the acceptance by the white public of Negro music and musicians not only demonstrated the ability of the race but also encouraged race pride. Yet coupled with this belief was his lack of contact with lower-class Negro culture and its music, as well as his firm commitment to accepted American values, musical and otherwise. Like Bob Cole, he wanted to maintain the racial identity of Negro music and at the same time "refine" and "elevate" it, thus bringing it into conformity with acceptable middle-class musical and moral standards. When it came to a choice between ragtime and classical music, Johnson obviously preferred Coleridge-Taylor's mundane but successful "white" oratorios to Joplin's unconventional and largely unpopular "black" rags.

In 1901 Johnson wrote an essay in which he asked if Negroes could preserve a distinctive racial identity and still advance themselves in American society. His reply to this rhetorical question was no.[51] His own musical achievements seemed to point to an ultimate loss of racial identity. In the lyrics of the most popular Cole and Johnson songs the team succeeded in cutting away the largely obnoxious racial stereotypes of the coon song, but they could only replace them with the equally stereotyped, though essentially non-racial, emotions of Tin Pan Alley.

Despite his basic commitment to the conventional, Johnson was one of the few middle-class Negroes of the period to recognize the artistic and racial importance of Negro folk music *and* of ragtime.[52] In his novel, *The Autobiography of an Ex-Colored Man,* written between 1906 and 1909, he predicted Negroes would ultimately recognize such music as a treasured heritage of their American past.[53] Yet Johnson made it clear in the novel that spirituals and ragtime compositions were "lower forms of art."[54] The octoroon hero of *The Autobiography of an Ex-Colored Man* is proud of "Negro" music, and he goes into the rural South to study it among the Negro folk. Yet his purpose is not to build in the musical idiom of the folk, but to select from it and assimilate it into the European classical tradition.[55] Though *The Autobiography* was a work of fiction, the hero's goal for Negro folk music was the same as Johnson's goal for ragtime and for the American Negro: assimilation into the culture and people of his country.

Notes

[1]"Fifty Years" first appeared in the *New York Times,* January 1, 1913, in commemoration of the anniversary of the signing of the Emancipation Proclamation.

[2]For example see Johnson's commencement address at Hampton Institute, June 1923, printed in *The Southern Workman,* III (July, 1923), 433-434. See also his *The Book of American Negro Spirituals* (New York, 1925), pp. 49-50, and *Book of American Negro Poetry* (Revised Edition, New York, 1931), p. 10.

[3]August Meier, *Negro Thought in America, 1880-1915* (Ann Arbor, 1963), pp. 50-58, 277-278.

[4]Booker T. Washington, *The Future of the American Negro* (Boston, 1900), p. 104.

[5]James Baldwin, *The Fire Next Time* (New York, 1963), p. 108.

[6]See James Weldon Johnson, *Along This Way* (New York, 1933), pp. 3-146, for his own largely descriptive account of his youth and early manhood.

[7]The move to Broadway was not as sudden as it might seem. He had been spending each summer since 1899 in New York working on song lyrics.

[8]R.C. Simmons, "Afro-Americans in the Musical World," *New York Age,* November 25, 1904.

[9]*New York Sun,* January 18, 1903; *New York Age,* October 9, 1913; James Weldon Johnson, *Black Manhattan* (New York, 1930), pp. 118-120.

[10]Edith Issacs, *The Negro in the American Theatre* (New York, 1947), pp. 12-23; Tom Fletcher, *100 Years of the Negro in Show Business* (New York, 1954), pp. 2-10.

[11]Carl Wittke, *Tambo and Bones* (Durham, N.C., 1930), pp. 91-92; Johnson, *Black Manhattan,* pp. 89-90.

[12]Rudi Blesh and Harriet Janis, *They All Played Ragtime* (Revised Edition, New York, 1959), pp. 128-129.

[13]The description of these early Negro variety shows is based on a number of unidentified newspaper clippings in "Old Timers Book," Johnson XI, Johnson Papers, Yale University Library. Johnson obviously thought such songs were better forgotten, for he did not mention them when writing of these groups in *Black Manhattan,* pp. 96-101.   [14]Unidentified newspaper clipping in "Old Times Book," Johnson XI, Johnson Papers.

[15] *New York Clipper,* January 4, 1899; *New York Sun,* April 1, 1900; Isaacs, *The Negro in the American Theatre,* pp. 30-35.

[16]Richard Bardolph, *The Negro Vanguard* (New York, 1961), pp. 236-37.

[17]Will Marion Cook, "Clorindy, The Origin of the Cake-Walk," *Theatre Arts,* XXX (September, 1947), 64.

[18] *Ibid.,* pp. 61-62.

[19] *Ibid.,* p. 65. Most of the major Broadway theatres of the era had gardens and theatres on the roof. There patrons could dine and watch lighter entertainment after the main attraction ended downstairs. *New York Times,* June 13, 27, 1899.

[20]Several versions of the libretto are in Johnson Manuscripts I, Johnson Papers.

[21]These and the following selections are from the first version of "Tolosa," Act I, in the Johnson Papers.

[22]Cecil Smith, *Musical Comedy in America* (New York, 1950), pp. 21, 51.

[23]Unless otherwise noted, all Cole and Johnson Brothers' songs were published by the self-styled "House of Hits," the New York firm of Edward B. Marks and Company. The Johnson Papers contain copies of the published sheet music of the trio's songs. May Irwin started the coon song craze in 1896 with her rendition of the Mississippi

River roustabout song, "I'm Lookin' for de Bully." Blesh and Janis, *They All Played Ragtime,* p. 93. See also Johnson, *Along This Way,* p. 153.

[24]Rupert Hughes, "A Eulogy of Rag-Time," *Musical Record,* No. 447 (April 1, 1899), 157-159. A copy of the Hughes article is in Johnson Manuscripts II, Johnson Papers.

[25]*Ibid.,* p. 157.

[26]Unidentified newspaper clipping in second scrapbook, Johnson Manuscripts II, Johnson Papers.

[27]*New York Sun,* August 25, 1903; *New York Telegraph,* December 21, 1902.

[28]*Washington Post,* February 15, 1903.

[29]*New York Sun,* February 17, 1903.

[30]*New York Telegram,* February 1, 1902.

[31]Edward B. Marks to Johnson, June 27, 1930, Johnson Papers.

[32]*Along This Way,* pp. 177-191.

[33]*New York Times,* October 30, 1900. The cover of the sheet music of "I Ain't Gwine Ter Work No Mo' " is reproduced in Mark Sullivan, *Our Times* (6 volumes, New York, 1930), III, 368.

[34]Rosamond was very positive on this point in the comments he wrote on the copy of "Under the Bamboo Tree" in the Johnson Papers.

[35]R.C. Simmons, "Europe's Reception to Negro Talent," *Colored American Magazine,* IX (November, 1905), 639.

[36]See Rosamond's comment on the copy of "Tell Me Dusky Maiden" in the Johnson Papers. This song, a parody of the theme song of the renowned Floradora Sextet, incorporated lines from Ernest Hogan's "All Coons Look Alike to Me."

[37]Unidentified newspaper clipping in second scrapbook, Johnson Manuscripts II, Johnson Papers.

[38]*Jacksonville Metropolis,* May 4, 1904, clipping in Johnson Papers.

[39]Undated clipping from the *Cleveland Plain Dealer,* second scrapbook, Johnson Manuscripts II, Johnson Papers.

[40]*New York Telegram,* February 22, 1903; Johnson, *Along This Way,* pp. 210-214

[41]In the comments he wrote on the copy of "Under the Bamboo Tree" in the Johnson Papers, Rosamond described their song as an "inversion" of "Nobody Knows de Trouble I See," but it is actually a variation on the spiritual's theme.

[42]*Vanity Fair,* XXXII (October 31, 1903), 18.

[43]National Negro Business League, *Fifth Annual Report* (Pensacola, Florida, 1904), pp. 11, 25, 36. See also Booker Washington to Johnson (telegram), August 29, 1904, Johnson II, second scrapbook, Johnson Papers. Johnson delivered an address when he introduced Washington as the principal speaker at the Emancipation Day celebration in Jacksonville in 1898. See the *Tuskegee Student,* January 20, 1898, where Johnson's speech is reprinted.

[44]Unidentified newspaper clipping in second scrapbook, Johnson Manuscripts III, Johnson papers.

[45]An undated clipping from the *Cleveland Plain Dealer,* Johnson Manuscripts II, Johnson Papers.

[46]The four songs in *The Evolution of Ragtime* were published in the *Ladies Home Journal* (May, 1905), p. 29; (June, 1905), p. 31; (July, 1905), p. 23; (August, 1905), p. 19.

[47]Unidentified newspaper clipping, second scrapbook, Johnson Manuscripts II, Johnson Papers.

48 Johnson, "The Negro of To-Day in Music," *Charities*, XV (October 7, 1905), 58-59.

49 For an extensive social history of ragtime, see Blesh and Janis, *They All Played Ragtime*, esp. pp. 14-127. For an analysis of the music, see Guy Waterman, "Ragtime," in Nat Hentoff and Albert McCarthy (eds.), *Jazz* (New York, 1961), pp. 45-57.

50 Ralph Ellison, *Shadow and Act* (New York: Signet Books, 1966), p. 261.

51 Johnson, "Should the Negro Be Given an Education Different from that Given to the Whites?" in Daniel Culp (ed.), *Twentieth Century Negro Literature; or, A Cyclopedia of Thought on the Vital Topics Relating to the American Negro* (Naperville, Illinois, 1902), pp. 74-75.

52 For example, see W.E.B. DuBois' distaste for ragtime in *Souls of Black Folk* (Chicago, 1903), p. 256.

53 *The Autobiography of an Ex-Colored Man* (Boston, 1912), p. 178.

54 *Ibid.*, pp. 84-85. See also Johnson, *The Book of American Negro Poetry*, p. 17.

55 *The Autobiography*, pp. 139, 144-145.

"Thou Witty": The Evolution and Triumph Of Style In Lyric Writing, 1890-1950

Timothy E. Scheurer

In 1906, Mike Salter, proprietor of Pelham's Cafe in New York, was faced with a crisis. Down the street, Callahan's, a rival eatery, was doing smash business because resident pianist, Al Piantadosi, had penned a dialect number entitled "My Muriuccia Take a Steamboat," and, as Michael Freedland writes, "In an age when immigrants were nostalgic about their home countries and native born Americans joked about the newcomers, a song like 'My Muriuccia' quickly became a hit" (25). Not to be outdone at Pelham's, Mike asked Israel Baline to whip something together to help their trade. As Freedland reports, composer Nick Nicholoson supplied music and Baline "scribbled the words on his celluloid cuffs" and sang them the very same evening. Two days later the song was published as "Marie From Sunny Italy," with lyrics by I. Berlin; it was a natural typographic mistake, but he decided to keep the name—he liked the sound of it.

In marked contrast to this, almost forty years later Oscar Hammerstein would spend two solid weeks working on the lyric for the "Soliloquy" number for *Carousel*. [1] That song, granted, is longer than Berlin's "Marie," but during the thirties and forties it was not unusual for a lyricist to labor for days or at least hours on a lyric. Ira Gershwin, for instance, describes how he struggled for two days with the tune of "It Ain't Necessarily So" from *Porgy and Bess* and then goes on to say how he and George worked the whole song out in a week (149).

These anecdotes serve to underscore a change that took place in lyric writing between 1890 and 1950. During this time period, the activity of lyric writing in popular music evolved from a relatively perfunctory activity to one that demanded some education and an awareness of the subtleties of language and literary style if one were to be successful. In the early days of Tin Pan Alley the attitude was "seize the moment", to lose that moment meant to lose money. Writers like Berlin, of limited literary and musical education, however, could score hit after hit if they were able to grasp the formula that was current on the Alley. Things would never be so simple after the teens. As we trace the evolution of lyric writing from the earliest days of Tin Pan Alley to the rise of rock 'n' roll, it changes from being an art form dealing with themes as diverse and as dynamic as the culture it mirrored and served, to a form of narrower thematic range, but of increasingly greater sophistication. Lyricists steadily grew more concerned with how to use the resources of language to revitalize the craft of lyric writing itself, and, consequently, there was a change from being concerned with *what* is said to being concerned with *how* something is said.

My purpose is this essay is, first, to describe and account for the changes in lyric writing style between the years 1890-1950, and second, to survey some of the major themes in Tin Pan Alley music. This second point is particularly important in understanding the role of music in the culture in the early years of the twentieth century, which, in turn, is important to our understanding what motivated the Tin Pan Alley songsmith and how he worked.

I

The songwriter at the turn-of-the-century could draw on two traditions in American music when crafting his lyrics. On the one hand there was what I would call the poetic tradition; the poetic tradition in lyric writing is akin to what Wiley Hitchcock calls the cultivated tradition in music. Music of the poetic tradition relies on poetic texts, often from great authors, or, more simply, it apes figurative language and lofty expression in an attempt to sound poetic. The inspiration for this style, according to Lehman Engel, was Viennese operetta. The high regard in which Viennese operetta was held was then "presented in highfalutin, bastardized English" (*Words* 100). During the glory days of Tin Pan Alley, the poetic tradition was perpetuated predominantly in the lyrics of operetta. In the Victor Herbert and Herbert Blossom song, "When You're Away" (1914), we find the following lines: "Ever I hear you, in seeming,/Whisp'ring soft love-words to me!" Transpositions such as, "Ever I hear you, in seeming," forced alliterations, and archaisms like these from "My Hero" from *The Chocolate Soldier* (1909) are hallmarks of the style: "Come! Come! naught can efface you,/My arms are aching now to embrace you,/Thou art divine."

The other tradition the songwriter drew from was the colloquial or vernacular style. This was a style closer to common speech patterns; it was a style associated with the minstrel show, with comedy songs, and ultimately with the stage plays of Harrigan and Hart and later George M. Cohan. It is distinctly American in its diction and syntax. A song such as Joe Howard's "Hello! Ma Baby" (1899) is a good example when he writes: "Send me a kiss by wire,/Baby my heart's on fire!" The style is breezy, confident and, for the most part, vibrant with American speech accents and expressions. The colloquial style held sway on Tin Pan Alley and would continue to dominate lyric writing, in fact, until the second golden age of rock when some songwriters, in the wake of Bob Dylan's success, associated lyric writing with poetic expression.

What was the philosophy of the Alleyman? What factors shaped the subject and style of songwriting in the years from 1890 to the end of World War I? First, there were the media available to the songwriter; there was, of course, Broadway and its variety of shows and genres (i.e., vaudeville, burlesque, musical comedy, operetta, and revue), there was the phonograph, the parlor piano, restaurants, and dance halls. With the exception of the phonograph, there was an immediacy to the entertainment because it was either live or, as in the case of the parlor piano, personally involving. These media, moreover, in large part catered to the tastes of the middle class and the growing body of immigrants. Second, there was the economy, shaped largely by an abiding faith in an entreprenurial spirit rooted in the success stories, ala Horatio Alger, of the nineteenth century. There was money to be made in this country, and it seemed at the turn-of-the-century as though the country was being reborn in the world; the city pulsed with life and offered the Alleyman a million possibilities for songs. The Alley can be seen today as a microcosm of the American Myth of Success. As a result, people like Charles K. Harris almost magically tapped into the system and pulled out unheard of wealth. Harris' success with "planting" "After the Ball" (1892) in a show served as a beacon to other songwriters. His motto, while still in Milwaukee, was "songs written to order," and after his success with "After the Ball," he moved to New York and there found an even richer seedbed in which to sow his craft. In time he spelled out the philosophy behind his success more clearly. He told songwriters to read newspaper headlines and be aware of trends that were in vogue; he then went on to offer the following nuggets of wisdom:

Watch your competitor. Note their success and failures; analyze the cause of either and profit thereby. Take note of public demand.

Avoid slang and vulgarism; they never succeed.

Many-syllabled words and those containing hard consonants, wherever possible, must be avoided.

In writing lyrics be concise; get to your point quickly, and then make it as strong as possible.

Simplicity in melody is one of the great secrets of success.

Let your melody musically convey the character andsentiment of the lyrics. (Hamm, 290)

How influential Harris was as the apologist for pop music is hard to determine; his success utilizing these techniques, however, seems to have struck a chord as we shall see when we begin examining the lyrics of the period. As one looks over Harris' comments, moreover, one notices that not much is said about style. He argues for a straightforward, perhaps archetypally American, plain-speaking style; a style perfectly adapted to the vicissitudes of "writing on demand."

It was a style, moreover, which by its nature placed more emphasis on the subject matter itself. Not until the first age of rock (the years 1955-1960) will one find the almost staggering diversity of themes that we encounter in the music of the pre-World War I era. There seems to have been virtually no subject the songwriter did not broach from the sinking of the Titanic to Red Cross nurses. The lyrics, furthermore, are rich in popular iconography and they ring with an immediacy and contemporaneity unmatched until the age of rock. Songwriters relied upon simple narrative techniques, concrete images, and language devices one associates with oral tradition. The music is filled with more symbols, epithets, motifs, and other verbal formulae than the music of the 1920's through the 1950's. It is a language, moreover, which, in its ability to tap the vein of our most cherished and most deeply held beliefs and myths, to paraphrase D.H. Lawrence, sloughs off the skin of the old world and jumps, both feet together, into the American century.

II

As we survey the themes in popular music from 1890-1920 it is difficult to know where to begin. Irish songs, songs about women, inventions, tragedies, exotic themes, and famous people, are but just a few of the preoccupations of the turn-of-the-century songwriter. It is not until we reach the teens that some new themes such as Dixie or Hawaiian songs and, naturally, World War I, enter the vocabulary of the Tin Pan Alley tunesmith. To begin, however, it might be interesting to examine a stereotype: the Irish in pop song. Of all the nationalities that flocked to the shores of the East Coast during the late nineteenth century, none were celebrated or derided more in song than the Irish. Oh yes, there were songs about blacks and Yiddish songs—in fact Yiddish and Irish are often interchangeable (i.e., in a verse one will find the singer can choose Abie Cohen or Mickey Malone, etc.), but the Irish clearly are the most visible and, perhaps, risible nationality in popular song.

From "My Wild Irish Rose" and "Sweet Rosie O'Grady" of the 1890's to "If I Knock the 'L' Out of Kelly" in the teens, the Irish enjoy one of the most schizophrenic portrayals in all of the popular arts. They are at once combative and tough ("Divil the man can say a word agin me" from George M. Cohan's "Harrigan") and filled with good humor; they also venerate mother and the homeland itself. Irish songs provide us with a crucible to examine attitudes towards immigrants in America. As I suggested above, the Irish are, on the one hand, the butt of countless jokes like the one in "If I Knock the 'L' Out of Kelly (It Would Still be Kelly to Me)" (1916) by Sam Lewis and Joe Young and Bert Grant. In the chorus we find: "Sure a single 'L-Y',/Should look just the same to an Irishman's eye." The song concludes by saying that if one knocks the "L" out of Kelly, "Sure he'd knock the 'L' out of me." There is the combativeness, with a touch of Irish earthiness in the double-entendre, not to mention the hint of dullness in the portrayal of the Irishman.

For every humorous Irish song, however, there are probably ten which nostalgically refer to Ireland. We find references to a fair green land, to waters kissing its shores, to the fairies and wishing wells, and, most notably, to angels and heaven. Among famous lines are "In the lilt of Irish laughter/You can hear the angels sing," and the famous "A Little Bit of Heaven" (1914) states that the Angels found it and, "Shure it looked so sweet and fair,/They said suppose we leave it, for it looks so peaceful there." In another Chauncey Olcott favorite, "Ireland Must Be Heaven" (1916), we find that indeed Ireland must be heaven "for an angel came from there" and that angel is none other than mother—a conflation of two durable symbols. In these songs one finds a yearning for one's roots and for home and for values that were undergoing change in a bustling and mechanized new world. The humorous stereotype is typical of our attempts to deal with people whose habits, speech, and lifestyle seem to lie slightly outside the norm (whatever that may be), but there is also something haunting for all listeners in the images of a green land kissed by angels and filled with simple values like home, mother, and an easy pace of life. There were in the Irish tunes reminders for all of our immigrant heritage and a nostalgic yearning for home and roots.

As the Irish theme suggests, there is a solid conservative mindset or system of values that characterizes most lyric writing through all the decades of the "melody years." And there is, as I suggested above, a sort of unspoken mythology that informs the message of popular music. This is particularly true of songs that deal with nostalgia. Although American life was expanding and the city was becoming the locus of the pursuit of the American Dream, there seems to have been some ambivalence if not downright regret over the growth of cities and the expansion of the industrial base of the economy, a fact reflected quite poignantly in many popular tunes. Songs such as "On The Banks of the Wabash" (1897) by Paul Dresser, "I Want to Go Back to Michigan (Down on the Farm)" (1914) by Irving Berlin, "When You and I Were Young Maggie" (1910) by J.A. Butterfield, "Down By the Old Mill Stream" (1910) by Tell Taylor, and "Down Where the Swanee River Flows" (1916) by Charles McCarron, Charles S. Alberte and Albert Von Tilzer all celebrate the rural and, in fact, set it in opposition to the city in a classic city vs. the garden conflict.

One of the devices songwriters used to highlight this conflict was evocative imagery. Dresser's "On the Banks of the Wabash" vividly summons the images of the moonlight "fair" on the river, the smell of new mown hay, and the sight of candlelights gleaming though the sycamores; the song is, furthermore, laden with regret as the narrator tells of leaving his loved one behind and she, like his simple life in Indiana, is gone. Narrators use images of the city as a springboard for reminiscences of days gone by as well as a counterpoint for bucolic settings of their innocent (almost edenic) pasts. For instance, the narrator of "Down Where the Swanee River Flows" sees a scene of his home town "While in a ten-cent photoplay"; while the narrator of "When You and I Were Young Maggie" wanders on a hill and looks at the spot where "The Creek and the creaking old mill" have now been supplanted by "polish'd white mansions of stone." Finally, the narrator of "I Want to Go Back to Michigan" states he is a "lonesome soul" and adds, "You can keep your cabarets"; it seems he's lost his rosy cheeks, and "That's the reason I'd rather have the country life for mine." The images and symbols of the city convey generally negative values and are placed in counterpoint to the rustic and innocent. These lyrics, consequently, reveal a profound sense of loss in the passing of the small town or rural way of life; most people know Cobb and Edward's "School Days" (1907) from its chorus, but the verse addresses this very point when narrator asks:

> 'Member the meadow so green dear,
> So fragrant with clover and maize,
> Into new city lots and preferred business plots,

They've cut them since those days.

The rustic setting, moreover, becomes emblematic of yet another concept: broken down mills and pastures once filled with birds are victims of progress and the ineluctable march of time, but they are also the setting for young love or the meeting of the lovers. And although time and progress have ravaged the mill and landscape, love remains eternal. Tell Taylor writes in the verse of "Down By the Old Mill Stream", "The old oak tree has withered, and lies there on the ground;/While you and I are Sweethearts, the same as days of yore."

There is, however, no better symbol for the past, no spot that resonates more with nostalgic feelings or utopian fantasy than Dixie. Dixie songs luxuriate in evocative images of nature and home—they are, in fact, *de rigeur* for the type. The narrator of "I Miss That Mississippi Miss That Misses Me" (1918) by Sam Lewis and Joe Young and Pete Wendling notes that "yesterday is miles away" and then goes on to catalog the things that he misses, among which are: "willows weepin'"; "woodland harmonies"; "The buzzin' of bees in melody lane"; "golden corn that used to wave 'howdy-do' "; honeysuckle; "dad and mother"; and, finally, that "Mississippi Miss that misses me." Berlin and Snyder similarly tell us that they want to be in Dixie because it's, "Where the hens are doggone glad to lay/Scrambled eggs in new mown hay." It is, however, "Rock-a-bye Your Baby With a Dixie Melody" (1918) by Sam Lewis and Joe Young and composer Jean Schwartz that best sums up all that Dixie is. The narrator states at the outset, "Mammy mine/Your little rollin' stone rolled away," establishing the theme of the prodigal and the centrality of mom; the song evokes the past, and Dixie, in essence, becomes symbolic of the past through the evocation of childhood memories ("A million baby kisses I'll deliver"). Dixie songs and the nostalgic song, in general, draw on rustic imagery, memories of childhood, or young love, to paint a picture of a dream-like world in our collective past, a world which probably never really existed, but one which maybe should have and one that people yearned for on the eve of the "great war."

There, were, however, worlds which did exist at the turn-of-the century and which provided inspiration for songwriters. Songs dealing with exotic places—most notably in the Mediterranean—and songs dealing with Hawaii were very popular during the teens. With America assuming its place as a world power in the late 19th century, it is natural that the range of subjects should have extended beyond our shores. The exotic song stresses the sounds and imagery popularly associated with their respective locales as a backdrop for romance. The songs feature camels, temple bells, sand, and mystery. Caravans are highlighted in Irving Berlin's "Araby" (1915), in Bobby Jones' and Jack Stern's "Turkestan" (1919), and in the best of all, "Hindustan" (1918) by Oliver Wallace and Harold Weeks. In the case of exotic songs the theme of escape is also present as the narrator usually yearns to return to see the one he fell in love with. The lyric writing, however, can be at best pedestrian as these lines from "Hindustan" bear witness to:

> Camel trappings jingle,
> Harp strings sweetly tingle,
> With a sweet voice mingle,
> Underneath the stars;

But the songs presage the era of Elinor Glyn, the Sheik, and provide good doses of passionate romance in exotic locales. The Hawaiian songs, similarly, stress the escapist theme and the theme of yearning to return. But perhaps the most interesting aspect of the Hawaiian songs from this period, as distinct from later tunes, is the emphasis on the "language" of the isles. For some reason the expressions "Yacki" and "Wicki" or "Hicki" have some mysterious resonance. In the Albert Von Tilzer classic "Oh! How She Could Yacki Hacki Wicki Wacki Woo (That's Love in Honolu)" (1916) we find the narrator, after having been a rover, returning to the islands; why?: "She had a Hula, Hula, Hicki, Boola, Boola in her walk,/She had a Ukalele Wicki, Waili in her talk." The islands, as we can see, are a magical paradise and, perhaps more than anything else, a novelty. For instance, many of the songs have phonetic spellings for words such as Ukalele ("Bird of Paradise") and Waikiki ("Yaaka, Hula Hickey Dula [Hawaiian Love Song]" from 1916). The exotic song, more importantly, allows the songwriter to indulge his penchant for sensuousness and passion, a penchant, moreover, which was being flaunted more in the teens in the wake of changing sexual mores. Thus, the chance meeting with the mystery woman on the caravan or on the islands is suggestive of more passion, sex if you will—as seen in the Hula, boola in her walk—than audiences had been previously exposed to in traditional love songs.

As the U.S. moved from being a purely national power to an international one during the years 1890-1920, the times were fraught with change and dramatic, sweeping technological advances. This type of atmosphere, while exciting, can also be slightly unsettling. Consequently, the social and mechanistic flux was, on the one hand, responsible for the rash of songs dealing with nostalgia, but, on the other hand, the minute a new invention hit, the songwriter, in typical Alley fashion, attempted to immortalize it in song. Among the inventions that captured the songwriter's fancy were the automobile, the airplane, and the victrola. It is, indeed, interesting to observe the songwriter attempting to integrate the new invention, or new technology, into the rituals and patterns of daily life and to make the invention part of the status quo. For instance, in the Cobb and Edwards gem, "In My Merry Oldsmobile" (1905), the car is used for the purposes of courting; such is also the case with the airplane. In the Albert Von Tilzer and Junie McCree song, "Take Me Up With You Dearie" (1909), Molly Ryan tells her beau, Barney, that she wants to fly ("aeroplane riding she dared"); well, Barney gets the plane and, "Then smiling with joy, she said to her boy,/You're the captain and I am the crew." Interestingly enough, we find out during the flight that they "Sail around the moon for a quiet spoon/Just the parson you and I." Where the parson came from is unexplained, but it certainly validates the morality of the machine. The final image in the song is of the lovers going "up up up as two and then come down as one." Similarly, marital bliss is a central theme in "They Start the Victrola (And Go Dancing Around the Floor)" (1914) by Grant Clarke and Maurice Abrahams, where a jealous husband buys a victrola so, "They never have to roam." But we find there is an ulterior motive as well: "And after dancing she's all out of breath,/loves to take her and hug her to death." In short, the Victrola encourages some serious "spooning" and ensures the closeness of the couple by making the young lady more susceptible to the young man's advances. If, on the other hand, there was ever a threat or problem posed by the technology it was treated humorously. "He'd Have to Get Under—Get Out and Get Under To Fix Up His Automobile" (1913) by Grant Clarke and Maurice Abrahams is a good example. In this song the auto gets in the way of spooning: "A dozen times they'd start to hug and kiss/And then the darned old engine it would miss." In the second verse our protagonist, Johnny O'Connor, is asked by a millionaire to court his daughter; when Johnny gets ready to pop the question, " 'Twas the old story again," and the chorus of he'd have to "get under" is repeated. In many songs the threat of the machine is mitigated through humor. Social mores relating to love and marriage are, moreover, validated—sometimes by the machine itself. In general, inventions provided songwriters novel ways to deal with the age old ritual of courting and romance; in the 20's and 30's, as we shall see, songwriters look less to objects or new subjects to revitalize the old themes and more to the fresh ways of saying something about the old rituals.

Finally, popular trends, fads, tragedies, and other popular phenomenon offered songwriters new challenges during the years 1890 to 1920. I would like to look at a couple of examples of this subject matter. The first has to do with a tragedy which recently captured public interest: the sinking of the Titanic. One might assume that this tragedy would have provided the songwriter a golden opportunity to moralize about technological hubris, but such is not entirely the case. The two major Titanic songs use the element of contrast between the luxuriousness of ship and passengers and the sinking itself for the basic structure; for instance, in "Just As the Boat Went Down" (The First Titanic Song) (1912) by Marvin Lee the verse reads: "Thousands on board were so gay and bright/And all was serene it seemed"; in due time, however, he writes, "Gladness and cheers turned to sadness and tears." In "Just As the Ship Went Down" (1912) by Edith Maida Lessing and Bernie Adler and Sidney Gibbons the reportage element is strong:

> A jar, a crash, a fearful clash,
> A sound like awful thunder,
> The dying groan, the living moan
> As the splendid ship went under.

Interestingly enough, both songs end with the now believed to be apocryphal image of the remaining passengers singing and shipboard band playing "Nearer My God To Thee"; each song captures the tragedy at its dramatic peak and then emphasizes the final cry to the Almighty for mercy as the ship goes down. Therefore, one can infer from this that no matter how mighty the ship or resplendent the company, in the face of tragedy, God is our only hope.

When we look at popular events or phenomena, no event elicited a greater or more varied response than World War I. What a moment for the Tin Pan Alleyman; he could be sentimental, chauvinistic, patriotic, humorous, and, if he chose, profound—sometimes all in the same song. In great Tin Pan Alley tradition, the Kaiser and all of Germany are poked fun at, and songwriters even had a good time dealing with those who might be shirkers, like Sammy Simpson:

> If Sammy's sister sewed some shirts for
> soldiers by the box
> Why shouldn't Sammy sail the sea and
> sew the sailors sox

It is an alliterative nightmare for singer and critic alike, but one can bet it had the desired effect in 1918. On the serious side we discover a real iconography in World War I songs, two dominant ones of which are God and Mother. There is hardly a song which does not allude to the Almighty; oftentimes, as in the case of the great "Hello Central, Give Me No Man's Land" (1918) (note the title's debt to Charles K. Harris) by Sam Lewis, Joe Young and Jean Schwartz, the allusion is wrapped in a child's prayer for her daddy "over there." This song works with familiar images and symbols: no man's land, the child paddling off in the middle of the night to call Daddy on the phone, and, finally the bedtime prayer: "I want to know why mamma starts to weep,/ When I say, 'Now I lay me down to sleep.' " The lyric's ability to suggest death and loss, as well as enunciate an innocence seemingly from another time, make this one of the great sentimental ballads of the War years. An interesting variation on the prayer theme is "Joan of Arc They Are Calling You" (1917) by Alfred Bryan and Willie Weston and Jack Wells, in which the spirit of the saint and martyr of the Hundred Years War is called upon to "Come with the flame in your glance;/Through the Gates of Heaven, with your sword in hand." Perhaps the most interesting use of God in a World War I song, however, occurs in that paean to the Red Cross nurse, "The Rose of No Man's Land" (1918) by Jack Caddigan and James A. Brennan. The writers inform us in the verse that "God in his mercy sent her" and in the chorus state: "It's the one red rose the soldier knows,/It's the work of the Master's hand." In this song, as well as others, one senses God as a presence on the battlefield; he seems very much to be the God of the Old Testament, aloof, but intimately concerned with the fate of his chosen people, in this case the Americans.

The earthly spirit summoned in war songs, on the other hand, was mother. There were hundreds of good-byes to mother in song, and, as an icon, she came to represent what one fought for: home, family, security, love, and, perhaps, tradition. In the verse of "So long, Mother" (1917) by Raymond Egan, Gus Kahn, and Egbert Van Alstyne the authors quickly note that: "On ev'ry mother's boy/From Maine to dear old Dixie shoulder arms with joy." There is no regret as they go to fight for Mom. Her presence, furthermore, added a potent emotional edge to the songs; unlike Euripides's Trojan women who curse the war for taking their sons, the American mother is depicted sentimentally making the ultimate sacrifice during a difficult time. In the second verse of "So Long, Mother" the authors note that some sweetheart may not be true—but not mother, and "That's why I'm mighty glad/For you're the only sweetheart that I ever had." Thus for the Tin Pan Alley tunesmith mother is definitely not a figure of tragedy but the handmaiden of heroism.

World War I also signalled some changes in the sexual behavior of Americans and these changes are recorded in the songs. By war's end, it was a tacit assumption that the "boys" had probably dallied with the mademoiselles; in fact, the narrator of "How Ya Gonna Keep 'Em Down on the Farm" opines the fact that her boy will be discontented with life at home because he can't "parlez-vous with a cow." And the narrator of "My Barney Lies Over the Ocean (Just the Way He Lied to Me)" (1919) by the incomparable Joe Young and Sam Lewis and composer Bert Grant says that her Barney, "...went to help the women/And I think he's helped himself to two or three"; although she is angry, it must be remembered that all this anger is treated humorously, thereby mitigating the element of moral outrage. Women, too, were subject to the same romantic inclinations as men, but the songs carefully reinforce the double standard. In "Oh! Frenchy" (1918) by Sam Ehrlich and Con Conrad, a nurse, Rosie Green, meets Jean; in the chorus of the song she assures Frenchy that he "won my love with [his] bravery" so he can "March on, March on, with any girl" he sees. The rather looser morality one finds in the World War I song presages the sexual revolution that would occur during what Fitzgerald called "The Big Party": the 1920's. The World War I song, in fact, represents something of an apotheosis for American popular music and Tin Pan Alley in particular. With the rise of radio, talking pictures and more quality Broadway productions following in the wake of Jerome Kern's Princess Theatre shows (1915-1917), the war is, in many respects, the last full flowering of the Alley and a particular and distinctive style of American songwriting.

III

Beginning in the 1920's, the mid-20's to be more exact, we encounter a change in lyric writing. Charles Hamm writes, "But somehow, as America moved into the 1920's and the 30's, the expressive range of popular song narrowed. Texts began dealing almost exclusively with personal emotions, almost never with events outside of the person. An increasingly large percentage of the most popular songs was concerned with one aspect or another of romantic love" (376). This is not to say that songwriters completely turned their backs on popular phenomena; we find, for instance motion pictures providing inspiration for tunes like "That Night in Araby" (1926) by Billy Rose and Ted Snyder (complete with Valentino on the cover). The song, however, does little more than recycle the old cliches of the exotic songs of the teens; and, after the death of Valentino, there was the song "There's a New Star in Heaven

Tonight," whose title was borrowed handily in 1937 by Nat Simon and Dick Sanford for "There's A Platinum Star in Heaven Tonight," commemorating the death of Jean Harlow. Lindberg's child was lauded in "Baby Lindy," and war hero Eddie Rickenbacker received some notoriety via a song for the car named after him. "In My Rickenbacker Car (Cracker Jacker Rickenbacker)" (1923) by Leo Wood suggests that the car is cheaper to maintain than a woman: "She's not a bit expensive like most sweethearts"; and, we find, the car is also more reliable: "Always there when I need her all I do is feed her."

About the only socio-cultural phenomena to engage the interest of later songwriters were prohibition and World War II. The Depression, for its devastating effect on life in the 1930's, was not a popular subject in song. Aside from "We're in the Money" (1933) (an oblique reference at that) and "Brother Can You Spare a Dime" (1932) there are just not that many songs actually dealing with the Depression.[2] Prohibition, on the other hand, gave us such classics as "What'll We Do On Saturday Night (When The Town Goes Dry)", "Give Me the Good Old Days" ("I'll take the headache with the morning after"), and Irving Berlin's "You Cannot Make Your Shimmy Shake on Tea" (1919) and "I'll See You in C-U-B-A," all of which, moreover, deal with the "problem" humorously. World War II songs, on the other hand, were not so numerous as those dealing with The Great War.

We see then that Hamm's assessment is indeed true: subject matter had narrowed; however, the period from 1920 to 1950 is considered to be the golden age of American song. These are the years of the Gershwins, Kern, Porter, Rodgers and Hart/Hammerstein, Dietz and Schwartz, Arlen and Harburg, Kurt Weill, and Harold Rome; even in motion pictures, where a high premium was not placed on inventiveness and art, we find such fine songwriters as Ralph Rainger and Leo Robin, Mack Gordon and Harry Revel, Al Dubin and Harry Warren, while a young Frank Loesser, and the team of Cahn and Styne began their songwriting apprenticeships at the studios. The greatness we encounter in the works of these men is attributable to the fact that they are no longer primarily concerned with novelty outside the lyric itself; they are, instead, concerned with intrinsic elements in the lyric, on how the lyric sounds as much as what it says.

The change in style is due to two factors: first, there is a natural evolution that occurs in any art; practitioners build on the work of the masters and attempt to improve on them or take the art in new directions. Such a thing occurred, quite naturally, in lyric writing. Along with a general discontent with the nature of lyric writing, the new generation of songwriters were, on the whole, better educated and more sensitive to the artistic aspect of their craft.[3] Second, a major cause for the change is found in the media the songwriter wrote for; as one looks over the best work of the decades from 1920 to 1950, one will find that the majority of songs were written for Broadway shows, with motion pictures coming in second. The writer's scope, to a certain degree, narrowed because of the demands of the medium itself. Musical comedy generally dealt with romance and, secondarily, with humor, and, consequently, the writer found that the greatest challenge came in making the standard dramatic situations fresh. This, ultimately, led songwriters to concentrate more on the qualities of wit, irony, sophistication in rhyme and metric schemes, and novel ways to make language come a live and work in the 32 bar world of the popular song.

The transitional figure in this move to a new lyric style seems to have been P.G. Wodehouse, by way of W.S. Gilbert, and channeled through Lorenz Hart and Ira Gershwin.[4] What Gilbert, and ultimately Wodehouse, Hart and Gershwin brought to the American song lyric was a concern for wit, the blending of humor and intelligence, and an interest in the sound and the potential of language for musical expression. Evidence of this concern can be found in Ira Gershwin's comments on the greatest challenge for a songwriter: "Wodehouse once told me that the greatest challenge (and greatest worry) to him in lyric-writing was to come across a section of a tune requiring three double rhymes" (290). Here is a problem that Charles Harris probably never would have imagined. It is interesting to note that the songs which presage the golden age come from the Princess Theatre shows which ran from 1915-1917. These shows, with music by Jerome Kern and lyrics mostly by Wodehouse, would have a dramatic impact on the shape and sound of American popular song.

What is there about Wodehouse's work that is new for this time period? Basically, he is a transition figure in that we find some archaisms in language (not many—not as many as Otto Harbach will ever use, in fact) but there is not the breathless rhyming and alliteration one finds in pre-Princess Theatre songwriting. In general, Wodehouse is able to use internal rhymes to give a sense of movement to the lyric without drawing undue attention to the rhyme; for instance, in the first line of the second verse of "Till the Clouds Roll By" (1917) we find: "What bad luck it's coming down in buckets"; one almost has to stop to see what he did there. Wodehouse also dared to use language understandable to someone other than an immigrant. One senses behind his lyrics, moreover, an active intelligence and love of language; as we look ahead to the great work of Hart, Gershwin, Porter, Dietz and Harburg, we find a similar concern for language. In fact, I think we can identify three broad areas which characterize the new style and emphasis in lyric writing of the golden age of songwriting: wit and, occasionally, irony; sophisticated rhyme schemes; and, finally, use of allusions to objects or ideas other than those of the immediate popular culture.

Where the Tin Pan Alley songsmith hearkened to familiar symbols or emblematic images to convey meaning, the songwriter of the golden age seems constantly in quest of the fresh turn of phrase to capture the moment. I think a song which typifies this new feeling is "Manhatten" (1925) by Rodgers and Hart; first of all, it does not nostalgically bemoan the passing of the rural life; the opening line of the verse makes this clear: "Summer journeys to Niag'ra,/ Seem to aggravate all our cares." The song instead, revels in what the city has to offer: the line, "The City's a great big toy," is typical of the song's sentiment. The lyricist during this period has concerns other than getting to the point fast (which he does anyway) and making it strong. Cole Porter, for instance, in his "DeLovely" (1936) describes the desire to get married as follows:

"Life seems so sweet that we decide/It's in the bag to get unified." Contrary to Charles K. Harris, Porter opts for a slang expression to convey meaning and in the process he slips in a wicked alliteration and what appears to be quadruple rhyme (seems, sweet, we, de-cide). Furthermore, in the verse, a part of the songwriting process he seems not to have liked and was not very good at, he overcomes his limitations with this bit of self-reflexive brilliance: "This verse I've started seems to me/The tin-pantithesis of melody". Indeed, his verses are not as good as the old Tin Pan Alley versions and they are, indeed, the antithesis of the melody in most songs, especially his.

One of the best examples of the new wit and sophistication in lyric writing is another Cole Porter Song, "I Get A Kick Out of You" (1934) from *Anything Goes*. The language, in keeping with Porter's best work, is sophisticated, i.e., "Fighting vainly the old ennui" would have pleased Wodehouse I am sure. But over and above this, is the unique, if not slightly cold, approach he assumes in treating the age-old theme of unrequited love. Unrequited love can be grim, as is the case in most torch songs—even the titles augur a grim experience, "Why Was I Born?", for example—but in Porter's hands it is almost tossed off, and, in fact, almost eludes the listener because he saves the message of the song for the bridge. In the two preceding "A" stanzas the narrator declares how she gets a kick out of the object of her affection, but it is in the bridge where the truth of the matter comes out when she notes she gets a kick seeing him before her "tho' it's clear to me/You obviously don't adore me." And then in the final "A" section the narrator, in a masterful bit of understatement, remarks: "Flying too high with some guy in the sky/Is my idea of nothing to do." In this stanza, however, the listener's response is tempered by the knowledge that the object of the narrator's affection does not reciprocate the feeling. Unlike the torch song, this song does not "grab" the emotions in a sentimental fashion; one senses, moreover, a certain emotional detachment because of the witty way he deals with the "reality" of the situation. The technical facility he displays is directed to the way things are being said almost more than what is said. Similarly, Ira Gershwin, in "Oh, Lady Be Good" (1924), when describing his desire to find the right girl, states: "I must win some winsome miss;/Can't go on like this"; in this case, as in the Porter song, the desperateness of the situation never is allowed full emotional play.

A second area where one notices a change in lyric writing style in the golden age is in the use of rhyme. In the early days of Tin Pan Alley, rhyme was handled at times in an almost perfunctory manner; one could almost count on the use of couplets with an occasional attempt at internal rhyme and rare attempts at triple rhyme. The rhyme, moreover, has a breathless quality as it seemingly cascades onward without any reason at times. Much of this changes, however, beginning in the 1920's when lyricists seem to be more confident about making a point and sustaining a rhythmic feel without rhyming every line. For instance, one of Hart's favorite rhyming techniques, as noted by Lehman Engel, is to use two adjacent words each which rhymes with a word in the preceding line and in the line ahead of that or a line after it. The important thing to remember in all of this is that these lyricists never once lose sight of the object of their song and, in fact, the lyric gains a rhythmic feel as well as unity and cohesiveness that one seldom finds in earlier songs. A brilliant example of language matching mood is in Ira Gershwin's "Bidin' My Time" (1930), a song sung by four lonesome cowpokes in the show *Girl Crazy*. He achieves that languorous and lazy quality we might associate with these cowpokes by exploiting the long "i" sound: "I'm Bidin' My Time/'Cause that's the kinda guy I'm."

Another one of the glories of the music of the golden age is the marriage of wit and rhyme. One of Gershwin's most stunning examples is in the last stanza of the second chorus of Ira Gershwin's "But Not For Me" (1930): "When ev'ry happy plot/Ends with a marriage knot—/And there's no knot for me." One seriously wonders, looking at those last two lines, if he was reading Donne before he wrote the lyric. The crowning touch here is the play on words which reiterates the title line but, because of the different spelling, with new meaning. In another example, Hart's "Bewitched" (1040), we see that an important ingredient in the marriage of wit and rhyme is a greater command of language. Here is part of the reprise verse: "Couldn't eat;/Was dyspeptic.../Now my heart's antiseptic...."The dyspeptic—Antiseptic rhyme is not a run of the mill rhyming dictionary example, and so it always gets a laugh and slight nod of recognition from audiences. One last example of language, wit and rhyme all coming together for great effect and humor is in Harold Rome's "It's Not Cricket to Picket" from *Pins and Needles* (1937); "Oh no, not 'Comme il faut' to picket,/You haven't any right you know; you're acting in great haste." One immediately appreciates the humor of the properness of the narrator's position, and the ingenious way in which Rome rhymes "Comme il faut" with "any right you know" shows a masterly touch.

A final way in which songwriters broke away from the style of their Tin Pan Alley forebears was in the use of allusions. In the period from 1890 to 1920 when songwriters made allusions they were usually to current popular events or people; if they made an allusion to high culture or serious art it was in the form of denigration. Berlin made occasional slaps at Verdi and Wagner; while George M. Cohan, in a patter lyric, states "Knock all the phoney cadenzas out of it"; of course, in this way the songwriter reaffirms middle class values and taste by taking a shot at the educated.

This, however, is not so with the lyricists of the golden age. Cole Porter, in fact, is almost phenomenal in his use of allusions; he alludes to the wealthy like Hearst, DuPont and Landy Mendl; among the places he alludes to are spots where one often finds wealthy Americans. Such as Taormina, Petti Palace, Il Duomo, The Riviera, and the Persian Room. If he refers to champagne it is Camembert (*Their Words* 15). The verse to "Just One of Those Things" (1935) rivals an epic catalog in its allusions to Dorothy Parker, Columbus, Abelard and Heloise, and Romeo and Juliet. One entire Porter song, "Always True to You in My Fashion" (1946), depends upon an allusion to fin-de-siecle English literature, Ernest Dowson's "Non Sum Qualis Eram Bonae Sub Regno Cynarae" ("I have been faithful to thee Cynara, in my fashion"), for its primary thematic message as well as its humor. Furthermore, in Porter as well as Hart,

Gershwin and the others, we find the allusions generally are meant to gain a knowing smile rather than a boffo laugh. For instance, in "Nobody's Chasing Me" (1950), Porter states that the dove grows bolder while a lark is singing "Ich Liebe Dich"; he finishes the stanza with the following: "Tristan is chasing Isolde/But nobody's chasing mich." In other music of the 30' and 40's one can find allusions to Greek tragedies, Cicero, and the Delphic oracle (*The Boys from Syracuse*, 1938 by Rodgers and Hart), Greek comedy in "Lysistrata's Oath" from Harburg and Arlen's *Bloomer Girl* (1944), and, finally, the bridge stanzas in the Gershwin's "Isn't It a Pity" (1932) make reference to reading Heine "somewhere in China," and that the narrator's nights "were sour,/Spent with Schopenhauer."

Now the question that arises is what did the average theatregoer or listener get from this? It is hard to determine, but clearly the songwriter seems less concerned than, let us say, Irving Berlin about public acceptance or response to the song. They would have had to allow for the fact that a large majority of Americans, then as now, hardly understand the significance of the allusion either in the context of the play or outside. Nonetheless, we see in the use of allusions by lyric writers of this period a desire to breathe fresh life into a potentially overworked medium. The allusions are, moreover, precise and, in the hands of these "masters," often insightful. They, on the one hand, allow the lyricist another tool to sharpen his wit and intelligence in the medium, yet, at the same time, they perhaps rob the lyric of some of its emotional import. In short, is the lyric still able to communicate on a basic emotional level that the average listener can respond to?

This last point opens up an interesting idea concerning the fate of popular music before the age of rock, one which I hinted at earlier: in the attempt to make the lyrics of popular music more literate and intelligent, more reflective of the craft of lyric writing itself, did the songwriter lose contact with the basic emotional needs of the audience? One can, at this point, only speculate, but it must be observed that in the case of some of the songs mentioned here the concern for how something is expressed, as opposed to what is said, can give a song an icy objectivity. Both Hart and Porter, for instance, have a tendency to desentimentalize potentially sentimental experiences, i.e., lost love; and the standard love songs themselves at times seem intent upon not saying I love you but finding a new way to express that emotion. It is perhaps because of this that Rodgers and Hammerstein's *Oklahoma!* produced so many hits; in a way, that score is a throwback to the "good old days" of Tin Pan Alley, this achieved in large part through the degree of what Lehman Engel calls particularization in the lyrics. The songs brim with ideas and images evocative of the 19th century, and, depending upon the narrator, they speak in language closer to that of the common man. When one, in fact, looks at the canon of Rodgers and Hammerstein, they find stories dealing with common folk, and my guess is if you judged their songs against Charles K. Harris' advice you might find large measure of agreement.

With the rise of rock 'n' roll in the mid-50's the traditions of Tin Pan Alley and Broadway slowly gave way to new lyric impulses, impulses, oddly enough, which are highly reminiscent of those that animated songwriters in the early days of Tin Pan Alley. We find songwriters picking up on the simplest nuances of teenagers, unabashedly dealing with young love, lost love, cars, and the entire panoply of icons that gave meaning to the youth of the 1950's and 1960's. The day of the carefully crafted lyric was gone with major practitioners confining their efforts to a declining musical theatre; some are still with us, such as Stephen Sondheim, but, in the main, they are of another generation. As we review the evolution of the lyric from its humble, if not crude, attempts at capturing and immortalizing those fleeting moments both in the life of man and in the culture, to its stature as almost a minor art form, where Oscar Hammerstein's labored for hours on a line, where a rhyme, an expression, a turn of phrase became a major focus in lyric writing, we can only wonder if the seeds of its obsolescence were not sown in its greatness.

Notes

[1]See Stanley Green, *The Rodgers and Hammerstein Story* (New York: DaCapo, 1963), p. 122.

[2]I would also mention here "Happy Days Are Here Again" (1929), however, it should be noted that this song was written before the "crash."

[3]As one looks over biographies of the composer and lyricists of the "Golden Age," one will notice that more composers had formal musical training, and many of the lyricists were college educated. Among composers with formal training are Jerome Kern, Cole Porter, Richard Rodgers, and Ray Henderson.

[4]See Earl Bargainnier's essay, "W.S. Gilbert and American Musical Theatre," *Journal of Popular Culture*, 12 (1978), 446-58 for the influence of Gilbert on theatre lyricists.

References

Engel, Lehman. *Their Words Are Music: The Great Theatre Lyricists and Their Lyrics.* New York: Crown Publishers, 1975.

_____ *Words with Music.* New York: MacMillan, 1972.

Freedland, Michael. *Irving Berlin.* New York: Stein and Day, 1974.

Gershwin, Ira. *Lyrics on Several Occasions.* New York: Viking, 1959, 1973.

Hamm, Charles. *Yesterdays: Popular Song in America.* New York: Norton, 1979.

W.S. Gilbert
and
American Musical Theatre

Earl F. Bargainnier

On 12 June 1976, a third group of ten creators and performers was inducted into the Entertainment Hall of Fame. As on the previous two occasions, five of those being honored "not for what they last did, but for what they did that will last" were no longer living, and among them and treated as one were Sir William Schwenk Gilbert and Sir Arthur Sullivan. During the ceremonies Gilbert and Sullivan were described as the Rodgers and Hammerstein, the Lerner and Loewe, and even the Simon and Garfunkel of their day. However inappropriate such comments may seem to some, it was certainly appropriate that Gilbert and Sullivan be among the first fifteen deceased "entertainers" so honored, for Sullivan's music and Gilbert's libretti combined to form the only body of British stageworks between Sheridan and Wilde still continually performed. Their international success for over one hundred years would seem to indicate that they must have influenced others in creating musical stageworks. Without minimizing Sullivan's equal role in the collaboration, this study is concerned with Gilbert's relationship to musical theatre in the United States.[1] That relationship includes four areas requiring examination: the original impact of the Gilbert and Sullivan operas on America, the imitations and burlesques of those works, the structure of musical plays and, most significantly, the writing of stage lyrics.

Gilbert and Sullivan's first great success was *H.M.S. Pinafore*. With the lack of copyright protection in the United States, that success in London in 1878 led immediately to unauthorized performances. Pirated productions were given in nearly every principal city from Boston to San Francisco long before the D'Oyly Carte company arrived from England with the authentic version. In 1878 and 1879 there were 150 different productions of *Pinafore* in the United States, most of which "bore little resemblance to the original opera."[2] These included a children's company, a black company, a performance on a real lake in Rhode Island, and a performance with the "Gloria" from Mozart's *Twelfth Mass* and the "Hallelujah Chorus" interpolated. People repeated lines

Reprinted with permission from the *Journal of Popular Culture*, Volume 12:3 (Winter 1978), pp. 446-58.

from the work under all circumstances, and cartoonists were quick to appropriate them for topical comment. Even before the D'Oyly Carte company arrived, the *American Register* could state on 10 May 1879 that "it is not improbable that this comparatively unimportant work may be the means of starting the great work of the generation of the modern stage in our native land."[3] That this was an accurate prophecy is indicated by the statement of a music historian seventy years later: "From *H.M.S. Pinafore* the American audience began to learn, whether it recognized the fact or not, the difference between hack work and first-class professional skill and integrity...Gilbert and Sullivan won an audience for not only their own works in America, but for transatlantic light music generally."[4]

Naturally desiring to profit from their own work, Gilbert and Sullivan came to America, and on 1 December 1879, Sullivan conducted the first "official" performance of *Pinafore*. Then to thwart the pirates of America, their new opera, *The Pirates of Penzance*, had its premiere in New York on 31 December 1879. It ran for only nine and a half weeks, but during that time, spies were sent to memorize the music, bribes were offered to the orchestra members, and the music had to be locked in a hotel safe each night to protect the author's and composer's rights. The two men even "instructed a chain of legal firms throughout the United States to protect their interests and apply for local injunctions" against unauthorized performances.[5] Six years later the *Pinafore* craze was repeated with the arrival of *The Mikado*. The 250 D'Oyle Carte performances in New York do not give a true indication of its popularity; "it is said that in one evening in 1886, 170 performances took place throughout the United States."[6] In fact, *The Mikado* swept the country as perhaps no other musical work has ever done. Its effect is summed up in a history of musical comedy in America:

All of the United States and Canada quickly went *Mikado*-mad. The rage for Japanese art, whose currency in England had prompted Gilbert's satire in the first place, swept the country. Nearly the entire text of *The Mikado* became household words; in due season the quips and lyrics were passed down from one generation to the next, and even today half the audience at a *Mikado* performance usually knows what the next line is going to be. Probably no other piece in the entire history of the American musical stage has settled so deep in the affections of thousands of perennial, unshakable devotees.[7]

Though Gilbert and Sullivan wrote fourteen operas together, America's favorites, by a wide margin, were *H.M.S. Pinafore* and *The Mikado*. These two works, and the unprecedented excitement they generated, were not the beginning of the American musical stage, but they gave it an impetus and a wide acceptance such as it had not had previously. One immediate reaction was the appearance of burlesques of the operas. Tony Pastor apparently presented the first, *The T.P. Canal Boat Pinafore*. Soon *The Pirates of Penzance* became *The Pirates of Pinafore* (an ironic title!) and Penn's *Aunts Among the Pirates*. The minstrel shows gave "musically serious parodies of Gilbert and Sullivan," as well as several burlesques of *The Mikado*, including *Black Mikado*, which ran for over 100 performances.[8] The latter was a forerunner of the several black versions in the 1930s and 1940s. Other burlesques of *The Mikado* included such characters as My-card-Oh, Bah-Pooh-Bah, Kat-with-Claw, Sing-a-Sing and Ko-Ko and Co. In another Nanki-Poo became Freddy-Pooh, Yum-Yum became (Lily) Langtry-Pooh, and Katisha became Vicky Shaw (a satirical presentation of Queen Victoria, played by a man).[9] J.F. Mitchell's successful *Mikado McAllister* of 1886 was another example of this short-lived but indicative genre.

There were imitations as well as burlesques. Willard Spenser's *The Little Tycoon* (1886), generally considered America's first comic opera, showed the "immediate influence of the Gilbert and Sullivan patter songs—particularly those in *The Mikado*."[10] In 1891 appeared the hugely popular *Wang*, whose composer, Woolson Morse, "so impressed W.S. Gilbert that he asked the American composer to become his collaborator after the split between Gilbert and Sullivan."[11] Morse declined the offer. The 760 performances of *The Geisha* (1896), by Sidney Jones, were largely due to its following the style of *The Mikado*. Theodore F. Morse, who set the words of "Hail, Hail, the Gang's All Here" to the second-act pirate chorus of *The Pirates of Penzance*, wrote "Hurray for Baffin Bay" for *The Wizard of Oz* (1903), and it "was altogether in the best Gilbert and Sullivan tradition."[12] Perhaps of more interest than these forgotten men and their works is the fact that Cole Porter's first stagework, *See America First* (1916) was, in the words of his biographer, "an American comic opera in the Gilbert and Sullivan tradition,"[13] Including such patter songs as "I've a Shooting-Box in Scotland" and a duet with lovers addressing each other as "Lady fair" and "Gentle Sir," the influence of Gilbert on it is unmistakable.[14]

Porter's first work introduces the modern American musical, and Gilbert's influence on it will be seen. But first it should be noted that burlesques and parodies began to appear again in that later period. Aside from numerous sketches and skits in revues, the major examples occurred in the late thirties and forties. In 1938-39 there were the Federal Theater Project's *The Swing Mikado* and Billy Rose's *The Hot Mikado*, both with black companies and both using jazz orchestration. At the same time, Harold Rome's socially-conscious *Pins and Needles* contained "The Red Mikado," a Gilbertian parody with a sharp topical sting: "Taking a jab at the recent barring of Marian Anderson from Constitution Hall by the DAR, the 'three little maids' became members of the Daughters of the American Revolution ('Three little DAR's are we/Filled to the brim with bigotry') who...spouted blue blood when treated to an application of the [Russian] Lord High Executioner's sword."[15] Six years later, there were two other shows, both using *Pinafore* as a basis: *Memphis Bound*, a black *Pinafore* set in the American south, and George S. Kaufman's *Hollywood Pinafore*. The latter, set at Pinafore Pictures, starred Victor Moore as Joseph W. Porter, the studio president; William Gaxton as agent Dick Live-Eye; and Shirley Booth as columnist Louhedda Hopsons, who sang "I'm called Little Butter-up." Some of these later burlesques succeeded and some failed, but all demonstrate that their planners realized that Gilbert and Sullivan had created a body of works which would be immediately recognized by audiences, no matter how distorted. The burlesques were compliments to the longevity and popularity of Gilbert and Sullivan opera.

The structure of a musical stagework is always the result of collaboration. The minimum number involved in creating such a work is nearly always two, as with Gilbert and Sullivan, but the tendency in twentieth-century America has been for there to be at least three: composer, lyricist and librettist. Authur Laurents, the librettist of *West Side Story* (1957), *Gypsy* (1959), and others, has said, "The first thing a librettist must be prepared to do is to sacrifice ego. You have to be prepared that you are going to be ignored." This situation is a partial explanation of the statement of Laurents' colleague, Stephen Sondheim, that "good bookwriting is the most underdeveloped part of the musical theater and the part that there is most to be learned about."[16] W.S. Gilbert was never willing to sacrifice his ego or be ignored in the preparation and performance of his works, and the unity of the operas is the result of his being lyricist *and* librettist—and director. However old-fashioned Gilbert's plots may seem to some in 1979, it must be granted that the best of them have a coherent structure; they are totalities, not melanges of unrelated songs and action. Gilbert's control of their production and his being the only writer not only greatly contributed to their success, but also set a standard for the integrated musical play.[17] However, with very few exceptions, such as the Kern-Hammerstein *Show Boat* (1927), American musical theatre did not really begin to practice his example until the 1940s.

Lehman Engel, who has conducted many Broadway musicals, says, "One of the advances made in modern theatre writing has been the dramatic integration of song and story, as opposed to songs that were formerly loosely inserted at random."[18] One hundred years ago, Gilbert recognized the necessity of that "dramatic integration." It is unfortunate for the reputation of musical theatre that he and Sullivan were alone in that recognition. They were solitary figures in realizing what could be done to make a musical stagework a truly coherent theatrical experience. Patrick J. Smith has most explicitly stated the debt musical theatre owes to Gilbert for his concept of an integrated work:

In most of the French light operas—as in the earlier English ballad operas—the sung moments were generally treated as "numbers," or moments of repose, between the twists and turns of the story. Gilbert, however, constantly interwove song and story into a unity, so that one not only "led into" another in the traditional "song cue" way but was dependent upon it.... Again and again in Gilbert's work this cohesiveness results in a shifting of emphasis from the dialogue to the sung portions as a *locus* of characterizational and developmental ideas, which gives these works their stature as librettos rather than stories with occasional lyrics.[19]

This statement of what Gilbert did also indicates what was ignored by American lyricists and librettists for so long that the musical play became a form to be considered on a lower level than the "legitimate" play.

As neglected as the integration of song and story has been the "book" of musical works. The Gilbert and Sullivan operas, as has been noted, "obey Aristotle in preferring plot to character."[20] And though Gilbert's characters may not be "three dimensional," both they and the plots were original at a time when adaptations were dominant on the stage of England (just as they have been in American musical comedy in this century). Gilbert's sources were the people, institutions and culture of late Victorian England; these he found around him and turned them topsyturvy. This topsyturviness—the systematic reversal of what is normal, accepted, approved or expected under a given set of circumstances—became with Gilbert a pattern to control an entire work, providing that work both unity and, through the satire produced, theme. He chose matter for his operas that would appeal to his audiences even before he did anything to it: the army, the navy, the melodrama, the aesthetic craze, etc. Then he satirized it with hilarity rather than bitterness to make the satire palatable to an unsatiric age, for, to use the words of Jack Point in *The Yeomen of the Guard*, he knew how to "gild the philosophic pill." Stephen Sondheim, America's most successful composer-lyricist today, says that "what make smash-hit musicals are stories that audiences want to hear—and it's always the same story. How everything turns out terrific in the end and the audience goes out thinking, That's what life is all about."[21] Gilbert would have agreed; he once told an American journalist, "I am not ambitious to write up to epicurean tastes, but contented to write down to everybody's comprehension."[22] By using contemporaneous subjects and mocking what was foolish about them, Gilbert did create works of wide appeal. His sense of structure, his particularity both of character and situation and in his use of words, and, most of all, his immense skill as a lyricist made his works successful and himself an influence on later writers of the musical theatre.

The writing of effective stage lyrics is not easy, for such songs have definite, even rigid, requirements. Gilbert is almost universally considered the greatest lyricist of the stage, and to understand his accomplishment and influence, some understanding of the stage lyric is required. E.Y. Harburg, lyricist of *Bloomer Girl* (1944) and *Finian's Rainbow* (1947), says, "A song is a song is a song...but a song in a stage musical is something special. It is a scene...an extension of the libretto...a development of character."[23] If the lyricist ignores these demands, he will surely fail, for the *meaning* of any song lies in its lyrics, the music providing its emotion. For example, a comic song is so because the words create a risible response; its music may be slow or fast, soft or loud. Also, when a song is in the context of a stagework, the lyricist must stage the song while writing it. He must also remember that the audience will hear the words only once or, if there is a reprise, twice. Finally, as Sondheim has noted, besides the music underlying the words, there are also "lights, costumes, scenery, characters, performers. There's a great deal to hear and get. Lyrics therefore have to be underwritten. They have to be simple in essence."[24] Ira Gershwin, one of America's most distinguished lyricists, has written of the difficulty of being successful in this craft: "Given a fondness for music, a feeling for rhyme, a sense of whimsey and humor, an eye for the balanced sentence, an ear for the current phrase, and the ability to imagine oneself a performer trying to put over the number in progress—given all this, I still would say it takes four or five years of collaborating with knowledgeable composers to become a well-rounded lyricist"; and he concludes that "if the lyricist who lasts isn't a W.S. Gilbert he is at least literate."[25] Gershwin's compliment to Gilbert is an illustration of the esteem in which he is held by most American lyricists, an esteem which has influenced the American musical theatre.

In his analysis of American stage lyrics, Lehman Engel finds that from 1900 to 1920 lyricists "were more influenced by poor English translations of Viennese operettas than by excellent English-language originals. The masterful lyrics of W.S. Gilbert had little effect on our new writers." Engel believes the reason for this neglect was the prevalent attitude then that Gilbert was passe. However, by 1930 Gilbert "had become fixed in history" and then assumed "his rightful position as a viable model." When American lyricists became more sophisticated, "they became acutely aware of W.S. Gilbert."[26]

Such major lyricists as Oscar Hammerstein II, Lorenz Hart, Ira Gershwin, E.Y. Harburg and Howard Dietz have made published statements of their respect for Gilbert. Hammerstein "greatly admired W.S. Gilbert and Lorenz Hart, and never felt that in the 'field of brilliant light verse' he could compete with them."[27] It is surprising that the often sentimental Hammerstein should pair his admiration of Gilbert with that of Hart, for both of them have been accused of cynicism in their satiric lyrics. It is also of interest that until Rodgers and Hart began collaborating in the 1920s, there had been no composer-lyricist team of equal billing since Gilbert and Sullivan; naturally, Rodgers and Hart were soon called "the Gilbert and Sullivan of America." In his book on American songwriters, Max Wilk tells how as a boy he was taken by his father to the matinees of the D'Oyly Carte performances in New York. There he was introduced to Hart. Afterwards, the following dialogue took place:

> "He writes pretty good stuff of his own," I complained to my father, "What's he doing *here* every week, listening to W.S. Gilbert's."
> "Homework," said my father. "You could say he was taking a refresher course."

Some years later Wilk told Hart of his father's remark. " 'Your old man was absolutely right!' said Larry. "I *was* there to study! Old man Gilbert was the greatest lyricist who ever turned a rhyme!' "[28] Hart's fondness for complicated "trick" rhymes, for incongruous juxtapositions in love songs, and for list or catalogue songs all reflect his study of Gilbert, "A Little Bit of Constitutional Fun," from *I'd Rather Be Right* (1937), "Zip" from *Pal Joey* (1940), and "Thou Swell," "Can't You Do a Friend a Favor?" and "To Keep My Love Alive" from the revised version of *A Connecticut Yankee* (1943) are just a few examples.

The first American musical to win the Pulitzer prize for drama was the Gershwins' *Of Thee I Sing* (1931). It has been said that until its appearance, "American musical comedy had never fully learned from Gilbert and Sullivan the art of arguing about public issues by means of laughter."[29] *Of Thee I Sing* and its less successful sequel *Let 'Em Eat Cake* (1933) both use Gilbertian libretti of hilarious satire on government and such songs as "Of Thee I Sing (Baby)," "Because, Because" and "Down With Ev'rything That's Up" are examples of the incongruously-worded love song, the comic song of explanation, and the topsyturvy satirical song so evident in Gilbert's work. Ira Gershwin has said that "Gilbert was the greatest, no question of that. If he were alive today, he'd be doing good musical-comedy songs."[30] Because of this admiration, Gershwin introduced his friend E.Y. Harburg to Gilbert and Sullivan during their college years. Harburg has recalled the event and its effect:

I remember once going up to the Gershwins' to hear the Victrola—that was a very new thing, Victrola records. That was the first time I heard W.S. Gilbert's lyrics set to Sullivan's music. Up to that time I thought he was simply a poet! Ira played *Pinafore* for me, and I had my eyes opened. I was starry-eyed for days. I couldn't sleep at night. It was that music—and the satire that came out with all the emotion that I never dreamed of before when I read the thing cold in print![31]

Harburg's enthusiasm has lasted for sixty years. In a recent letter he gave Gilbert and Sullivan as the principal influence on his work as lyricist and librettist: "Though many other versifiers have added a considerable portion to this evolvement, i.e. Herrick, Calverley, Dorothy Parker, Heine, Wodehouse and Taylor, the major gratitude goes to Gilbert and Sullivan." And he adds that, in his opinion, "the American musical as an art form received its major stimulation from these two ingenious gentlemen. . . ."[32] The songs from *Finian's Rainbow*, particularly "When the Idle Poor Become the Idle Rich," and those from the film *The Wizard of Oz* (1939), as well as others in other shows, demonstrate that Gilbert has been a significant and beneficent influence on this outstanding American lyricist.

Still another important lyricist who has expressed his admiration for Gilbert is Howard Dietz, writer of songs and sketches for America's most successful revues, including *The Bandwagon* (1931). In his autobiography, besides alluding to the operas frequently, Dietz says that when a student at Columbia University, "My 'by-heart' knowledge was French verse, W.S. Gilbert and Lewis Carroll." Perhaps his greatest praise of Gilbert occurs in his discussion of translation, especially as he himself has translated into English *Die Fledermaus* and *La Boheme* for the Metropolitan Opera: "When a work is perfect in its original form, when the language has the handwriting of an individual poet, it had better be left alone. I would shudder at the idea of foreign adaptations of the Gilbert and Sullivan operas even though they are light works. There is often more poetry in these so-called light works than in those operas with large tonnage."[33] "Hottentot Potentate" of *At Home Abroad* (1935), "Triplets" of *Between the Devil* (1937), "Rhode Island is Famous for You" and "At the Mardi Gras" of *Inside U.S.A.* (1948) and "That's Entertainment" from the film version of *The Band Wagon* (1953) are just a few of Dietz's songs which illustrate his long attachment to Gilbert and Sullivan. He writes, "When I was young, I was thrilled when I discovered Gilbert and Sullivan, and I still consider them non pareil. I still know most of the lyrics and melodies by heart." He also thinks that "one of the reasons that American musicals are better" is that "Gilbert and Sullivan have had more influence on the American musical theatre than on the English" (14 October 1975).

Cole Porter's *See America First* has already been noted as Gilbertian, and though no direct comments by Porter are available as to his view of Gilbert and Sullivan, he is the most Gilbertian lyricist of the American musical theatre. In his rhymes, his use of words as words, his patter songs, his satiric contemporaneity and his approach to the love song, Porter is a twentieth-century sophisticated Gilbert. Gilbert could rhyme "you shun her" and "executioner" or "lottery" and "terracottery"; Porter matches him with "cutie pie, a tryst" and "you try a tryst" and "bin of manure, a" and "Duke of Verdura." Instances could be multiplied by the hundreds. Similarly Porter's playing with words, as in "It's delightful, it's delicious,/ It's delectable, it's delirious,'It's dilemma, it's delimit, it's deluxe, it's delovely" (*Red, Hot and Blue* 1936), is simply a progression from Gilbert's "Our Lordly Style" (*Iolanthe*), "So Go to Him and Say to Him" (*Patience*), or the trio in *The Mikado* ending with "Awaiting the sensation of a short, sharp shock/From a cheap and chippy chopper on a big black block!" Gilbert is considered the master of the patter song—the long-lined, rapid-fire comic song—and one of his favorite types was the song which utilizes lists of people, places and things, often incongruously juxtaposed, as in "My Name is John Wellington Wells" (*The Corcerer*), "The Colonel's Song" (*Patience*), and "I've Got a Little List" (*The Mikado*). This same type has become practically a trademark of Porter's; a few examples from many include "Let's Do It" (*Paris*, 1928), "You're The Top" (*Anything Goes*, 1934), "Brush Up Your Shakespeare" (*Kiss Me, Kate*, 1949), and "Cherry Pies Ought to Be You" (*Out of This World*, 1950). These list songs also provide Porter a vehicle for satirizing contemporary persons, institutions, fads and follies, just as they did Gilbert. Finally, many of Porter's love songs underplay or invert usual sentiments in the same manner as Gilbert's "Refrain Audacious Tar" (*Pinafore*), "There Is Beauty in the Billow of the Blast" (*The Mikado*), and "In Sailing O'er Life's Ocean Wide" (*Ruddigore*). Examples of Porter's use of this technique include "What Is This Thing Called Love?" (*Wake Up and Dream*, 1929), "I Get a Kick Out of You" (*Anything Goes*), "Just One of Those Things" (*Jubilee*, 1935), "Always True to You in My Fashion" (*Kiss Me, Kate*), and "It's All Right With Me" (*Can-Can*, 1935). Perhaps Porter would still have written in the manner he did if Gilbert had not existed, but Gilbert's example as a lyricist must have been a factor in his development.

Not all those working in musical theatre today see Gilbert and Sullivan as an influence. Abe Burrows, librettist of such successes as *Can-Can, Guys and Dolls* (1950) and *How to Succeed in Business Without Really Trying* (1961), says, "I've always been a great admirer of Gilbert and Sullivan and we still spend a lot of evenings at my home singing their songs." However, Burrows does not think their influence is "as great as some people think. Gilbert and Sullivan did Operettas...I think the modern American musical in a *new* form. It's a marriage of dialogue and music in which the music is used to express emotions and thoughts that can't be conveyed by the dialogue" (4 November 1974). Similarly, Charles Strouse, composer of *Bye Bye Birdie* (1960) and *Applause* (1970), feels that Gilbert and Sullivan "represented a kind of topping to much of the 'serious' music preceding them, rather than a precursor to music or theater after them. . . .For me, then, Gilbert & Sullivan remain parodists of the first order—of Rossini, of opera in general—while American Musical Theater took another course" (undated; received 26 October 1975). Stephen Sondheim writes that "I don't much like Gilbert and Sullivan. I find the lyrics too fussy and too often sacrificing sense for rhyme. I enjoy the music but I don't respond very enthusiastically." Nor does Sondheim believe that Gilbert and Sullivan have had any influence on American musicals, which he sees as "a development out of the mid-European tradition, not the British." Nevertheless, he can use their work for his own purposes: "I've recently done a parody of 'I Am the Very Model of a Modern Major-General' in 'Pacific Overtures.' I did this to fix the time and attitude of the British Admiral who visits Japan in the second half of the 19th century" (30 January 1976). Also, Sondheim describes "A Weekend in the Country," the first-act finale of *A Little Night Music* (1973), as "a Gilbert and Sullivan-type operetta ending."[34]

Burrows, Strouse and Sondheim are in the minority in their views. Differing from them—besides those already quoted—are Johnny Mercer, Betty Comden, Richard Rodgers, Sammy Cahn, Burton Lane, Harold Rome, Sheldon Harnick, Lee Adams, Jule Styne and Leonard Bernstein. It is unfortunately impossible to present the full and detailed statements provided this writer by these distinguished figures in American theatre, but at least a few of their comments can show the general attitude toward Gilbert's (and Sullivan's) relationship to that theatre. Lee Adams, lyricist of *Bye Bye Birdie* and *Applause*, disagrees with his collaborator, Charles Strouse:

As a working theatrical lyricist, my opinion of Lyricist William S. Gilbert could not be higher. Together with his talented. . .collaborator, they created the first truly modern "musicals." Gilbert's wit and erudition, his style and taste, have always inspired me. . . . No lyricist who ever tried to write a clever patter song could fail to be influenced by Gilbert, whose patter was the greatest. Obviously, G & S have had an influence on me. From the time I appeared in a summer camp production of *The Mikado* I have appreciated and read Gilbert's work (20 November 1975)

Leonard Bernstein reports that when he discovered *The Mikado* at sixteen, he immediately produced and directed a version with friends, "not only singing Nanki-Pooh but also playing the piano offstage whenever I could get there. From then to now, the incredible inventiveness and stylistic brilliance of those two gentlemen have enriched my life, and, I dare say, not a few pages of my theatre works" (17 December 1976). The work of Bernstein's whose pages most reflect Gilbert and Sullivan is his "Comic Operetta" *Candide* (1956), written with Lillian Hellman as librettist and Richard Wilbur as lyricist.

Bernstein is not the only composer who thinks of Gilbert and Sullivan with respect. Probably the most distinguished composer of musicals today is Richard Rodgers, who believes that Gilbert and Sullivan "have had, and still have, a great influence on the American musical theatre and I believe I have been equally influenced in my own career by listening to their works. I feel that they have moved all American writers for the theatre to as great extent as anyone in their field" (6 October 1975). The composer of *High Button Shoes*

(1947), *Gentlemen Prefer Blondes* (1949), *Gypsy, Funny Girl* (1964) and many other successes, Jule Styne, feels that Gilbert and Sullivan "laid the groundwork in a large way for our modern trend in musical comedy or musical drama." He credits Sullivan with "the major part of making this team so successful," but specifically praises Gilbert for his "tremendous influence on the rhyming patterns that we find and found in the American musical comedy. I would go as far as to say that Lorenz Hart, E.Y. Harburg and parts of Ira Gershwin could be called contemporaries of Gilbert" (17 February 1976). Likewise, Burton Lane, composer of *Finian's Rainbow* and *On a Clear Day You can See Forever* (1965), writes that "I had always taken for granted" the influence of Gilbert and Sullivan, for "One has only to listen to some of the great music scores by George and Ira Gershwin, Rodgers and Hart, Cole Porter, and E.Y. Harburg and Harold Arlen, just to mention a few, to observe the Gilbert and Sullivan influence." Lane gives more credit to Gilbert, calling him "a genius" and Sullivan "very competent. But together they made magic" (19 February 1976).

As a transition from composers to lyricists the remarks of Harold Rome, who is both, are opposite. Rome believes, "There is no question that they have had a profound influence on the American musical theatre, setting a precedent in musical treatment, style, fantasy and satire which has contributed to the growth and coming of age of the American musicals." On the personal level, Rome writes, "Since I have known and loved the works of Gilbert and Sullivan from an early age, I am sure that consciously or unconsciously they have helped me to understand what the right combination of words and music can do in the theatre and encouraged me in my early days to attempt works of social significance and taught me how to mix satire and humor" (23 February 1976).

Another personal statement is that of Sammy Cahn, lyricist of *High Button Shoes* and many musical films, who was introduced to Gilbert and Sullivan by fellow lyricist Johnny Burke: "Of their influence on my work, it may seem immodest but if there is any hint of a really felicitous or elegant rhyme you can be sure it can be attributed to all of the classics that are G & S" (2 November 1975). One of the most successful writing teams in the musical theatre has been Betty Comden and Adolph Green. Their lyrics and libretti for such shows as *On The Town* (1944) and *Bells Are Ringing* (1956), as well as their scripts for *Singin' in the Rain* (1952) and other M-G-M musicals have all been witty and satirical. Ms. Comden says of Gilbert and Sullivan, "Their influence in American musical theatre exists wherever there is musical satire." Her first exposure to their works occurred when she was ten, after which "I saw the shows, read them, listened to them, studied them, responded to them, memorized them, got and still get enormous pleasure from them.... Of course they had an influence. Adolph and I began as writers of topical material, little revues.... They were not political revues, but dealt mainly with social foibles, and aspects of the arts and journalism. Our patter songs of comment owed a debt to Gilbert and Sullivan, and later on in our shows for the theatre, there have always been some satirical elements with Gilbert and Sullivan roots" (6 March 1976). As a final comment, a complete letter from Sheldon Harnick,

Pulitzer Prize-winning lyricist of *Fiorello!* (1959) and of the longest running of all Broadway musicals as of (1978), *Fiddler on the Roof* (1964), is presented as an appendix, for Harnick's analysis of both the general and personal influence is masterfully clear.

Other lyricists could be named who show Gilbertian tendencies, two of prominence being Frank Loesser, with *Where's Charley* (1948) and *How to Succeed in Business Without Really Trying*, and Alan Jay Lerner, with *My Fair Lady* (1956). But enough comments by the professionals of the American musical theatre have been given to substantiate the view that Gilbert (and Sullivan) have had a considerable impact on that theatre. The first performances of the works in the United States, at least of *H.M.S. Pinafore* and *The Mikado*, immediately established the "book musical" as a leading stage form. The burlesques which appeared of the works indicate the widespread popular acceptance of them, and the direct imitations and adaptations for the next seventy-five years demonstrate the longevity of that popular acceptance. Gilbert's creation of unified musical stageworks, with total integration of song and dialogue, set a standard which—though not always followed—has remained a criterion of judgment ever since. Most importantly, Gilbert's satiric libretti and his mastery of the stage lyric—his single most lasting contribution—inspired many American writers to emulate his craftmanship in their own works. Whether there has been direct influence or simply the inspiration of the standards Gilbert and Sullivan set, s Betty Comden has written, "It is hard to think of anybody who has written for the musical theatre as not having been influenced by Gilbert and Sullivan in some way."

Appendix

October 8th, '75

Dear Mr. Bargainnier:

If I had any class I would have put my answer to your letter in the form of a Gilbert and Sullivan patter song. However. To comment on your three questions:

1) I love Gilbert and Sullivan. I discovered them at the age of 15 or 16 when I played violin in the pit orchestra of an amateur production of *The Mikado* (or was it *Pinafore?*). I fell in love with their work and have remained steadfast through the years, so much so that I wish I had several days at my disposal to give proper, considered answers to your questions. Since I don't, I can only give you my immediate responses. I love Gilbert and Sullivan because, in a word, I think the lyrics are astoundingly rich and eternally fresh and the music is marked by elegant craftsmanship and an abundance of engaging melodies.

2) and 3). It's easier to discuss your second and third points as part of one answer, rather than considering them separately.

As a budding lyricist, I responded initially to Gilbert's lyrics more intensely than to Sullivan's music. I accepted the music as the natural complement to the lyrics without thinking too much about it. Years later I began to realize the extent of Sullivan's accomplishment. I was first impressed (bowled over, is more accurate) by Gilbert's virtuosity, particularly in the patter songs. When I began seriously to write songs and to try to find my own individual voice, I know I was greatly influenced by Gilbert albeit it was a submerged influence. The more readily identifiable influences were (in high school) Larry Hart and (in college) "Yip" Harburg. But I suspect, although I don't know for sure, that Hart and Harburg were great admirers of Gilbert and Sullivan (hereafter 'G & S') too, so the Gilbert influence probably reached me through their lyrics. The Gilbert influence emerged in pure form whenever I tackled a lyric with an element of patter to it. Also, I think that once one has been exposed to Gilbert's droll, impish wit, his sharp satire, his effective use of paradox, and his remarkable lovers—unsentimental, comic, dryly perceptive, yet nonetheless endearing—once one has been exposed (and responded appreciatively) to these things, one has been forever influenced.

I still find occasional echoes of G & S in my work. For instance, in *Fiddler On The Roof* in the first act dream sequence, there is a line which is pure G & S. It may even be a trifle out of character for the shtetl dwellers, but since they were figures in a dream I couldn't resist: when they see Fruma-Sarah appear, they sing:

"WHAT WOMAN IS THIS
BY RIGHTEOUS ANGER SHAKEN?"

In addition to the foregoing, I find that there is (in my work) an 'ongoing' influence, if that's the right word. Always, in a special place somewhere in the back of my mind, is the *idea* of G & S, i.e. the notion that there is a body of work of such sustained excellence (the level of intelligence, wit, taste, inventiveness, originality, etc.) provides a constant yardstick, a constant mark to shoot at. Also, I frequently look back admiringly at the extended musical sequences in G & S (and Offenbach and others, too) as examples of what can be done on the musical stage which approaches opera but remains popular entertainment. I haven't attempted as much in this direction as I would like (and intend) to, but others have, notably Stephen Sondheim (whether or not G & S influenced him at all).

Hardest of all is to pinpoint the G & S influence on American theater. Unquestionably, the influence was strong and obvious in late 19th century and early 20th century American operettas. But it's harder to discern in those shows (that began appearing soon after the turn of the century) which reflected the desire to break away from the European operetta tradition and utilize a breezier, jazzier musical idiom we've come to think of as the American musical comedy style. Since these shows made a point of breaking away from the operetta style, the G & S influence (among others) is, naturally, harder to spot, (except in those numbers written intentionally in the G & S style to make some point or other). My guess would be that the influence on yesterday's and today's musical theatre would be, for the most part, indirect and even unconscious but nonetheless real for all that. And it would come about through writers who have been affected in the same ways I have. (I'm sure I'm not the only current writer who acknowledges G & S as giants, and one is inevitably influenced by the giants, however subtly, in one's own line of work).

Yours truly,

Sheldon Harnick (signed)

P.S. It strikes me that the popularity of the Marx Brothers shows little signs of diminishing. And the songs and musical sequences in many of their films were enormously influenced by G & S. So it's quite possible that youngsters who don't know the operettas of G & S but who are becoming acquainted with the Marx Bros. films, will be influenced by G & S at one remove![35]

Notes

[1]As I am not a musician, I cannot evaluate the influence of Sullivan's music; rather, while admiring it, I take the view of Sir Arthur Quiller-Couch, addressing a group of undergraduates in 1929 on the success of the joint works: "Offenbach's music was as tunable as Sullivan's and belonged to its age as closely. But Offenbach lacked good librettists, and for this reason you do not stand in long files to buy tickets for Offenbach" ("W.S. Gilbert," reprinted in *W.S. Gilbert: A Century of Scholarship and Commentary*, ed. John Bush Jones, New York, 1970, p. 161).

[2]Colin Prestige, "D'Oyly Carte and the Pirates: The Original New York Productions of Gilbert and Sullivan," in *Gilbert and Sullivan: Papers Presented at the International Conference*, ed. James Helyar, Lawrence, Kansas, 1971, p. 116. This article is the most detailed study of the Gilbert and Sullivan phenomenon in the United States in the 1870s and 1880s, and my discussion of the matter is greatly indebted to it.

[3]Quoted in Prestige, p. 115.

[4]Cecil Smith, *Musical Comedy in America* (New York, 1950), p. 126.

[5]Prestige, p. 126.

[6]Prestige, p. 137.

[7]Smith, p. 90.

[8]Robert C. Toll, *Blacking Up: The Minstrel Show in Nineteenth-Century America* (New York 1974), pp. 150 & 172.

[9]Prestige, p. 137.

[10]Smith, p. 77.

[11]Smith, p. 99.

[12]Sigmund Spaeth, A *History of Popular Music in America* (New York, 1948), p. 338.

[13]George Eells, *The Life That Late He Led* (New York), 1967, p. 49. Cecil Smith says of *See America First* that its "story about a 'back-to-nature' debutante and a cowboy-duke underlay Porter's attempt to 'combine Gilbert and Sullivan wit with college musical spirit'...(216).

[14]Complete lyrics for these songs may be found in *Cole*, ed. Robert Kimball (New York, 1971), pp. 35-36 & 38.

[15]Frederick S. Roffmann, "D'Oyly Carte Tradition vs. 'The Hot Mikado'" *The New York Times* (2 May 1976), 2: 15.

[16]Both quoted in Craig Zadan, *Sondheim & Co.* (New York), 1974, p. 69.

[17]For Gilbert's methods of composition and stage-management, see my doctoral thesis: "W.S. Gilbert and Nineteenth Century Drama," University of North Carolina (Chapel Hill, 1969), pp. 129-163.

[18]*Their Words Are Music: The Great Theatre Lyricists and Their Lyrics* (New York, 1975), p. 147.

[19]"W.S. Gilbert and the Musical," *Yale/Theatre*, 4:3 (1973), 22 & 23.

[20]Quiller-Couch, p. 165. Patrick J. Smith says that "Gilbert's most conspicuous weakness as a librettist is his lack of rounded characters" (25). This same weakness seems to inflict nearly all librettists for "light music," British, American or otherwise. One reason is given by Stephen Sondheim: "The rigidity of lyric writing is like sonnets,

and onstage this rigidity makes creating characters difficult, because characters, if they are to be alive, don't tend to talk in well-rounded phrases" (Quoted in Zadan, p. 217).

[21]Quoted in Zadan, p. 59.

[22]Quoted in Joseph Anderson, "Gilbert the Librettist," Boston *Transcript* (18 January 1895), p. 11.

[23]"Theater Music: Seven Views," in *Playwrights, Lyricists, Composers on Theater,* ed. Otis L. Guernsey, Jr. (New York), 1974, p. 139.

[24]Quoted in Zadan, p. 217.

[25]*Lyrics on Several Occasions* (New York, 1959), pp. 120 & 362.

[26]Engel, p. 1.

[27]Engel, p. 41.

[28]*They're Playing Our Song* (New York), 1973, pp. 51-52.

[29]Cecil Smith, p. 281.

[30]Quoted in Wilk, p. 88.

[31]Quoted in Wilk, pp. 219-220.

[32]Letter of E.Y. Harburg to this writer, dated 18 December 1975. I wish to express my sincere gratitude to all of the composers, lyricists and librettists who have generously given me their views on Gilbert and Sullivan, on any influence those two men may have had on American musical theatre, and on any influence on their own works. They are George Abbott, Lee Adams, Leonard Bernstein, Abe Burrows, Sammy Cahn, Betty Comden, Howard Dietz, Sherman Edwards, George Furth, E.Y. Harburg, Sheldon Harnick, Burton Lane, Arthur Laurents, Richard Rodgers, Harold Rome, Stephen Sondheim, Charles Strouse and Jule Styne. My deep appreciation goes also to Mrs. Johnny Mercer for replying, during Mr. Mercer's tragic illness, through Marshall Robbins of Mercer Music. I have respected the wishes of the two persons who do not wish to be quoted. All quotations from the others will be cited in the text, using the date of the individual's letter to me.

[33]*Dancing in the Dark* (New York), 1974, pp. 23 & 293.

[34]Quoted in Zadan, p. 206.

[35]Betty Comden provides a comment to Harnick's view of the Marx brothers: "Groucho Marx...is a Big G. and S. enthusiast, and not too long ago would go driving around Beverly Hills with a copy of The Collected Works on the front seat next to him, so that when he came to a light he could glance in it at random and either read a bit, or sing out loud till the light changed. One evening at dinner, we had some argument about a lyric, and all we had to do was run outside and look in the car" (6 March 1976).

"Welfare Store Blues"—Blues Recordings and The Great Depression

John S. Otto
and
Augustus M. Burns

As the radio industry enjoyed its first period of dramatic growth in the early 1920's, phonograph recording companies became fearful that radio competition would threaten their markets. To meet the new challenge, record companies began searching for buyers. They found an untapped and promising market among black Americans. Advertising their releases as "race records," the companies began issuing recordings by black artists—gospel singers, jazzmen, and blues performers.

The earliest blues releases featured women vocalists accompanied by jazz bands and pianos. Generally, these women artists sang vaudeville blues composed by professional songwriters. But after 1924, the companies also began recording "downhome" blues sung by male and female vocalists accompanying themselves with guitars and pianos.[1] These indigenous blues musicians often composed their own songs, drawing from a body of traditional formulaic verses or commenting on widely-shared experiences in the black community.[2] Thus, downhome blues were commercial folksongs sung in a folk idiom which expressed the interests of the folk—in this case working class blacks.[3]

Record companies issued literally thousands of downhome blues recordings between 1924 and 1942. These issues constitute a significant body of social documents from the interwar years.[4] Although the written records of black workers from this period are relatively scant, blues musicians, who served as the voices for working class blacks, have left these oral records.[5] Mistreatment and hard times were the principal subjects of these downhome blues. Admittedly, most blues dealt with mistreating lovers, but other blues commented on topical problems in black life. Farming, migration to the cities, crowded urban life, factory work, and unemployment were all themes in various downhome blues recordings. And unlike interviews collected from elderly informants, these topical blues are not reminiscences. Rather, they are contemporary commentaries on events and situations of the day. Originally issued on fragile 78 pm shellac

Reprinted with permission from *Popular Music and Society* Volume 7:2 (1980) pp. 95—102.

discs, hundreds of these oral documents have now been reissued on long-playing microgroove albums which are readily available to historians.

Despite the preponderance of romantic and fantastic themes in downhome blues, there remains a sizable body of topical blues which comment on life situations in the interwar years. These topical blues represent a potential source of oral history from the period which encompassed both the Great Depression and the New Deal. Since they were subject to few constraints in the recording studios,[7] Depression-era blues singers commented openly on the hard times and New Deal policies. Frequently, they based their topical blues on personal experience, since blues musicians lost jobs, went on relief, or worked on government projects. In other cases, they sang about the experiences of friends, and fellow workers.[8] Providing us with insights into black experience and attitudes, such topical blues could be used in conjunction with Federal Writers' Project life histories and current oral histories to study working class perceptions of the Depression and New Deal.[9]

As working class blacks felt the first shocks of the Depression, one of their first responses was to cut back on record purchases. A few months after the Crash, the race record market began to contract. Some companies collapsed, others merged, and most cut record prices drastically.[10] In a further effort to cut costs, the companies recorded fewer blues musicians, turning to performers whose "lyric inventiveness was such that they could meet the demands of the consumer market."[11] Thus, the blues of the 1930's "was sometimes less rich musically than it had been hitherto, but the content of the verses, which mattered greatly to those who bought the discs, was of more immediate social relevance than at any previous time."[12] Moreover, the blues of the 1930's reflected urban concerns as the recording companies focused on blues singers living in cities such as Chicago and St. Louis, foregoing the expensive field recording caravans which had once toured the South searching for new blues talent.[13]

Within a year after the Crash, black musicians had recorded a number of "hard times" blues. Unemployment for blacks appeared earlier, came with greater intensity, and lasted longer than elsewhere in the community. In addition, many black workers experienced discriminatory layoffs as whites sought jobs formerly reserved for blacks.[14] With no paycheck coming in, unemployed blacks faced eviction and destitution:

> The times are getting tighter,
>   getting tighter day by day (2x)
> But the rent man comes as usual
>   when he knows that we can't pay.
>
> I stood him off so long,
>   until I'm afraid to facing him now (2x)
> Because I know when I do facing him,
>   there's going to be a row.
>
> (Now) my coal bin is empty,
>   not a lump there can you find (2x)

> I would buy coal by the bushel,
>> if I only had the dime.
>
> Just a (lonely?) alley where my
>> baby used to find some wood (2x)
> But now she can't find a splinter,
>> no one in that neighborhood.
>
> Now the times is so tight
>> they keep you walking up and down the street (2x)
> With all these debts a coming in,
>> not a one of them can we meet.[15]

Rather than passively accepting hard times, one bluesman chided black Republicans for having elected Herbert Hoover:

> Just before election,
>> you's talking how you was going to vote (2x)
> And after election was over,
>> your head down like a billy goat.[16]

Hoover's insistence on relying on local relief agencies and private charities inadvertently created hardships for unemployed workers.[17] In "Starvation Blues," Charley Jordan sardonically commented on the inability of local relief agencies to aid the destitute:

> Lord, Lord, starvation is at my door (2x)
> Well, there ain't no need of running,
>> because I ain't got no place to go.
> Now, I almost had a square meal the
>> other day (2x)
> But the garbage man come,
>> and he moved the can away.[18]

In 1933, however, Franklin Roosevelt, cognizant of the limited resources of local agencies, instituted the Federal Emergency Relief Administration (F.E.R.A.), which provided grants to state and local relief agencies. By October 1933, 18% of all blacks were on the relief rolls.[19] Unemployed blacks lined up at relief offices, hoping for fair treatment but expecting the worst:

> (Now) I'm going down to the relief, I want a order today (2x)
> If I don't get some groceries, my baby'll run away.
>
> (Now) Uncle Sam is helping millions, seems like he'd help poor me. (2x)
> Now, I'm going down there tomorrow morning, and ask for sympathy.
>
> Now if they deny me,
>> and they won't help me none (2x)
> I'm going to help myself with

my .32-20 and my .41 (pistols).

The F.E.R.A. program, however, did little to alleviate unemployment. Consequently, the Roosevelt administration planned to shift from direct relief to federally-sponsored work relief.[21] During the difficult transition from direct relief to work relief, Carl Martin, a Chicago bluesman, impatiently sang "Let's Have a New Deal:"

> Now, everybody's crying, 'Let's Have a New Deal.'
> Relief station is closing down, I know
>   just how you feel....
>
> Now, I woke up this morning, doggone my soul,
> My flour barrel was empty, I swear I
>   didn't have no coal....
>
> Now, you go to your [case] worker,
>   and put in your complaint,
> Eight times out of ten, you know they'll
>   say I can't....
>
> They don't wanna give you no dough,
>   won't hardly pay your rent,
> And it ain't costing them one doggoned cent....
>
> Refrain: Everybody's crying: 'Let's Have a New Deal,'
> 'Cause I've got to make a living, if I
>   to rob and steal.[22]

One of the most important work relief agencies for blacks was the Public Works Administration (P.W.A.). The P.W.A. assumed control of major construction projects, low-rent housing projects, and slum clearance. Harold Ickes, the director of the agency, insisted that blacks be well-represented in P.W.A. payrolls. Furthermore, P.W.A. projects included schools, hospitals, and housing tracts for blacks. Of all the New Deal agencies, the P.W.A. was perhaps the most concerned with black needs.[23] Understandably, the P.W.A. became the subject of laudatory blues recordings.:

> Lord, Mister President, listen to what
> I'm going to say (2x)
> You can take away all the alphabet,
>   but please leave the P.W.A.
>
> Now, you're in Mister President
> and I hope you're there to stay (2x)
> But whatever changes you make,
> please keep the P.W.A.
>
> P.W.A. is the best old friend I ever seen (2x)

> Since the job ain't hard,
> and the boss ain't mean.
>
> I went to the poll and voted,
> and I know I voted the right way (2x)
> Now, I'm praying to you Mr. President,
> please keep the P.W.A.[24]

But federally-funded slum clearance projects often outstripped the building of low-rent housing projects, creating overcrowding in black neighborhoods. Moreover, many of the people ousted by slum clearance were not eligible for the new housing projects; or, they could not afford the rents. Blacks crowded into the remaining slums as landlords subdivided multi-room apartments into one-room "kitchenettes."[25] Bluesman Bill Weldon sang of the consequences of slum clearance:

> Everybody's working in this town,
> and this worries me night and day (2x)
> Yes, that mean working crew that works for the W.P.A.
>
> Well, well, the landlord came this mornin',
> and he knocked on my door.
> He asked me if I was going to pay my rent no more.
> He said: 'You have to move if you can't pay.'
> And then he turned, and he walked slowly away.
>
> So I have to try, find me some other place to stay.
> That house-wrecking crew's comin' from that W.P.A.
> Well, well, I went to the relief station,
> and I didn't have a cent.
> They said: '(Sit still?) where you staying,
> you don't have to pay no rent.'
> So when I got back home,
> they was tacking a notice on my door.
> This house is condemned, and you can't live here no more.
>
> So a notion struck me, I'd better be on my way.
> They're gonna tear my house down, ooh, that crew from the W.P.A.
>
> Well, well, I went out next morning; I put a lock on my door.
> I swore I would move, but I have no place to go.
> The real estate people they all done got sore.
> They don't rent to no relief clients no more.
> So I know I have to walk the streets night and day,
> Because that wrecking crew's coming, ooh, from that W.P.A.[26]

By 1936, the Works Progress Administration (W.P.A.), not the P.W.A., had become the dominant work relief agency. Drawing 90% of its workers from relief rolls, the WPA was responsible for an incredible variety of small works projects. Though the percentage of black WPA workers exceeded their percentage of the national population, there were charges of racial discrimination. Black wages were generally inferior to those of whites; blacks were usually found in the unskilled wage categories; and there were few black WPA administrators and supervisors.[27] And even with WPA work, many blacks found it necessary to turn to local relief agencies in order to make ends meet.

> I was working on the project,
> > begging the relief for shoes (2x)
> Because the rock and concrete...
> > giving my feet the blues.

> Working on the project with holes
> > all in my clothes (2x)
> Trying to make me a dime...to keep
> > the rent man from putting me outdoors.

> I am working on the project,
> > trying to make both end meet (2x)
> But the payday is so long...until
> > the grocery man won't let me eat....

> Working on the project with pay-day
> > three or four weeks away (2x)
> Now, how can you make ends meet...when
> you can't get no pay.[28]

With the liquidation of F.E.R.A. in 1935, general relief again became the responsibility of local governments, although the federal government did provide surplus commodities. Due to their higher unemployment rate and lower wages, blacks were disproportionately represented on the general relief rolls. Black people on general relief lined up at warehouses and welfare stores to receive surplus food and clothing. Direct distribution of surplus commodities, however, was a humiliating experience for relief clients, and often there were shortages of needed items.[29]

> Now, me and my baby we talked last night,
> > and we talked for nearly an hour.
> She wants me to go down to the welfare store,
> > and get a sack of that welfare flour....

> Now, you need to get you some real white man,
> > you know, to sign your little note.
> They give you a pair of them keen-toed shoes
> > and one of those pinch-backed soldier coats....

> President Roosevelt said them welfare people,
> > they going to treat everybody right.
> Says they'll give you a can of them beans

and a can or two of them old tripe.

But I told her no, baby, and I sure
don't want to go.
I say I'll do anything in the world for you,
but I don't want to go down to that
welfare store.[36]

Sonny Boy Williamson's "Welfare Store Blues" is one of the most striking documents from the 1930's. On the one hand, "Welfare Store Blues" served as entertainment providing dance music with its rollicking piano, guitar, and harmonica accompaniment. It was a way of "laughing off" the Depression.[31] But on the other hand, "Welfare Store Blues" was a crushing indictment of the local discrimination which hindered federal attempts to aid the poor. In addition, the song anticipated the historian's discovery of the ambivalent legacy of New Deal efforts to aid blacks in relief and recovery programs.

Blues songs from the Depression era not only entertained. They also defined social situations and offered ways of coping with them. The body of blues lyrics may thus be broadly viewed as history—"a cycle of journeys in search of fair treatment and better times."[32] By recording topical blues about the Depression, blues musicians not only mirrored black experiences, but they also helped shape the attitudes and actions of black people.

Notes

[1]Robert Dixon and John Goodrich, *Recording the Blues* (London, 1970), 9-33; Jeff Todd Titon, *Early Downhome Blues: A Musical and Cultural Analysis* (Urbana, 1977), xii-xvii, 64-65. In black English, the term "downhome" does not refer to a geographic region but rather to a way of life: black tenant farming culture and its partial extension to the cities. Jeff Todd Titon, "Thematic Pattern in Downhome Blues Lyrics," *Journal of American Folklore*, 90 (1977), 318.

[2]William Ferris, "Blues Roots and Development," *The Black Perspective in Music* 2, (1974), 124; David Evans, "Techniques of Blues Composition Among Black Folksingers," *Journal of American Folklore*, 87 (1974), 240-249; Titon, *Early Downhome Blues*, 37-42; William Ferris, *Blues From the Delta* (New York, 1978), 57-75. Blues songs generally have a twelve-bar structure, three-line verses with an AAB rhyme scheme, and tonic, subdominant, dominant chord progressive patterns. See Peter Guralnick, *Feel Like Going Home: Portraits in Blues and Rock 'n' Roll* (New York, 1971), 22. 24.

[3]John Greenway, *American Folksongs of Protest* (New York, 1953), 8. Perhaps the most succinct definition of a folksong was offered by Aunt Molly Jackson, a Depression-era union organizer: "This is what a folksong really is; the folks composes (sic) there (sic) own songs about there (sic) own lives (sic) there (sic) home folks that live around them." *Ibid.*

[4]For a complete listing of downhome blues records from the interwar years, see John Godrich and Robert Dixon, *Blues and Gospel Records 1902-1942* (London, 1969). Discographical information for records cited in this article is taken from above.

[5]Charles Johnson, *Shadow of the Plantation* (Chicago, 1934), 129; Titon, *Early Downhome Blues*, 59-60.

[6]Ferris, "Blues Roots and Development," 124; Titon, "Thematic Pattern in Downhome Blues Lyrics," 315; Paul Oliver, *The Meaning of the Blues* (New York, 1960); Paul Oliver, *The Story of the Blues* (Radnor, Penn., 1969, 103-104.

[7]Titon, *Early Downhome Blues*, 64.

[8]Oliver, *Story of the Blues*, 106; Titon, *Early Downhome Blues*, 43-44.

[9]See Jacquelyn Dowd Hall, "Documenting Diversity: The Southern Experience," *The Oral History Review* (1976), 23; W.T. Couch, ed., *These Are Our Lives* (Chapel Hill, 1939); Studs Terkel, *Hard Times: An Oral History of the Great Depression* (New York, 1970); David Culbert, "The Infinite Variety of Mass Experience: The Great Depression, W.P.A. Interviews, and Student Family History Projects," *Louisiana History*, 19 (1978), 43-64.

[10]Dixon and Godrich, *Recording the Blues*, 64-77.

[11]Oliver, *Story of the Blues*, 106.

[12]*Ibid.*, 103.

[13]Paul Oliver, *The Meaning of the Blues* (New York, 1960), 27; Mike Rowe, *Chicago Breakdown* (London, 1973), 15; Michael Stewart and Don Kent, Album Notes to "Hard Times Blues: St. Louis 1933-1940," Mamlish 53806.

[14]Robert Weaver, *The Negro Ghetto* (New York, 1948), 54; Raymond Wolters, *Negroes and the Great Depression: The Problem of Economic Recovery* (Westport, Conn., 1970), 113-114.

[15]Charley Jordan, "Tough Time Blues," Vocalion 1568 (Chicago, 1930). This recording has been reissued on "Hard Time Blues", Mamlish 53806, mistitled as "Tight Time Blues."

[16]"Barbecue" Bob Hicks, "We Sure Got Hard Times Now," Columbia 14558-D (Atlanta, 1930). Reissued on "Hard Times" Rounder 4007.

[17]Searle Charles, *minister of Relief: Harry Hopkins and the Great Depression* (Syracuse, 1963), 15, 18, 21.

[18]Charley Jordan, "Starvation Blues," 1627 (Chicago, 1931). Reissued on "Hard Times" Rounder 4007.

[19]Charles, *Minister of Relief*, 27.

[20]Blind (Teddy) Darby, "Meat and Bread Blues (Relief Blues)," Vocalion 02988 (Chicago, 1935). Reissued on "Savannah Syncopators," CBS 52799.

[21]Richard Sterner, *The Negro's Share: A Study of Income, Consumption, Housing and Public Assistance* (New York, 1943), 218; Charles, *Minister of Relief*, 101.

[22]Carl Martin, "Let's Have a New Deal," Decca 7114 (Chicago, 1935). Reissued on "Country Blues Classics: Vol. 4," Blues Classics 14.

[23]Wolters, *Negroes and the Great Depression*, 197-200.

[24]Jimmie Gordon, "Don't Take Away My P.W.A.," Decca 7230 (Chicago, 1936). Lyrics transcribed in Oliver, *Meaning of the Blues*, 60.

[25]Sterner, *The Negro's Share*, 323; Weaver, *The Negro Ghetto*, 67-68.

[26]"Casey" Bill Weldon, "W.P.A. Blues," Vocalion 03186 (Chicago, 1936). Reissued on "Country Blues Classics: Vol. 3," Blues Classics 7.

[27]Charles, *Minister of Relief*, 120, 145-146; Sterner, *The Negro's Share*, 249, 251-252.

[28]"Peetie Wheatstraw" (William Bunch), "Working on the Project," Decca 7311 (Chicago, 1937). Reissued on "Kokomo Arnold/Pettie Wheatstraw," Blues Classics 4.

[29]Sterner, *The Negro's Share*, 218, 287, 291; Also, see Couch, ed., *These Are Our Lives*, 365-368.

[30]John Lee "Sonny Boy" Williamson, "Welfare Store Blues," Bluebird B8610 (Chicago, 1940). Reissued on "Sonny Boy Williamson," Blues Classics 3.

[31]Robert Springer, "The Regulatory Function of the Blues," *The Black Perspective in Music*, 4 (1976), 278.

[32]Titon, "Thematic Pattern in Downhome Blues Lyrics," 317, 329.

A Word About Whiteman

Russel B. Nye

Paul Whiteman was born in 1890, died in 1967, and during the twenties—whether he deserved the title "King of Jazz" or not—personified popular music to the public. Exactly where he belongs in the history of jazz and popular music is still a subject of controversy, and sometimes a heated one. Actually, his importance in the field diminished rather rapidly after 1930, so that forty years later it ought to be possible to assess his influence on popular music of the twenties, one way or another, with some degree of objectivity. Unfortunately, the majority of jazz critics and historians seem to have made up their minds some time ago. The purpose of this paper is to take another look at him and his music.

Whiteman was born in Denver into a musical family; his father was director of musical education in the public schools and his mother a well-known vocalist. Paul learned to play violin quite well by ten; by his own account he then developed an intense dislike of music, and not until his mid-teens did he return to it. He was good enough at seventeen to play in the Denver Symphony, and, planning a career as a professional musician, went to San Francisco to join the World's Fair Orchestra. Here he heard jazz for the first time and unlike most symphony musicians, was fascinated by it. During the war he served with the Navy as a bandmaster, and after it collected a few musicians to play dance dates—thus being one of the first to take advantage of the postwar dance craze. Finding an eager market for dance music, Whiteman (who had an acute business sense) organized a number of dance bands and booked them out quite profitably around California. His own band he took to Los Angeles, where he became the toast of the Hollywood movie colony.[1]

S.W. Straus, who was about to open the new Ambassador Hotel in Atlantic City, heard Whiteman's group and offered him $600 a week to come East. Neither he nor his Californians liked the idea, but the pay was attractive. They were a hit in Atlantic City, so much so that the Palais Royal, New York's smartest dance club, offered him $1800 a week to come to the city. He did, opening on October 1, 1920, and soon was drawing $2750 a week, double the rate paid any other band. (Vincent Lopez, brought in from Long Island as

Reprinted with permission from *Popular Music and Society*, Volume 1:4 (Summer, 1972), pp. 231-41.

competition, got $1200 a week.) When the Palais Royal closed for remodeling in 1922, Whiteman took his band to the Trianon in Chicago for six nights at $25,000, the highest price paid to a dance band to that time.[2]

The Whiteman band's popularity soared. In 1923 he visited London for a triumphal stay, and back in New York later that year planned, quite daringly, the famous (and later misunderstood) Aeolian Hall "jazz concert" of February 12, 1924. His purpose was frankly educational. "My idea," he said,[3]

was to show these skeptical people the advance which had been made in popular music from the day of discordant early jazz to the melodious form of the present.

Meanwhile, Whiteman signed with Victor Records and produced dozens of records a year. "Wang Wang Blues," his first (released September, 1920) sold well, but "Whispering," recorded the same year, sold the staggering total of 1,800,000 within a year, and later, with his recordings of "Avalon" and "Three O'Clock in the Morning," reached three million. He eventually had from twenty to thirty bands operating under his name, starred in five movies, and had steady work in radio. He made money fast and spent it fast until the bottom dropped out of the business in the early thirties.[4] He kept on, however, with radio and occasional theater tours, and in 1943 became musical director of the "Blue" network, later ABC. He tried television in the fifties, not very successfully, and as late as 1962 he led a band for a month at Las Vegas. But he had many other interests—auto racing for one—and remained mostly out of music before his death in 1967.

The denigration of Whiteman began during his lifetime, not by musicians but by critics. Some, entranced by negritude, attacked his music because of his color; others, especially the hard core purists, attacked him personally as an insensitive, commercially-minded destroyer of artists—a tempter who lured creative men away from true art with regular salaries. Much sport was made of his use of the title, "King of Jazz," neglecting to note that the use of grandiose names for publicity purposes—including titles like "Duke" and "Count"— was common in the twenties; or, that Benny Goodman was not averse to being called "The King of Swing" a few years later. He "temporarily neutralized" real jazz men, wrote one critic, "by waving hundred dollar bills in their faces." Others accused him of corrupting musical purity by "opening his checkbook...and pandering" to the lowest musical tastes.[5] Except for a judicious footnote by Gunther Schuller in 1968, few historians of popular music or jazz critics have questioned such judgments.[6]

The fact is that Paul Whiteman and his music represented a direct, timely response to the cultural needs of the nineteen twenties, and he should be judged in that context. It is far too easy, and not a little arrogant, for the modern jazz writer to take advantage of forty-odd years of musical sophistication in order to derogate the taste of the public who liked Whiteman, and to criticize him and the men who played and arranged for him.[7] It must be recognized first of all that the nature of popular music changed swiftly in the twenties as the nature of the market changed. The shift of dancing styles away from the waltz and other traditional forms toward the foxtrot and its variations—which began during the World War I years—meant that dance music had to alter with it, as the saxophone replaced the violin in the European-type string ensemble and the small jazz-oriented dance combination emerged. The popularity of dancing, the rise of the recording industry, and the introduction of radio influenced all varieties of popular music in the twenties, quickly and irrevocably. A successful orchestra had to play music that was danceable *and* listenable; it had to meet the demands of thousands of people who flocked to hotels, dancehalls, and clubs, as well as those of other hundreds of thousands who listened to records and radios at home. The buying public mattered to musicians as it never had before.

The music business responded with three-million-seller records, travelling dance bands, theater concerts, and nightly broadcasts from every major (and most lesser) cities. The dance market, however, was the critical factor in making the band an organized unit. Until about 1910 music for dancing was provided by a group hired for the job, which might disband until the next job. The rise of the public dancehall, after 1915 or so, furnished a market large and consistent enough to maintain a band that moved from job to job as a group.

There appeared also in the twenties a new generation of musicians—black and white—young, well-trained in fundamentals, musically sophisticated, well aware of the market and willing to work creatively within it. The day of the jazz innocent was more or less over; as George Morrison, the black band leader and arranger told young jazzmen, "Get all the Bach, all the Haydn, all the technique you can get." Fletcher Henderson, Don Redman, Duke Ellington, Bennie Carter, Jimmy Lunceford, and Mary Lou Williams, for example, were musically trained; so were white arrangers like Lenny Hayton, Fud Livingston, Bill Challis, Russ Morgan, Glenn Miller, and others. The five-piece Dixie combo, playing old standards, did not fit the bill. The big, danceable, listenable band did—which meant both skilled musicians and arrangers.

Whiteman was among the first to make his music fit the market. His was the first band to be successful in all three categories of popular music—dancing, recording, and broadcasting. Others followed his lead—Vincent Lopez, Edgar Benson's, Sam Lanin, Nat Shilkret, Ben Selvin, and dozens more. Black bands like McKinney's, Henderson, Sissle, Basie, Kirk, Lunceford, or Ellington played white dances no differently than Casa Loma, Goldkette, the Dorseys, Whiteman, or any others. It is impossible to identify the first *organized* danceband of professional musicians playing jazz, but the trend in the market was clear by 1918—Ark Hickman (1913?), Ted Lewis (1916), Paul Specht (1916), Meyer Davis (1916), Isham Jones (1916), George Olsen (1917), Vincent Lopez (1917), Jan Garber (1918) etc. Whiteman organized his Fairmont Hotel group in 1918 and moved to the Alexandria in Los Angeles in 1919. His may not have been the first of the big dancebands, but his instant success in New York made his band the model for those who followed.[8]

Whiteman's book for his band in the mid-twenties furnishes an excellent example of what the public expected from a big, popular jazz orchestra. It included novelty tunes, straight dance tunes, tunes from shows like the Follies or the Scandals, and "symphonic" or light classic numbers. Whiteman, or any band so equipped, could play a dance job, a theater appearance, a radio hour, or a record date out of the book by choosing what fitted the occasion and the medium. In the first category would be numbers like "Charleston" or "Yes, We Have No Bananas;" in the second "Poor Butterfly" or "Changes;" in the third songs from *Showboat* or *The Little Show*; in the fourth "Vienna Waltzes" or "Song of India." A Whiteman specialty was the simple popular song arranged in semi-symphonic style—"Sweet Sue," "Among My Souvenirs," etc.[9] All big bands carried similar books, adding specialties of their own—Ellington's, for example, included "mood" or "blues" tunes like "Mood Indigo," whereas Lunceford was known for his "killer-diller" arrangements and Wayne King for waltzes. The point was, however, and Whiteman saw it clearly, that there were sweeping changes taking place in the musical tastes of this great new audience that the older jazz and the traditional dance music could not satisfy.

The success of Whiteman's California group, when transferred to the Palais Royal, was a perfect example of giving the public what it wanted, and doing it with style, ingenuity, and taste. Most important of all, Whiteman was one of the first to recognize the importance of arrangements, and by reason of his emphasis on *arranged* dancing and listening music permanently changed the character of popular music. "I could never understand," he wrote later,[10]

why jazz had to be a haphazard thing. I couldn't see why it shouldn't have form and consistency. I recall that during my stay in San Francisco I heard bands render one jazz number in excellent style and another in the worst possible manner. The players were faking, or as we say today, jamming. It occurred to me that scores to these numbers could be written.

Exactly who first "arranged" jazz cannot, of course, be accurately determined. Obviously musicians agreed to do certain things at certain times during a number long before anyone wrote down directions, and undoubtedly some musicians who could do so must have used rudiment musical notations. Art Hickman and other dance bands worked from arrangements before 1920, and by 1922 practically all dance bands used fairly formal charts. Nonetheless, it was Whiteman who insisted on the discipline and order of arranged jazz, and he who (before he left California) recognized more clearly, perhaps, than many others, the importance of controlling popular music in performance.[11] Arrangements not only gave jazz consistency and form, but made it possible to increase both the number of musicians and the variety of instruments in a jazz group. With arrangements the big band became possible; what musicians played could be rehearsed and controlled, and more complex and imaginative musical effects could be obtained than before. What Whiteman did, actually, far from *confining* jazz, was to take it out of the "You take the next chorus, Joe" category and open it up to far greater freedom. Arrangements and augmented instrumentation meant the creation of sections—brass, reed, rhythm—and the development of harmonies, block writing, statement and response patterns, and a whole range of musical possibilities unavailable to the traditional five-or six-man group. Transferring to jazz some of the formal control of the traditional orchestra gave it a new kind of sound; Whiteman made the arranger a key figure in jazz (which he still is) and the jazz band itself a more varied and disciplined unit. He was careful to point out that a jazz arrangement, unlike a symphony's, did not "tell all," as he put it, but left ample room for improvisation, reflecting the player's mood and talent. Jazz, he wrote, "is not the thing said; it is the manner of saying it."[12]

The basic pattern of Whiteman's method of arranging (later amplified and extended, of course, by many others) was musically simple, yet extremely effective. A good popular song, he said, was built about one good melody. (The popular song writer, as he explained, who had two good melodies, unlike the classical composer, made two songs out of them.) Whiteman took the one good melody and provided counter-melodies for each repeat of it. Thus he escaped what he felt was the chief weakness of most contemporary jazz, that is, repetitions of the same melody over and over. The counter-melodies might be variations of the melody, themes from other songs (even from the classics) or different related melodies composed by the arranger. An early Whiteman arrangement, then, introduced the song's melody and then alternated repeats of it with counter-melodies, leading to a conclusion and restatement of the original. This is what he brought East with him, and by 1921 music publishing houses were getting so many requests for stock arrangements for 4-12 man orchestras that most of them hired staff arrangers to write them wholesale. "For a year now," commented a writer in the New York *Times* in 1922, "all the dance orchestras have been modelling themselves on Whiteman."[13]

Certainly two of Whiteman's additional contributions to jazz, non-musical though they may be, were that he helped to make it respectable, and that he helped to make it profitable. One must remember that jazz, when Whiteman came East, was still regarded by large segments of the public and by many in the musical world as a kind of smallpox of the arts. Professor Herman Derry of Detroit was quoted in 1922 to the effect that "the jazz-band view of life is wrecking the American home," while Dr. E. Elliott Rawlings of New York told the press in 1923 that jazz had "the same effect as a drug, and one may become addicted to it"—quotations that could be multiplied by the dozen through the early twenties.[14] Whiteman's concerts, his sponsorship of serious music, his attempts at "symphonic" jazz, and his demands for impeccable musicianship in his own bands did much to make jazz reputable. He did it so well that *Etude* magazine, the most prestigious of musical journals, when it decided in 1924 that jazz was "worthy of serious attention," invited him to write an essay for its pages. In the argument over jazz-whether it should be abolished, encouraged, or simply disregarded—Whiteman was by far the most influential of its spokesmen. Few articles on jazz during the twenties, on either side, failed to mention him; he was always available for comment, for he knew the value of public relations, but he was also sincerely committed to gaining public relations, but he was also sincerely committed to gaining public acceptance for jazz music. When the powerful English music critic Ernest Newman published a blistering attack, "The Case Against Jazz," in 1927, advising jazz musicians to "keep their dirty paws" off good music, it was Whiteman who wrote an able and authoritative reply in the New York *Times*.[15]

In addition, musicians had good reason to appreciate his contributions to the economics of the profession. The salaries he paid became the standards by which other bands operated; he was fair to his men, and because of him many musicians ate regularly who would not have otherwise. They called him "Pops," "Fatho," and the like, and he was always an easy mark for a hard-luck story. Whiteman critics might well have listened to Joe Venuti, who spoke for musicians of the twenties:[16]

Don't make fun of Paul Whiteman. He did great things for American music. He took pride in having the finest musicians in the world as sidemen, and he paid the highest salaries of the period.

Whiteman's contributions to jazz were more than economic, of course. He took jazz seriously and believed it should be conceived and played well. He demanded that musicians treat their craft with respect, and he would not accept second-rate performances from men he knew could do better, thereby helping in a significant way to bring discipline to a somewhat disorganized and raffish profession. He searched out and hired the best musicians and arrangers, paid them well, and provided outlets for their talents. Literally dozens of famous names passed through the Whiteman organization—singers like Bing Crosby and Mildred Bailey, arrangers and songwriters like Challis and Johnny Mercer, great musicians like Lang, Venuti, Rank, Trumbauer, the Dorseys, Teagarden, Beiderbecke, and many others.[17]

Musically, a Whiteman concert or recording session was a skilled, highly professional exhibition. He was willing to have his arrangers experiment freely (if not always successfully) with new instrumental combinations, musical effects, and ideas, with the result that the better Whiteman performances were interesting, original, and something more than merely saleable. His arrangements asked musicians to give their best; they made full use of the richness, variety, and color of the instruments and made the listener aware of the complexity and originality of what was going on. Actually, one of Whiteman's great contributions to jazz was that he made the public *listen* to popular music as it never had before. For all the derogation of his "symphonic" jazz, it ought to be noted that others from Ellington to Kenton to Mancini to Evans have also tested the potentials of the jazz idiom. In addition, Whiteman's emphasis on technique and musicianship, which led him to make permanent members of highly skilled men such as Ross Gorman, Charles Strickfadden, Chester Hazlett, Roy Bargy, and Harry Goldfield, among others, presaged the development of the similarly skilled bands of today. Nor should schools of music which teach courses in jazz arranging forget who started it. Paul Whiteman was not afraid to be experimental; he admired all that was musically praiseworthy in jazz, and did his best to develop it. The popular music world owes him a great deal, and it is time this was recognized.

Notes

The author expresses his appreciation to William   (Bill) Challis, staff arranger for Paul Whiteman 1927-30, and to Bill Rank and Chauncey Morehouse, former members of the Whiteman orchestra, for information used in this essay.

[1]Chaplin, Mabel Normand, C.B. DeMille, and Harold Lloyd were his particular friends. Wallace Reid sat in occasionally on drums; Whiteman thought him particularly bad. Whiteman's *Jazz* (New York, 1926, with Mary Margaret McBride) is the best biographical source.

[2]In 1924, Whiteman received $10,000 for six hours of music at Clarence Mackay's famous garden party for the Prince of Wales at Mackay's Long Island estate.

[3]Chapter IV of *Jazz* gives a full account of the concert, which he titled "An Experiment in Modern Music," Heifetz, Kreisler, Stokowski, and Rachmaninoff were among its patrons; the concert introduced, of course, Gershwin's "Rhapsody in Blue," which Whiteman had especially commissioned for it. He lost $7,000 on the concert. Lopez actually beat Whiteman to it by giving a program of "contemporary popular music" at the Anderson Galleries, with a commentary by Professor Edwin B. Hill, on February 10, two days earlier, which received only minor notice. Lopez later gave a concert at the Metropolitan, while Whiteman repeated his concert at Carnegie Hall later in 1924 and gave another at the Metropolitan in 1925.

[4]His gross income in 1929, for example, was $648,000; he and his band received $440,000 for the *King of Jazz* movie; and he charged $6,000 an hour for radio work. See James Gillespie and Wesley Stout, "Hot Music," *Saturday Evening Post*, March 19, 1932. Whiteman made over 600 records with Victor, the last in 1938.

[5]H.O. Brun, *The Story of the Original Dixieland Jazz Band* (Baton Rouge, 1960); Hugues Panassie and Madeleine Gauthier, *Dictionary of Jazz* (London, 1956); Dave Dexter, *The Jazz Story* (Englewood Cliffs, 1964); Sinclair Traill, ed., *Concerning Jazz* (London, 1957). See especially Rudi Blesh, *They All Played Ragtime* (New York, 1966), and Benny Green's uncharacteristically violent criticism in *The Reluctant Art* (New York, 1963). Panassie, of course, takes a strong racist line, defining jazz as exclusively Negro music, imitated successfully by only a few white men. How he would classify the great black band of George Morrison, who called himself "The Colored Paul Whiteman," boggles the mind.

[6]*Early Jazz: Its Roots and Early Development* (New York, 1968) 192.

[7]Green, for example, *op. cit.*, 40-43, called the Whiteman organization "a clumsy group," which it assuredly was not, whose records were "horrors and travesties." It was clear to those who heard such records as "Among My Souvenirs" and "Washboard Blues" when they appeared, that they were experimental and not automatically to be rejected for so being. Louis Armstrong, among others, was a Whiteman admirer.

[8]See Albert McCarthy, *The Dance Band Era* (New York, 1972). Such dates are of course difficult to pinpoint but these are more or less accurate. Isham Jones began his long residency at the Hotel Sherman's College Inn in 1921, when Whiteman was at the Palais Royal.

[9]Frede Grofé specialized in symphonic arrangements, and staff arrangers like Lenny Hayton, Tom Satterfield, and Bill Challis in jazz-style and concert-orchestra combinations. Challis' "Sweet Sue," for example, is an excellent illustration of the latter. "San," "Dardanella," and "Sugar" are superb examples of the kind of creative arranging they did; to see how the Whiteman staff handled a routine commercial assignment with

skill and originality, see Challis' "Forget Me Not," done for Whiteman's big band in 1928.

[10]"This Thing Called Jazz," *Rotarian*, June, 1939, 34.

[11]Leonard Feather's statement in *The Book of Jazz* (New York, 1965) 192-6 that Don Redman was "the first jazz arranger of influence and importance" and that Elmer Schoebel was "the first white composer and arranger to document jazz" seems too positive for accuracy. Isham Jones, for example, was arranging for his own dance band in 1916.

[12]*Jazz*, op. cit., 35, 116. His definition of jazz is still interesting: "Jazz is a musical treatment consisting largely of question and answer, sound and echo. It is what I call unacademic counterpoint. It includes rhythmic, harmonic, and melodic invention. . . . The great art in a jazz orchestra is a counterbalancing of time values and their placement."

[13]For Whiteman's arranging and its effect on the music business, see Helen B. Lowry, "Putting the Music into Jazz," New York *Times*, February 19, 1922.

[14]As late as 1937 an instructor at the New York Schools for Music charged that swing was responsible for a current wave of sex crimes, a conclusion reached after a series of psychological experiments with young people of opposite sexes placed in a room and subjected to jazz and classical music alternately. See *Downbeat*, December, 1937.

[15]"What is Jazz Doing to American Music?" *Etude* XLII (August, 1924) 523-25. Whiteman concluded that jazz contributed freshness, variety, and new instrumental techniques to music. Newman's article appeared in the New York *Times*, March 6, 1927, and Whiteman's reply March 13, 1927. Olin Downes, the *Times'* regular music critic, respected Whiteman and often quoted him.

[16]Nat Shapiro and Nat Hentoff, *Hear Me Talkin' To Ya* (New York, 1955) 277. Whiteman's payroll for one month in 1928 showed a range of $150 to $350 a week, unusually high for the times. Whiteman's discipline gave rise to many stories. He once fired (though temporarily) the great clarinetist Chester Hazlett for an inadequate performance at a concert in New Orleans, and suspended Jack Teagarden for missing an afternoon concert in Madison, Wisconsin, to buy a dog. On the other hand, Whiteman was too softhearted to make his discipline stick when good men were involved. His kindness to Bix Beiderbecke is well known; he paid Bix's salary during the whole of his absence from the band during his illness.

[17]*Ibid.*

"Hot Jazz," The Jitterbug, and Misunderstanding: The Generation Gap in Swing 1935-1945

J. Frederick MacDonald

In the area of popular musical preferences there is much evidence to support the notion that each generation, as it accepts new musical forms, must contend with the criticism and general disapproval of the older, established generation before it is able to indulge its tastes openly. At different points in time, this generational conflict over popular music centered about the cakewalk, ragtime, jazz, rock and roll, and even contemporary "progressive rock." In each case youthful appreciators of the new musical style had to defend their preference from the condemnation of the adult generation. Such defiance of the parental position took forms ranging from discreet indulgence in private surroundings to the more open social rebellion such as that which occurred among white middle-class Americans in the 1920's. In each historical instance, however, the debate over musical freedom was keenly felt and the contending generations loyally argued their convictions.

During the period 1935-45, a decade posthumously termed the "swing era," American youth and its supporters rallied their energies to defend swing music and dance from a persistent and variegated attack by the adult generation. Although, as Neil Leonard has shown, the generational conflict was not as intense as it had been over jazz in the 1920's,[1] a study of newspaper and magazine materials of the swing era reveals a deep trepidation in the older generation caused by the enormous popularity of swing. The parents of the "jitterbugs," "hep cats," and "alligators" looked upon the antics of their offspring with incomprehension and mistrust. Whether these parents referred to the pure swing, or "hot jazz," of a Benny Goodman or Artie Shaw which through 1938 dominated the era; whether they discussed the moderate variant, or "sweet jazz," which Glenn Miller began to popularize in 1939; or whether they analyzed an offshoot of swing such as boogie-woogie, the older critics tended to see swing as a perverted musical form which was dangerously debasing the moral and physical character of American youth. Due, moreover, to certain technical advancements

Reprinted with permission from *Popular Music and Society*, Volume 2:1 (Fall 1972), pp. 43-55.

(improvements in radio programming, development of the jukebox, and proliferation of dance-hall facilities), the parental critique of swing became all the more harried as swing music was diffused throughout the United States on an unprecedented scale.

I

Swing music and dance forms were assailed for numerous reasons, but one of the strongest and most constant arguments during the decade was an attack upon the psychological implications of swing. This assault was more damaging because it was often conducted by members of the scientific and academic communities. One psychologist reported that swing was an insidious influence upon youngsters "unfamiliar with the ways of the world"; he claimed, moreover, that its rhythms produced in American youth a "mental epidemic" which in turn created a "break down [in] conventions and led to moral weakness."[2] On much the same theme, a psychiatrist in Chicago argued that swing should be treated as an epidemic. He felt that the most effective treatment would be to separate the "victim" from the infectious "jitterbug," and he advised that "this would be a wise thing for many parents to do if their children are innocent bystanders who are being drawn into the craze."[3] Speaking in November, 1938, one month after German troops had marched into Czechoslovakia, a professor of economics at Barnard College told an audience more threateningly that swing music could possibly lead to "musical Hitlerism." Chiding American education for stressing specialization to the point of "emotional starvation," the professor prophetically warned that this condition might give rise to someone "from commercialized entertainment or commercialized politics, a man on horseback, to give us emotional outlets in mass demonstration and other ways."[4]

The findings of scientific research could also be used to reassure those who distrusted and disliked swing. Such a conclusion came out of an experiment conducted in 1939 by the department of psychology of Columbia University. It revealed that when several hundred humans were exposed to various forms of music, including "hot jazz," they liked "swing music very much but they tired of it more quickly than any other type of music."[5] Nevertheless, on the insidious side, another writer reported that in a closed experiment with an unsuspecting man and woman, researchers observed that when classical music and light waltzes were played the couple was "friendly, but that was all," but when the man and woman suddenly heard swing, they "become much bolder, both of them" and "the progress of the experiment brought brow-raising confirmation of scientific fears."[6]

Attacks upon swing music and dance by scientists and academicians affected even supporters of the musical fad. One such writer, epitomizing much of the criticism of academicians, admitted wryly that to "some historians and sociologists the boisterous vitality of swing is but a specious agitation concealing the intellectual aridity and jaded senses of the effete modern mind." Interestingly, this writer projected swing music into the historiographical debate over the decline of the West, noting that "Spenglerites, no doubt, hail swing as a fitting danse macabre for a society tobogganing to its grave."[7]

Many times in the decade the assault upon swing received the strong endorsement of leading figures in American cultural life. In 1938 the Broadway composer, Meredith Wilson, confidently predicted that within one year swing would be outdated. He assured the public that it would be replaced by the return of the Virginia Reel and other community dances.[8] The eminent conductor, Bruno Walter, admitted to interviewers that although he found the rhythmic variety of jazz interesting, "it is drowned by wildness of sound; my ears become unhappy."[9] These criticisms were mild, however, in comparison with the attack upon boogie-woogie launched in 1944 by Arthur Rodzinski. This form of jazz (which one writer correctly and simply defined as a "style of piano playing,"[10]), according to the conductor of the New York Philharmonic, was "the greatest single contributing factor to juvenile delinquency among American youth today." With many fathers in the armed services, Rodzinski argued, "parental supervision is lacking and this type of music leads to war degeneracy."[11] William Allen White, however, was much more descriptive and compelling when he condemned swing music as

merely syncopated, blood raw emotion, without harmony, without consistent rhythm, and with no more tune than the yearnful bellowing of a lonely, yearning and romantic cow in the pastures, or the raucous staccatic meditation of a bulldog barking in a barrel.[12]

Jitterbugging, jam sessions, and the other socializing activities of swing music even drew rebuke from Church leaders. In fact, one of the strongest condemnations of swing was issued by the Roman Catholic Archbishop of Dubuque, Iowa. Speaking in 1938 before the National Council of Catholic Women, the Reverend Francis J.L. Beckman blasted modern popular music as "evil and malicious" and "communistic." According to the Church official, "We permit...jam sessions, jitterbug and cannibalistic rhythmic orgies to occupy a place in our social scheme of things, wooing our youth along the primrose path to hell." In his well-received speech, the Archbishop contended that although the Church was pursuing "as zealously as ever she has in the past her policy of motivating, conserving and drawing to herself the best of modern art," swing music was among the "evil forces...hard at work to undermine its Christian status, debauch its high purposes and harness it to serve individual diabolical ends."[13]

Regardless of the elements of society from which the criticism of swing music and dance emanated, those who derided the fad generally emphasized several recurrent themes. In studying the pronouncements of the more outspoken critics during the swing era, three principal types of criticism are noticeable. The first type of disparagement was enunciated by those who regarded swing music and dance artistically displeasing. To such critics, swing was an irreverent and raucous cacophony. William Allen White felt the music "squaked and shrieked and roared and bellowed in syncopated savagery."[14] With the increasing popularity of swingtime versions of melodies from classical composers, many musicians and music lovers assailed swing as debasing the quality of classical music. In 1938, A.L. Dennis, as President of the Bach Society of New Jersey, requested that the Federal Communications Commission penalize radio stations that broadcast "jazzed-up" versions of the classics.[15] Another critic sardonically wondered what the reaction of the audience would be "if the players of the Philadelphia Orchestra 'got religion' in the middle of the Fifth Symphony and started to improve upon Beethoven."[16] Reflective of this attack upon swing as an art form was the reorganization in December, 1938, of the National Star Spangled Banner Association for the purpose of preventing dance orchestras from improvising upon the national anthem.[17]

Just as the music of the swing era was condemned as unartistic, so too were swing dances and dancers castigated. One dance expert reproached the most popular dance form when he claimed that there was "little or no display of natural grace in good jitterbug."[18] This opinion was graphically substantiated by another writer who described the average jitterbug as having "a spinal column like a macaroni, the head, neck, and shoulders of a jack-in-the-box, and the legs of a young kangaroo."[19] Music critic Jack Gould protested that jitterbug dancers resembled "a chimpanzee suffering from delirium tremens."[20] Even advocates of swing could be less than reassuring in their assessments of jitterbug. Although one such proponent praised it for everything from keeping American youth mentally alert, to helping young dancers develop their leg muscles, her picture of a typical dance floor as being "wildly catapulting, bobbing, stamping, leaping, surging"[21] was not likely to convince uncertain parents to approve their children's tastes. Another supporter also depreciated his argument when he informed readers that "social dancing is for the most part a mild sex experience," and "the humorous possibilities of jazz have made it susceptible to a certain amount of surreptitious obscenity."[22] Even Benny Goodman admitted that the young "tempo fiends" who heard him perform did act immaturely. He likened their dancing to "track meets and sitting-up exercises" on the dance floor.[23]

A second type of criticism of swing music centered about the detrimental effect that the music was having upon society. The essence of this argument was that swing and its performers threatened the moral fiber of the nation because they popularized the use of alcohol and drugs, and their music represented a direct and irresponsible appeal to the sensual and erotic nature of the citizenry. Charges of alcoholism and marijuana usage were made frequently against swing musicians. Even when a prestigious personality such as Paul Whiteman sought to deny these allegations, he was compelled to admit that a "great many people think that a swing musician has to fight his way through a fog of marijuana smoke before he can play a hot lick." Although he added that a "reefer man or a man whose technique comes out of a bottle couldn't last two nights with one of our first-rate swing bands,"[24] "Whiteman's defense apparently did not include the hundreds of second-and third-rate bands which flooded the nation. The usual critique was to the effect that 'cup and the weed' were integral aspects of the life of the 'ordinary hipster' operating in dives all over the land."[25] Critics argued that artificial stimuli were necessary to the average swing musician because of the exhaustive lifestyle he followed. One apologist, describing the typical aspiring musician, confessed that "on the whole, jazz musicians probably do go in for a good deal more heavy drinking and 'reefer' smoking than, say, the Wellesley class of '39." He contended, however, that this was not due to "congenital depravity," but was the result of "the atmosphere surrounding him and the emotional strain and physical disturbance involved in playing an instrument." Nevertheless, this writer recommended that "a field to stay out of is music."[26]

Because of the emphasis of swing upon rhythm, and because of the wild abandon which the jitterbug often approached, the charge frequently was made that swing was an erotic attack upon conventional sexual mores. One analyst in 1938 asserted that swing was a "degenerated" musical form in which the youth of the United States had found "neurotic and erotic expressions of physical activity."[27] The eminent violinist, Fritz Kreisler, contended jazz in general was "the expression of primeval instincts."[28] The methodology of William Allen White reiterated this theme more poignantly when he claimed jitterbugging was the "same old stuff that mating animals have used far down the zoological line through the beasts of the field, the birds of the air, and the lightning bugs on a summer evening."[29] The methodology of modern science was also used to prove the sexually stimulating nature of swing.[30] One defender of swing claimed there was a greater sexual potential in cheek-to-cheek dancing than in jitterbugging which was far too athletic an occupation for dancers to have time for "sexual experimentation." He was, however, forced to preface his defense with the remark that on the surface the "shaking and swaying" of swing "impresses the non-initiate as something not quite nice, even shameful."[31]

A third type of reproach of swing was the argument that the music and dance were ultimately primitive and barbaric manifestations foreign to American civilization. This attack contained an obvious racist undertone. Despite the swarm of white orchestras, it was difficult for many critics of swing to overlook the fact that jazz and swing originated among black musicians. This caused some to suggest that the rhythm of swing was the beat of African savagery. One analyst felt the roots of swing to be in "the rhythmic jungle chants of the descendents of Africans, from the coon songs of the early 1900's—watered-down pablum for the white man."[32] A.L. Dennis was intolerant of the "savage slurring of the saxophone and the jungled discords of the clarinet."[33] Another critic stressed his opinion that "the frantic fervor with which many of the players perform seems more like the religious orgies of very primitive peoples." He also contended that "Swing, after all, is at times very near to the jungle."[34] And the implications of primitiveness in swing were not dispelled by Bruno Walter when he remarked that "swing hits the lower strings of mankind and sets them in vibration."[35] Although no writer overtly attacked swing as a Negro subversion of white American social values, the implications of phrases such as "cannibalistic rhythmic orgies" and "syncopated savagery" reveal a racist ground tone in much of the criticism. This mentality was even expressed in the prestigious *Christian Science Monitor* which, remarking on the musical programs presented on radio for American troops during the Second World

War, noted that "If it is true that jazz music is jungle music, then the jungle is getting it back, in Burma and on the Pacific Islands. At any rate, the natives react enthusiastically to good swing."[36]

II

Given the rapidity and thoroughness with which swing was accepted by American youth during the Depression, and given the persistent criticism of swing coming from articulate members of the older generation, it is little wonder that the proponents of swing music and dance had a difficult time trying to understand the nature of the swing era. In order to defend swing, many writers tried to explain the phenomenon. Several historical analysts concentrated upon tracing the origins of swing. Although most agreed that its roots were in the jazz music of the American Negroes, others traced it in part to classical Greece, to seventeenth-century England, and to Western mining camps. To one writer, swing was simply "the grand-daughter of the Cakewalk";[37] another contended that "there wouldn't be any of their beloved swing in 1937 if we had not taken rag-time to our hearts so rapturously in 1912."[38] Others sought to comprehend the reasons for the success of swing. To one journalist, the invention of the juke box was primarily responsible for the popularity of swing.[39] Nevertheless, an earlier researcher suggested several psychological theories, among them the fact that with the repeal of prohibition in 1933, the country needed a "madder music to go with its stronger wine." This writer, assessing swing in light of the Depression, added that the mission of swing was to "liven-up the general post-crash bender."[40]

Conversely, some sought to explain the swing fad as a sociological phenomenon embodying the response of the younger generation to the dislocation of the contemporary world. Larry Clinton, one of the more popular band leaders of the era, maintained swing was a "reflection of a restless, tense world." He noted that "Young people always need an outlet for physical energy. Here is a strenuous outlet in a strenuous age."[41] Another writer felt that after the "darkest despair" of the early years of the Depression, a time in which youngsters were "straying about the dance floor as if they didn't care if they lived or died," jitterbugs were now daring "to assert the right of youth to enjoy itself in dance." She added that "It's not cricket to be bored by swing. Swing is serious...it has made it smart to care to give a hang about what you're doing."[42] Music critic Irving Kolodin also sought to allay parental misgivings about swing. He chided adults who regarded swing music "as merely raucous and noisy because it diverges so strongly from the dance music with which they grew up." He argued that the popularity of swing with American youth could be explained in psychological and sociological terms: "the youngsters who have reached adolescence during its vogue recognize it as something of their own, an exciting and stimulating sound to which they react spontaneously." According to Kolodin, swing was an expression of "the immortal right of adolescence to assert itself."[43]

To still other supporters of swing, the phenomenon was the product and expression of urbanity. According to one musical expert, just as folk music expresses the spirit of rural people, "Tin Pan Alley music has a definite place in our musical expression. It is the music of the cities."[44] Violinist Misha Elman defended jitterbug dancing as "merely the social outlet for our city just as folk dancing goes on in the country."[45] The insights by knowledgeable defenders of swing were overshadowed, however, by a letter in the *New York Times:*

Why all this disapproval of swing? It seems incredible to me that in our modern society where people are supposed to be educated, they should not realize that ideas change with the times. What is this thing called swing? Swing is the voice of youth striving to be heard in this fast-moving world of ours. Swing is the tempo of our time. Swing is real. Swing is alive....The older folk may be more conservative and truly shocked at swing, but they should realize that our fast-moving world makes swing acceptable. If they must do away with swing, then they must do away with everything that is fast. Give us a slow-moving era if you want to see the minuet.[46]

Despite the defenses of swing along historical and sociological lines, the proponents of swing had to contend more directly with the substantive allegations of immorality and indecency in swing music and dance. This was a charge levelled more often at jitterbug dance forms. Whether youthful dancers did the Big Apple, Dartmouth Dip, St. Louis Shuffle, Truckin', Susie-Que, Collegiate Shag, or any of the various styles, they were always open to parental condemnation for devious activity. In countering such charges, Larry Clinton claimed that to most youth "swing is no more than a game—a good strenuous game after eight hours in an office or good solid study in a classroom."[47] Kolodin also urged patience among the older generation. He maintained that jitterbug was "participation in the performance," and that promiscuousness among jitterbugs was unlikely since "A partnership that embraces leaps and bounds, bodies flung through the air and other hair-raising exploits really doesn't permit much distraction."[48]

Defenders of jitterbug also cautioned that swing dance was physically and socially salutary. One writer, critical of the "vigilantes of public health and morals," berated the adult generation for not realizing that when the jitterbugs were finished dancing, there stood "two abundantly healthy young kids, winded and perspiring, perfectly happy and mentally sound."[49] This point was also urged by Benny Goodman who maintained that "Kids want to blow off steam. They like our music because it's spontaneous just like themselves."[50] That swing dancing could lead to better understanding among ethnic and racial groups within the society was a point argued by several teenagers during a round-table discussion on delinquency sponsored in 1944 by the *New York Times.* Most of the participants agreed that juvenile delinquency was fostered by "boredom and not knowing what to do with yourself." Therefore, to one representative, jitterburg gave a teenager something to do and promoted understanding among youth of differing backgrounds. According to this speaker, if "everyone learned to dance boogie-woogie, more young people would get together and understand one another better."[51]

The artistic value of both swing music and dance was also proposed by supporters of swing. The reknowned composer Leopold Stokowski declared that "Modern American music—boogie woogie, jive and swing—will in time be absorbed into American art music." He praised the individualistic phrasing of Frank Sinatra, and the virtuosity of Harry James in declaring that "Art is not based on imitation, but initiative."[52] To one writer, jitterbug dancing was also a definite art form. She contended that such was "the younger set's answer to the challenge of the improvisations of the music." She argued that jitterbug was "pedal dexterity on the dance floor to match the digital flourishes of the band. It's translating hot licks into hot steps."[53] Benny Goodman carried that artistic theme one step further when he compared the reactions of adults at symphonic concerts and teenagers at swing concerts. "The difference," he argued, "is that the sensitive concertgoer doesn't move a muscle. He just sits there and gets goose-pimples." On the other hand, according to Goodman, the foot-tapping youth "hasn't attended enough concerts or received enough dirty looks to stop his unashamed rhythmic movements. When he does, he'll sublimate them into goose-pimples."[54]

III

Analysis of journalistic materials from the period 1935-45 has shown that a heated generational conflict over the merits of swing music and dance existed throughout the decade. Faced by a barrage of critics from the Church, the arts, and public leadership, the defenders of swing had to resort to pedagogic, defensive pronouncements to dissuade the parental generation from believing that its children's tastes in popular music were pernicious and subversive. Usually the supporters of swing stressed historical, psychological, or sociological arguments in attempting to allay the fears of anxious parents. Lexicons of swing slang were often printed, and important music critics constantly assured readers that swing virtuosi could also play classic compositions well. In this regard, it is interesting to note that although someone like Neil Leonard feels that the controversy over swing was relatively moderate, and that the swing period marks "the beginnings of general acceptance" of jazz forms,[55] the assault upon swing was of such magnitude that throughout the decade defenders were compelled to announce publicly and strongly their support of the phenomenon and their displeasure with those who assailed swing musical and dance forms.

Perhaps of interest to the student of popular music is what was not said during the debate over swing. Neither the critics nor the defenders of swing discussed lyric content in support of their respective positions. If anything, the lyrics of swing tunes were extremely traditionalistic with strong overtones of morality, loyalty, and conservatism. Ironically, moreover, the swing decade embraced both the Depression and World War II, two developments from which one might expect to find popular songs espousing radical social causes. Nevertheless, the fact that both sides in the controversy overlooked lyric content seems to illustrate the relative unimportance of content analysis in understanding the popular music of an era. In the present disagreement over the merits of content analysis, the example of the swing era appears to confirm the opinion of those who discount reliance upon the words of a song.

Finally, the historical recurrence of the generational dispute over tastes in popular music needs a much more thorough and consistent analysis than has heretofore been afforded. Although jazz in the 1920's has received masterful analysis, there is much that needs to be done with the generational controversy in the decades before the Jazz Age, and with similar patterns of disagreement of more recent vintages. From such investigation could come important explanations of not only the debate over musical preferences, but also significant insights into the general and persistent existence of social tension between the adolescent and parental generations.

Notes

[1]Neil Leonard, *Jazz and the White Americans: The Acceptance of a New Art Form* (Chicago, 1962) pp. 150-153.

[2]Gama Gilbert, "Higher Soars the Swing Fever," *The New York Times Magazine* (cited hereafter as *NYTM*), August 14, 1938. p. 18.

[3]*Ibid.*

[4]*The New York Times* (cited hereafter as *Times*), November 2, 1938. This theme also appeared in Gilbert, p. 16. Interestingly, in 1937 the Nazi Labor service condemned swing as a product of degeneration comparable in its malign influence to "Bolshevist culture" in literature and art; "Swing could only have originated in a country where dances are executed in front of altars during divine service, and where there will soon be swing dancing between tombstones at funerals." *Times*, September 5, 1937.

[5]*Ibid.*, April 16, 1939.

[6]Gilbert, p. 18.

[7]Gama Gilbert, "Swing It! And Even in a Temple of Music,"*NYTM*, January 16, 1938, p. 21.

[8]*Times*, August 14, 1938.

[9]*Ibid.*, March 26, 1939.

[10]John Martin, "Inquiry into Boogie Woogie," *NYTM*, July 16, 1944, p. 18.

[11]*Times*, August 14, 1938.

[12]"A Sage Looks at Swing," *Time*, May 20, 1940, p. 41.

[13]*Times*, October 26, 1938.

[14]"A Sage Looks at Swing," p. 41.

[15]*Times*, October 27, 1938.

[16]William Roberts Tilford, "Swing!, Swing!, Swing!," *The Etude*, December 1937, p. 835.

[17]*Times*, December 21, 1938.

[18]*Ibid.*, July 27, 1938.

[19]Gilbert, "Higher Soars the Swing Fever," p. 19.

[20]*Times*, August 7, 1938.

[21]Cecilia Ager, "Swing Dance," *Variety*, January 6, 1937, p. 188.

[22]Reed Dickerson, "Hot Music, Rediscovering Jazz," *Harper's Monthly Magazine*, April, 1936, p. 570.

[23]*Times*, December 8, 1940.

[24]Paul Whiteman, "The All-American Swing Band," *Collier's*, September 10, 1938, p. 9.

[25]Gilbert, "Higher Soars the Swing Fever," p. 19.

[26]Lewis Bergman, "Small-Time Musician," *NYTM*, September 10, 1939, pp. 6, 16.

[27]*Times*, July 27, 1938.

[28]*Ibid*, October 9, 1936.

[29]"A Sage Looks at Swing," p. 41.

[30]*Supra*, note 7.

[31]Irving Kolodin, "What About Swing?" *The Parents' Magazine*, August, 1939, pp. 18-19, 59.

[32]James H.S. Moynahan, "Ragtime to Swing," *The Saturday Evening Post*, February 13, 1937, p. 15.

[33]*Times*, October 27, 1938.

[34]Tilford, pp. 778, 835.

[35]*Times*, March 26, 1939.

[36]Nicholas Slominsky, "Jazz, Swing, and Boogie Woogie," *The Christian Science Monitor* (Weekly Magazine Section), May 20, 1944, p. 5.

[37]Richard Williams, "Basic Swing-lish or How to Know What the Younger Generation is Talking About," *House Beautiful*, February, 1944, p. 27.

[38]*Times*, April 25, 1937.

[39]Barry Ulanov, "The Jukes Take Over Swing," *The American Mercury*, October, 1940, pp. 172-177.

[40]Frank Norris, "The Music Goes 'Round and Around," *The New Republic*, January 29, 1936, p. 334.

[41]Larry Clinton, "Swing Grows Up, A Prophecy for Days to Come," *Good Housekeeping*, October, 1938, p. 13.

[42]Ager, p. 188.

[43]Kolodin, p. 18.

[44]*Times*, May 5, 1937.

[45]*Ibid.*, January 24, 1944.

[46]*Ibid.*, February 26, 1939.

[47]Clinton, p. 13.

[48]Kolodin, p. 59.

[49]Gilbert, "Higher Soars the Swing Fever," p. 19.

[50]Cited in Kolodin, p. 19.

[51]*Times*, January 29, 1944.

[52]*Ibid.*, January 23, 1944.

[53]Ager, p. 188.

[54]*Times*, December 8, 1940.

[55]Leonard, chapter 7.

Oh, What a Beautiful Mornin':
The Musical, *Oklahoma!*
and the Popular Mind in 1943

Timothy P. Donovan

The last day of March, 1943, in New York City had been the kind of day that is so characteristic of the early spring. While winter could still be found in the chill of early morning temperatures, the afternoon contained hints of summer in the warmer air that covered the city and the weather forecast promised more of the same until the weekend. To those who attended the opening of the Theater Guild's new musical play that night at the St. James Theater the feeling of spring in the offing was confirmed for everything about *Oklahoma!* from the simple lyrics of Oscar Hammerstein II and the enchanting music of Richard Rodgers to the energetic choreography of Agnes de Mille suggested those things usually associated with springtime: youth, hope, and love. The play became an immediate hit, not only because it seemed synchronized with the season but also because in a very special way it reflected the popular mood of America in the war year of 1943.

Oklahoma! was not just an overnight sensation; it proved to be the most successful Broadway musical in history although its records have since been surpassed by *My Fair Lady, Hello, Dolly,* and *Fiddler on the Roof.* A look at some of the musical's box office accomplishments makes the point very clear. During its first year run it played to 580,000 people and already had a road company on tour which, in itself, was somewhat a rarity for such a new show. By the time of *Oklahoma!*'s second anniversary 1,336,974 people had attended the New York performances, another 1,073,000 had seen the touring production. Over 5 1/2 million dollars had been taken in by the producers and thousands of servicemen had seen a special U.S.O. company which took the show overseas.[1]

By the end of its fifth year in 1948, *Oklahoma!*'s statistics were even more impressive. Both the New York and road companies were still going strong and it was estimated that the musical had already been seen by over eight million people. More than 500,000 albums of the original cast recording had

Reprinted with permission from the *Journal of Popular Culture,* Volume 8:3 (Winter 1974), pp. 477-488.

been purchased and two million copies of the sheet music sold.[2] When the initial Rodgers and Hammerstein production finally closed its unprecedented run of 2,248 consecutive performances,[3] it had grossed seven million dollars in New York alone and original investors in the show had realized a 5,000 percent profit. Touring companies had taken the play to every country in western Europe and Scandinavia, South Africa, Australia, and various islands in the South Pacific. It was a hit everywhere. At London's famous Drury Lane Theatre *Oklahoma!* had the longest run in the history of that ancient playhouse. Altogether, *Oklahoma!* earned over one hundred million dollars, and in so doing rescued the Theater Guild from near bankruptcy and made a million dollars each for Richard Rodgers and Oscar Hammerstein.[4] That *Oklahoma!* was an extraordinarily popular presentation is apparent. What makes its public acceptance the more remarkable was the large number of drawbacks it carried into opening night. Not many associated with the production had much confidence in the ability of the musical to surmount what knowledgeable theater people believed would prove fatal.

In the first place there were no recognized stars in the cast; neither Alfred Drake nor Joan Roberts, the male and female leads, had ever seen their names at the top of marquees, and the show business world was increasingly dominated by the emphasis Hollywood had given to the star system. Nor could *Oklahoma!* use the play itself as a substitute. It had been adapted from Lynn Riggs' "Green Grow the Lilacs" which the Theater Guild had staged earlier as straight folk-drama; it had collapsed after 64 performances in 1931. The names, Rodgers and Hammerstein, added a certain luster but were no guarantees of success. Richard Rodgers was working for the first time with a collaborator other than Lorenz Hart whose increasing unpredictability and approaching final illness had removed him from Broadway to Florida. Hammerstein was a well-known lyricist but he had not authored a hit show for a decade.

There were other problems as well. The director, Rouben Mamoulian, had little experience with musical comedy—his only previous effort being the direction of Gershwin's *Porgy and Bess* which while an artistic triumph had been a financial failure. Additionally, *Oklahoma!* violated some of the conventional canons concerning musical comedy; it had very little structured humor, certainly few burlesque-style gag lines; it lacked as well that most staple ingredient of all musical shows, the chorus line. No one since the days of Ziegfeld and his Follies had believed it possible to lure customers past the box office without the promise of high-kicking girls. To compound the sin *Oklahoma!* had the effrontery to use a ballet troupe instead. This was considered deliberately high-brow, especially when extended musical sequences frequently interrupted the flow of the narrative. Inexperience and innovation were *Oklahoma!*'s hallmarks, and neither characteristic was considered an asset in prolonging a play's welcome.

Pessimism about the success of the show deepened as the pre-Broadway tryouts in New Haven and Boston were not received with much enthusiasm. Plagued with problems of every sort, it was decided to change the title from *Away We Go* to *Oklahoma!* and to reorganize the finale with the title song as centerpiece. Typical of the difficulties encountered was the pigeon escapade in Boston. For over a month 16 pigeons had been coached by a professional trainer to fly across the stage as the curtain came up on the opening scene. Evidently the idea was to provide the proper bucolic atmosphere appropriate for a frontier territory at the turn of the century. The pigeons had performed like veteran troupers in rehearsal but when they were released in front of an audience for the first time, they scattered to the four corners of Boston's Colonial Theater. Two were never recovered and the idea had to be abandoned.[5]

If errant birds were only a minor catastrophe, a more serious problem involved Marc Platt, the lead member of the ballet chorus. Platt, who was well-known for his dancing with both the Ballet Russe and the Monte Carlo Ballet, had been unable to participate in the show's tryout run because of a bone injury in his foot. On opening night in New York the ballet star received an injection of pain killer only thirty minutes before curtain time. In that memorable performance it was Platt's number which received the lengthiest ovation.[6] All signs prior to March 31 certainly did not point to success. *Oklahoma!* had as much going against it as any previous musical comedy. A starless cast, a composing duo working together for the first time, an inexperienced director, all working on a financial shoestring with a story devoid of either subtle plot or bawdy lines seemed destined for a short engagement at best. That the reverse occurred can be explained by a variety of factors, not the least of which was the lean narrative of the play, the simple story which so many had feared could not support the musical score.

The plot of *Oklahoma!* was an old and familiar one. It is a love triangle with hero, heroine, and villain occupying the three sides. The setting is northeastern Oklahoma in the years just before statehood when the conflict between rancher and farmer over land usage was gradually being reconciled. Curly McLain, the story's protagonist, is a light-hearted cowboy in love with Laurey Williams, who lives with her Aunt Eller Murphy on a small farm. Both Curly and Laurey initially feign indifference to each other, pretending interest in others. For Laurey this is Jud Fry, the transient hired man on her aunt's farm. Fry is the opposite of Curly: sullen, a loner about whom clings the odor of evil. His intentions toward Laurey are clearly malevolent as his wall cover of "dirty pictures" is intended to emphasize. The contest for Laurey's love reaches its climax at an old-fashioned box supper in which Curly sells everything he owns to outbid Jud for the pleasure of purchasing the supper she has prepared. At this point Laurey and Curly realize their love for each other and decide upon marriage. In a final attempt at vengeance Jud attacks the new bridegroom and in the ensuing struggle falls on his own knife and is killed. A trial is held on the spot; Curly is acquitted; and the young couple drive off on their honeymoon "in the surrey with the fringe on top." Another triangle forms a sub-plot in the persons of Ado Annie Carnes, the girl who "cain't say no," her impecunious suitor, Will Parker, and the unwilling fiancé, Ali Hakim, the Persian peddler. Their confusions and mixups provide a comic counterpoint to the more serious fight for the love of Laurey.

Lynn Riggs originally intended for his story to be a folk drama, and some *Oklahoma!* enthusiasts claimed that the Rodgers-Hammerstein adaptation was a folk opera.[7] That claim is probably extravagant, but there is no question that it was the perfect integration of the music into the narrative that elevates *Oklahoma!* to something more than traditional musical comedy. It is the Rodgers' melodies and the Hammerstein lyrics, above everything else which transform the simplistic plot into a near magical myth.

The mood is established in the opening scene. Ignoring the theater wisdom that all musicals must open with a chorus and chorus line, *Oklahoma!* began with Aunt Eller alone on stage churning butter while in the distance the strains of "Oh, What a Beautiful Mornin' " are being sung by the approaching Curly. The first words of that song, "All the sounds of the earth are like music," effectively establish the sunny, optimistic atmosphere which pervades the entire play.

The scene was by no means fortuitous; it was deliberate and well planned. Rodgers and Hammerstein had discussed the matter at length and both wanted to retain the spirit of Riggs' original work. At his "Highland Farm" near Doylestown, Pennsylvania, the methodical librettist composed the lyrics to "Oh, What a Beautiful Mornin' " in less than an hour. The only line which gave him difficulty was the one which states that "the corn is as high as an elephant's eye." Looking out his study window upon a Pennsylvania cornfield, Hammerstein at first compared the height of the corn to a "cow pony's eye" but he was dissatisfied with the analogy because the corn seemed higher. After a brief flirtation with giraffe, the writer settled for elephant while rejecting the impulse to call the Philadelphia zoo for precise measurements.[8] When Hammerstein took the lyrics to Rodgers in New York, the composer immediately put the words into the familiar music in a single attempt. Later, both explained their feelings about that opening scene. Rodgers said that

> Such a course was experimental, amounting almost to a breach
> of implied contract with a musical comedy audience....
> Once we had made the decision everything seemed to work
> right, and we had the inner confidence people feel when they
> have adopted the direct and honest approach to a problem.[9]

The song, argued Hammerstein,

> sums up the mood of the whole performance and tells the
> audience, 'Come on, relax and have fun. Everything's going
> to be swell for a couple of hours!' And they do. You couldn't
> possibly get the same effect with dialogue, having the boy say,
> 'Gee, it's a swell day. I'll bet something nice is going to
> happen'[10]

Practically, every song in the show was a hit and each acted as functional instrument to advance the narrative. The very popular, "People Will Say We're in Love," sung by Alfred Drake as Curly and Joan Roberts as Laurey, demonstrates vividly the subtle relationship between the two—that of real but undeclared love. Ado Annie's character is capsulized in "I Cain't Say No" and "All er Nuthin" while the excitement of fresh beginnings can be felt in the rousing title song, "Oklahoma," in Will's belief that "Everything's Up to Date in Kansas City," and in the flippant, "Many a New Day." Not all of the music was as quickly put together as "Oh, What a Beautiful Mornin'." Rodgers took several days to find the first eight bars of "People Will Say We're in Love."[11] But all of the score including the hauntingly beautiful ballet number, "Out of My Dreams," was used either to advance or inform the plot. Today, such correlation between story and song is commonplace; in 1943 it was bold innovation.

With a single exception reviewers afforded *Oklahoma!* superlative notices. Most pointed to the qualities of gayety, freshness, and simplicity as the play's best assets. Lewis Nichols termed the show, "wonderful" with a "fresh and infectious gayety." Howard Barnes in the *New York Herald Tribune* thought *Oklahoma!* "a jubilant and enchanting musical." *Time* declared that the title "pretty much deserves its exclamation point" and that the show "is thoroughly refreshing without being oppressively rustic." The same magazine believed the story to be passé and insisted that Hammerstein's lyrics lacked polish, left-handedly emphasizing *Oklahoma!*'s simplicity. *Newsweek* credited the play's charm to "good taste and smart showmanship" but Flora Rheta Schreiber was closer to the mark in her analysis for *The Player's Magazine* when she noted especially the combination of naivete and adultness. "It is naive all right, but neither naive stupid nor naive pretentious. It is naive earthy."[12]

Wolcott Gibbs in *The New Yorker* and Joseph Wood Krutch in *The Nation* wrote perceptive reviews which saw *Oklahoma!* as both the representative of a new art form and as a logical extension of the limits of American musical comedy. Krutch labelled the show a "comic opera" that had discovered "a fresh source of themes." He found the show "one of the most lively, entertaining, and colorful musical comedies it has ever been my privilege to see." Gibbs was uncustomarily overwhelmed. "There is, in fact, so much to admire about *Oklahoma!* that I don't quite know how to sort it all out for you." He was particularly impressed with the choreography of Agner de Mille and the sets created by Lemuel Ayres whose designs reminded him of the art of Thomas Benton and Grant Wood and "give the stage depth and brightness and the audience a conviction that the red barns and green fields and yellow roads must be what America really looked like at the turn of the century." Freshness, newness, simplicity, happiness, then, were the characteristics which impressed most critics who hailed *Oklahoma!* as refreshing.[13]

More critical was George Jean Nathan, whose popularity as sophisticated critic had deteriorated along with that of his celebrated partner, H.L. Mencken, from their pontifical pinnacles of the old *American Mercury* days in the twenties. Although finding the Rodgers and Hammerstein effort "agreeable entertainment," Nathan thought the de Mille dances "too arty" and the plot "dubious." Yet, he agreed that *Oklahoma!* had "more body to it than the usual Broadway musical-comedy book." The only reviewer who was completely negative in his appraisal was James Vaughan who said, "As a play I will put it down at once at zero value." Vaughan's view did not go unchallenged by his readers. A letter appearing in the May 7, 1943 issue of *Commonweal* called Mr. Vaughan to account and compared *Oklahoma!* in its "clean, fresh, newness to the old George M. Cohan shows."[14]

In the thirty years that have elapsed since *Oklahoma!*'s debut historians of American musical comedy have periodically reassessed the factors involved with making the show such an instant success. For the most part their explanations have not gone very far beyond those offered in 1943. Yet, almost from the beginning there has been a feeling that attributing *Oklahoma!*'s popularity to the enchanting music or the simplicity of the libretto was inadequate.[15] Obviously, there was something about the show which transcended the ordinary, and several reasons have been advanced to account for the fact.

Some evaluators argued that it was the "decency" of the musical play that made it so appealing. Its humor was earthy rather than risque; its emotions honest rather than contrived. The off-color joke, the *double entendre*, the sight gags which musical comedy had borrowed from burlesque were eschewed by Hammerstein in his writing of the book. Richard Rodgers, himself, reflected in 1945 that he thought *Oklahoma!*'s success proved "that the public wants a decent meal, not all ice cream and soda."[16] Decency did not imply a return to comstockery or a Pollyannish presentation, pruned of concern with sex. Certainly, the suggestive lyrics of "I Cain't Say No" disprove this. But "decency" did imply that human and universal emotions ought to be treated with an honesty and straight-forwardness that did not diminish the moral stature of the characters.

It was in fact, the concern of the play with people in recognizable emotional situations that also was saluted by later observers as contributing much to the longevity of *Oklahoma!* Brooks Atkinson, commenting on the development of the American Theater over a half-century, declared that the genius of Rodgers and Hammerstein was "their insight into character and their sympathy for the common dilemmas of people." He admitted that more than any others the famous team were masters of technique. "But they also believed in human beings."[17] It was this universality, a real interest in people as people, that came across the footlights. "It suggested," said Cecil Smith, a "folk feeling," and *Life* magazine, only a year into *Oklahoma!*'s fantastic run, attributed the show's continuing enchantment for its audiences to its "genuine feeling for America."[18]

As good a word as any to describe this facet of *Oklahoma!*'s attractiveness is authenticity. Everything—the scenery, the songs, the dialogue, the dances—,mesh perfectly to convey what William Beyer has termed a "lyric-dramatic validity."[19] *Oklahoma!* is simple but not juvenile; it is art without being "arty." It is true musical theater as opposed to musical comedy, and like good theater at any time or place aims at something larger than the temporal-spatial limitations of its immediate environment. The target was life itself.[20] Richard Rodgers, perhaps, articulated this feeling best when he explained why he thought *Oklahoma!* was so popular. After pointing to the happy integration of plot, music, and dance, to the naturalness of the costumes and sets, the composer concluded by saying: "The audience simply knows the show makes it 'feel good' and it tells its friends to buy tickets."[21]

For audiences, however, to feel as good as they obviously did after seeing *Oklahoma!* there had to be a closer identification than any of the aforementioned factors explained. What most critics overlooked was the state of the popular mind in 1943. Popular culture can frequently be a subtle barometer of the nation's mood, registering its highs and lows. When the popular mind discovers something—a play, book, or movie—that expresses what it is feeling the result is best seller or box office smash. In the spring of 1943 the popular mind in America was optimistic and hopeful for the future. *Oklahoma!* reminded Americans of the "sunnier days that were so much a part of [their] heritage."[22] The hopes of Curly and Laurey duplicated the deep anticipations that most Americans felt in the middle of World War II.

At first inspection it appears paradoxical to claim 1943 or any year of the forties as one of hope. A decade which brought to the world its greatest war in history, the horror of mass extermination camps, the use of atomic weapons, and the onset of a cold war which always threatens to erupt into nuclear catastrophe can hardly be described as one of mankind's more fruitful ten years. With the advantage of retrospect most students would agree with the assessment of Warren I. French:

The Forties constituted one of the longest, unloveliest, and ominously significant decades in human history. Like the most dread kind of visitor, they arrived early, stayed late, and made an awful mess of the place.[23]

A recent collection of documentary selections for the forties bears the title, *The 1940's: Profile of a Nation in Crisis,* and the editor of this volume employs that much used theme, the loss of innocence, as his principal motif.[24] Yet, a random sampling of American public opinion in 1943 reveals quite a contrasting perspective. It reveals an America truly confident of victory in the war for the first time and determined that the establishment of peace would be permanent. Believing the crusade against Hitler to be a clear case of good fighting evil, Americans had taken their cue from President Roosevelt's declaration of unconditional surrender at the Casablanca Conference in January. By March the war appeared to be turning around. The Nazis had been checked at Stalingrad; the Anglo-American forces had invaded North Africa and were only six weeks away from pushing Rommel's desert troops out of Tunisia. In the Pacific the Solomons, campaign which had seemed so precarious in the fall of 1942 now was assured of success. In Winston Churchill's apt phrase "closing the ring" had begun. Still in the future were the lengthening casualty lists that characterized 1944, the revelations of Dachau and Auschwitz, and the terror of Hiroshima and Nagasaki. 1943 was the summit of American idealism concerning the world's future: Wendell Willkie's paean to internationalism, *One World,* was one of the nation's all-time best sellers; participation in a peace-keeping organization once the war was over had been assured with the passage by overwhelming majorities in the Congress of the Fulbright-Connolly

Resolutions. In the words of an earlier popular song, "The White Cliffs of Dover," that "tomorrow when the world is free" seemed near at hand.

Domestic conditions also contributed to a growing confidence. The commodity price index went over 100 for the first time since 1929. The last of the New Deal relief agencies, the National Youth Administration, was liquidated. Minor discontents over rationing and price control could not obscure the comforting fact that the depression was at long last over. Even serious racial troubles, like the Detroit and Harlem riots, were dismissed as probably the work of Nazi agents. The United States of America was more united in spirit and purpose than at any time since the "hundred days" following Roosevelt's inauguration in 1933 or than it would be for the ensuing quarter-century.

That a spirit of optimism pervaded the country is confirmed by both editorial opinion and public opinion polls. In a New Year's message Major George Fielding Eliot, military writer for the *New York Herald Tribune*, looked forward "to a year which is full of hope." Confident of growing American strength he urged his compatriots "to show ourselves worthy of the favor of Heaven, . . . to make the armed power of the American people a thing of dread to tyrants and would-be tyrants for generations to come." The same issue of the *herald Tribune* editorialized that the war was being "waged to set up the fixed sign-posts of decency and peace and order in human relations. . . . It is a war which a year ago was being lost, which today. . . is beginning to be won." The *Washington Post*, echoing the same sentiment stated "that the tide of war had really turned at last."[25]

A Field public opinion poll, taken in January, 1943, demonstrated how strongly most Americans believed the war against Germany to be entering its last stage. 47.6% of those questioned thought Hitler would be defeated within the year and 35% thought only one additional year would be required to bring Japan to her knees. While the percentages declined somewhat during the year and the much-anticipated second front did not materialize, they remained significantly high.[26] Even the anti-administration *Saturday Evening Post* under the skeptical editorship of Ben Hibbs found the spring of 1943 "the most hopeful since the totalitarian revolution first challenged our complacency." By 1943 Americans were sure enough of final victory that merchants in Spencer, Indiana, displayed window signs which read "Will be Closed on the Day of Hitler's Funeral."[27] In the May 22 issue of the *Saturday Evening Post* the lead article claimed that German prisoners-of-war in the United States knew they were beaten. Significantly, the same issue carried an article by Harold Stassen on the need for world government.

A fundamental factor in the prevailing optimism of 1943 was the belief that future wars would be prevented through the creation of an international agency dedicated to keeping the peace. Viewing history as a simple and repetitive process, most Americans accepted the thesis that World War II cold have been prevented had only the League of Nations been strong enough to resist fascist aggression. A corollary of this postulate was that the failure of the United States to join the League had been its fatal defect. That was all going to be remedied after the current conflagration, and the remedy was simplicity itself—this time the United States would join an assembly of nations and supply the power which the League had so clearly lacked. Nothing more permeates the atmosphere of 1943 than this clear, if naive conviction.

A poll taken early in the year showed that 69.5% of the population believed that it would be a good idea for the United States to join a union of nations after the war to preserve the peace. 64% believed that the administration should make immediate plans for the establishment of a world organization. An even larger number, 76% felt the United States must not return to isolationism but remain active in world affairs once the war was over.[28] The findings of the pollsters were likewise mirrored in numerous editorials across the country from Walter Lippmann to Anne O'Hare McCormick. The former argued that Americans would not be satisfied "with a peace that is a mere cessation of hostilities" and the latter declared that the war had convinced Americans to accept "the essential postulates of international cooperation for peace...."[29] A quick glance at that widely circulated cultural breviary of the common man, *The Reader's Digest*, for 1943, suggests a preoccupation with postwar security. Almost every month's edition carried article condensations concerning the peace; Robert Moses' "The Average American and the Postwar World" in the February issue was typical.

Nor was the surety of a secure postwar world confined to the civilian population. Both *Stars and Stripes* and *Yank* editorialized frequently about war aims. A common theme was emphasized for the G.I. readers. In an approving report of the Casablanca Conference *Yank* demanded that "the peace must prevent the reappearance of the kind of men and ideas that jaggle our world for their own selfish benefit." As an example of the euphoria which followed the Moscow Foreign Ministers Conference in October, *Yank* hailed the creation of international peace-keeping machinery so "that the world in general gets a chance to live in peace—even if peace has to be crammed down a few throats."[30]

In expressing enthusiasm for the Allied commitment to a United Nations at Moscow, *Yank*, inadvertently, perhaps, touched upon the most enigmatic part of postwar projections. Could the Soviet Union be trusted? That selfsame question was put to respondents by a Gallup poll in April of 1943. By a margin of 44% to 34% the answer was in the affirmative. Only a year before the public had been evenly divided on the question.[31] Indeed, 1943 represented the most sanguine beliefs entertained by Americans concerning Russia during any wartime year. Admiration for the fighting capabilities of the Red Army was chiefly responsible for the growing confidence that the two powers could cooperate in maintaining the peace. Wendell Wilkie had held such cooperation absolutely essential in his 1943 best seller, *One World* and such 1943 films as *Mission to Moscow* and *The North Star* buttressed the propaganda image of capitalists and communists as being just democratic brothers under the skin. Even the Army did its part by producing the *Why We Fight* series for troop indoctrination which depicted the Russians as fighting for the ideals of the Atlantic Charter, the four freedoms. American-Soviet relations would never again seem so friendly and promising as they did in 1943. The Teheran Conference in December with its toasts of amity and friendship seemed a fitting climax to the year and seemed also to promise the beginning of a new era of friendship and cooperation.

Oklahoma! was a resounding hit not only because it fulfilled the necessary esthetic requirements but also because its atmosphere and mood so closely matched the prevailing public mood. Just as the play cleanly divided the "good guy" and the "bad guy" so had the war against Hitler achieved a similar dichotomy. Those longtime enemies, the farmers and the ranchers, had come together in common purpose. The same counsel applied to the United States and the Soviet Union. Old antagonisms had to be forgotten if a new era of responsibility was to be initiated; for the show it was Oklahoma statehood; for the world it was the promise of peace in the United Nations.

Indeed, a major characteristic of *Oklahoma!* was its insistent theme of new beginnings and fresh starts. It can be seen in the exhilarating music of the title song and in its exultant lyrics which declared "that the land you belong to is grand." It can be seen in the wonders of "Kansas City" where "you can walk to privies in the rain and never wet your feet." It can be seen in the magnificent surrey which symbolizes all that Curly wishes for Laurey. In fact, Curly effectively summarizes the feelings of optimism and hope in a speech he delivers after he and Laurey have finally admitted their love for each other. After kissing her, Curly says:

I'll be the happiest man alive soon as we're married. Oh, I got to learn to be a farmer, I see that! Quit thinkin' about th'owing the rope, and start in to git my hands blistered a new way! Oh, things is changin' right and left!...They gonna make a state outa this, they gonna put it in the Union! Country a-changin', got to change with it! Bring up a pair of boys, new stock to keep up with the way things is goin' in this here crazy country! Now I got you to he'p me—I'll mount to sump'n yet.[32]

Yet, in the final analysis it was the humanity of *Oklahoma!* which triumphed: its ability to place into song and dance the faith of people in their own survival and to capture in sets and speech their universal aspirations for a better world just ahead. This is what America felt so poignantly in 1943. This is what Aunt Eller meant when she advised Laurey

Oh, lots of things happen to folks. Sickness, er bein' pore and hungry. Even bein' old and afeared to die. That's the way of it, cradle to grave. And you can stand it. They's one way. You gotta be hearty, you got to be. You cain't deserve the sweet and tender things in life less'n you're tough.[33]

Americans in the springtime of 1943 were convinced of their heartiness and their toughness. They were equally sure that the sweet and tender things of life were soon to be theirs, sometime during the new day that had begun with such a beautiful morning.

Notes

[1]Lewis Nichols, "Oh, What a Beautiful Morning—and Matinee," *New York Times Magazine*, March 25, 1945, p. 19.

[2]*Time* April 12, 1948, p. 75. The figures for albums and sheet music were records at that time.

[3]There is a discrepancy about the number of consecutive performances. Some give the figure of 2,208 rather than 2.248. This is explained by either counting or not counting 40 matinees given for servicemen. See Abe Laufe, *Broadway's Greatest Musicals* (New York: Funk and Wagnalls, 1970), p. 65.

[4]David Ewen, *The New Complete Book of the American Musical Theater* (New York: Holt, Rinehart, and Winston, 1970), p. 384.

[5]Leonard Lyons in *Washington Post*. April 11, 1943, p. 12.

[6]*Ibid*, April 5, 1943, p. 12.

[7]For example, Lewis Nichols in his review declared, "Possibly in addition to being a musical play, "Oklahoma!" could be called a folk operetta...." See *New York Times*, April 1, 1943, p. 27.

[8]*Life*, May 29, 1944, p. 104. See also pp. 109-10.

[9]Quoted in Ewen, *New Complete Book*, p. 380.

[10]*Life*, May 29, 1944, p. 104. See also Oscar Hammerstein, II, "Where the Song Begins," *Saturday Review of Literature* (December 3, 1949), p. 13.

[11]Gertrude Samuels, "Success Story Set to Music," *New York Times Magazine* (January 21, 1945), p. 14.

[12]Lewis Nichols in *New York Times*, April 1, 1943, p. 27; Howard Barnes, "The Theater," *New York Herald Tribune*, April 1, 1943, p. 14; *Time*, April 12, 1943, p. 73 *Newsweek*, April 12, 1943, p. 84; Flora Rheta Schreiber, "New York Calling," *The Player's Magazine*, 20 (October 1943), p. 6.

[13]Wolcott Gibbs, "With Thanks," *The New Yorker* (April 10, 1943), p. 34; Joseph Wood Krutch, "High, Wide, and Handsome," *The Nation* (April 17, 1943), p. 572.

[14]George Jean Nathan, *The Theatre Book of the Year, 1942-1943* (New York: Alfred A. Knopf Co., 1943), pp. 269-70; James N. Vaughan, "The Stage and Screen," *Commonweal* (April 16, 1943), p. 642.

[15]Nichols, "Oh, What a Beautiful Morning—and Matinee," p. 18.

[16]*Ibid.*, p. 19; quoted in Samuels, "Success Story Set to Music," p. 39.

[17]Brooks Atkinson, *Broadway* (New York: Macmillan Co., 1970), p. 341.

[18]Cecil Smith, *Musical Comedy in America* (New York: Theater Arts Books, 1950), p. 343; *Life*, March 6, 1944, p. 82; See also *Life*, May 15, 1950, p. 103.

[19]William Beyer, "The State of the Theater: New Trends in Musicals and Revivals," *School and Society*, 67 (June 26, 1948), pp. 475-76.

[20]The following summarize quite well the fusion of artistic elements in *Oklahoma!* Edith J.R. Isaacs and Rosamond Gilder, "American Musical Comedy: Credit it to Broadway," *Theater Arts*, 29 (August 1945), p. 493; Jackson R. Bryer, " 'A Nightly Miracle': The Early Musical Dramas of Rodgers and Hammerstein," in Warren I. French (ed.), *The Forties* (DeLand, Fla.; Everett/Edwards, 1969), p. 128.

[21]Richard Rodgers, "Theater Music," *American Mercury*, 59 (September 1944), p. 280.

[22]Stanley Green, *The World of Musical Comedy* (New York: Ziff-Davis Pub. Co., 1960) p. 245.

[23]French (ed.), *The Forties*, p. 1.

[24]Chester E. Eisinger (ed.), *The 1940's: Profile of a Nation in Crisis* (Garden City, N.Y.: Doubleday and Co., 1969).

[25]*New York Herald Tribune*, Jan. 1, 1943, pp. 1, 21; *Washington Post*, January 1, 1943, p. 8.

[26]*Public Opinion Quarterly*, 7 (Summer 1943), p. 329.

[27]Editorial, *Saturday Evening Post* (May 22, 1943), p. 108; Margaret Weymouth Jackson, "So We Don't Know There's a War," *Saturday Evening Post*, May 15, 1943, p. 17.

[28]*Public Opinion Quarterly*, 7 (Summer 1943), pp. 331-33.

[29]Walter Lippmann, "Today and Tomorrow," *Washington Post*, January 2, 1943, p. 7; Anne O'Hare McCormick, "America's New Mood," *Reader's Digest* (March 1943), p. 37.

[30]*Yank*, February 10, 1943, p. 19 and November 26, 1943, p. 15.

[31]*Public Opinion Quarterly* 7 (Summer 1943), p. 334.

[32]From Act 2, Scene 2. See Burns Mantle (ed.), *The Best Plays of 1942-43* (New York: Dodd, Mead, and Co., 1943), p. 405.

[33]From Act 2, Scene 3. See *Ibid.*, p. 408.

The Changing Popular Song:
An Historical Overview*

Paul Hirsch
John Robinson
Elizabeth Keogh Taylor
Stephen B. Withey

In order to estimate the probable impact on teenagers of changes in the values and ideology expressed in popular song lyrics, it is first necessary to estimate reliably the extent to which today's songs differ from their predecessors. How different are current popular songs from their counterparts of five, ten, or twenty years ago? What types of changes have occurred?

The content of popular songs has been analyzed periodically in professional journals since the early 1940's. Concentrating specifically on song lyrics, researchers generally have found that popular songs' "messages" reinforce an idealized set of traditional values, avoid any commentary on subjects of possible controversy, and are concerned almost exclusively with various phases in the "drama of courtship."[1]

Several writers have traced the heavy predominance of lyrics about "moon and June" in popular songs to the power and influence exerted by "Tin Pan Alley" and its ASCAP-affiliated composers over the entire music industry through the middle 1950's.[2] By 1955, however, the power of these organizations was weakened severely by three notable changes in the structure of the popular music industry: (1) ASCAP's monopoly power in the music industry was broken: (2) television successfully "stole" many adult listeners from once-popular radio stations; and (3) the advent of high-fidelity long-play records discouraged many adults from buying "hit singles." First, the American Society of Composers, Artists, and Publishers (ASCAP) lost a lawsuit initiated by non-member songwriters, and was found guilty of discriminatory admissions practices and illegally barring the access of non-members to recording channels and to radio broadcasting of their songs. H.F. Mooney suggests a direct relationship between

Reprinted with permission from *Popular Music and Society*, Volume 1:2 (Winter 1972), pp. 83-93.

*This project was supported by Grant 1-R01-MH17064-01 from the National Institute of Mental Health.

the rise of rock and roll and ASCAP's loss of control over the direction and content of American popular music:

> Into the vacuum created by the 'death of Tin Pan Alley'...exploded the rock-folks and soul shouts from a score of urban slums throughout the country...Encouraged by the breakdown of ASCAP's hegemony and by prosperous new markets among formerly depressed and minority groups, rival publishing and recording companies had arisen by 1950 in many other, frequently less sophisticated localities [than New York-based Tin Pan Alley]...Negro and country music fused into [rock and roll].[3]

Second, the radio medium in the early 1950's lost much of its adult audience to competition from television, forcing its programmers to seek out new listener markets. One audience market, previously neglected, consisted of the rapidly-growing teenage population: youth-oriented "Top 40" radio stations were inaugurated. Finally, around this same time, the introduction of long playing, better quality records resulted in a shift by adults away from the "hit singles" market. By 1956, raucous "rock and roll" records were seriously competing with recordings of popular songs in the more traditional genre for consumer and listener support. Radio stations were free to select "rock" records for air-play only after ASCAP lost its monopoly power over the music industry.

What values are disseminated through the mass medium of rock and roll records? What images of good and bad? Of successful and unsuccessful roles? How has the role of the vocalist been affected? What "messages," explicit or implied, are contained in the songs' lyrics? What changes have occurred over time?

To develop some answers to these questions, we compiled a list of the three "most popular" records in the United States in the last week of every month over the twenty year period from January 1950 through December 1969. Our source was *Billboard* magazine, the music industry's influential weekly trade paper. Currently, *Billboard's* relative ranking of 45 rpm singles' popularity is based on a weighted sample of 65 retail record stores and ten record distributors in twenty-one major record markets, selected randomly each week from a list of 2000 possible respondent firms. Based primarily on record *sales*, it is supplemented by information on which records are played by fifty-four radio stations in both major and secondary markets.[4] (In the period 1950-1969, various other methods for ranking records' popularity were employed by *Billboard*.) We have also listed, in addition to each "hit" record's title, the name(s) of the performer(s,) the number of weeks each record remained on *Billboard's* "chart," and the record label on which each hit song appeared.

Four trends of possible interest can be found on examination of our listing of hit records over the twenty year period:

1. Male singers have dominated the "charts" consistently throughout the entire twenty year period. Since 1964, there has been a drastic reduction, however, in the number of hit records recorded by single vocalists, with groups having replaced the individual singers.[5] The "causes" of this shift[6] seem less interesting to us than one of its probable "effects": a reduction in the clarity of song lyrics to listeners.

2. A corollary of the trend towards group renditions of song hits is likely to be a decrease in the clarity of recorded song lyrics. Many observers, comparing recent songs to tunes recorded in earlier years, have noted a sharp increase in the number of records whose message is "drowned out" by noisy and/or complex vocal and instrumental arrangements. For example:

[By the 1960's] love lyrics were often so hopelessly submerged in and mangled by arrangements aimed primarily at rhythmic effect that observers could easily conclude that the love song as they remembered it had all but disappeared.[7]

3. The turnover of hit records has increased over time. Songs remain popular for shorter time periods, as more and more records succeed in attaining the top three positions on the "charts." Our monthly sample of three most popular records shows that between 1950 and 1956, all 36 possible "slots" for each month's top three records (12 months x 3 hits per month) were occupied by an average of 18 records annually. Each record thus remained in a top position for an average of two months (18 records / 36 chart positions). On the basis of our monthly sample, the largest number of different records to reach the Top Three in a single year between 1950 and 1956 was 20. Since 1957, the average annual number of records per month attaining positions one, two or three has risen to 28, with a range of 23 (in 1958) to 34 (in 1965). Each record now averages just over five weeks in the Top Three, compared to the previous (1950-1956) average of eight weeks.

4. Until 1955, over eighty percent of all top hit songs were manufactured and distributed by only five record companies: RCA Victor, Columbia, Mercury, Decca and Capitol. The advent of rock and roll also brought a large number of competing firms into the picture. Our listing shows, for example, that by 1959, the "Big Five" companies produced only 47% of the year's Top Three singles; in 1969, they produced only 37%. It appears that the "Big Five" were taken unawares by the receptivity of radio station programmers to rock and roll music in the middle 1950's and by the enthusiastic reaction of young people, once they were provided access to this music. We suggest that much of the change in message content which has occurred in song lyrics is not due simply to changes in "youth values," but rather can be traced to the major record companies' loss of legal control over the selection of songs chosen by performing artists to record.[8]

Changes in Message Content Over Time

Four independent content analyses of recent popular song lyrics, completed between 1967 and 1970, have come to our attention in the last year.[9] Each study performs a similar quantitative analysis of the "messages" contained in popular song lyrics, and arrives at a set of conclusions similar to those reached by the other three. Each study serves as a check upon the reliability of the others. Their findings confirm the general impression that song lyrics have changed substantially over the last fifteen years. Specifically, (1) the song lyrics of recent years deal more frankly with a wider set of issues than their predecessors, and (2) attitudes expressed about relations between the sexes are more openly favorable towards physical contact and individual autonomy.

(1) Greater Diversity of Themes and Topics

In 1955, nearly 85% of all popular songs still concerned different stages in the "drama of courtship."[10] The remaining 15% "range widely and show no clear-cut focus. They include song dances, general narrative ballads on love themes, religious songs, comic songs, and others which could not be classified."[11] By 1966, only 65% of popular song hits concerned stages in the courtship process.[12] The remaining songs' lyrics "reveal more specific concerns;" a crucial area of concern has become the role of the individual in the conventional world.

Will he become part of the conventional world or will he drop out and create his own scene? The decision to do something about one's life, to think for one's self, no matter what the consequences, is generally enjoined.[13]

More specifically, a rising proportion of best-selling popular songs contain lyrics which comment on controversial subjects previously avoided by song writers. Frequently, but not always, these songs criticize conventional modes of behavior and celebrate values which many segments of our society find offensive. The issue of the individual's relation to *society*, rather than only to his peers, is now the generator of controversy. For example, in 1952, at the height of the Korean conflict, no popular song hit even alluded to the war in Asia.[14] In contrast, during the last five years, one or more hit songs each year has contributed to an ongoing musical debate over the morality of war between youthful "hawks" and "doves." This argument was initiated late in 1965 when "The Eve of Destruction" (a trenchant condemnation of war in general and American society in particular) rose to the number one position on the national hit parade charts. Several months later, a patriotic ("pro-war") song, "Ballad of the Green Berets," was the number one hit. Both songs provoked a great deal of public comment and controversy, for in treating the individual in his relation to *societal* concerns, each song came out in support of a strong position on a politically sensitive issue.[15]

Two other social issues traditionally avoided by popular song writers, but more recently treated in songs on the hit parade are race relations (*e.g.*, "We're Movin' on Up," "Society's Child") and drug usage; critics and proponents both agree, for example, that references to marijuana or other drugs are contained in such song hits as "Puff the Magic Dragon," "Mr. Tambourine Man," "Incense and Peppermints,," "White Rabbit," and "Eight Miles High." As a result of 1971 statements by the Federal Communications Commission, however, concerning the acceptability and "public interest" nature of possibly drug-related song lyrics, many radio stations may cut back on the airplay of such records.

A number of writers have categorized as "social protest" all hit songs whose lyrics are concerned with controversial themes surrounding the morality of war, relations between different racial groups, and drug usage, as well as any song whose lyrics are critical of widely accepted values or legitimate roles in American society.[16] The common dimension running through each of these themes is the song's placement of individuals in relation to society, rather than to their peers. Most "protest" songs are either implicitly or explicitly critical of generally accepted values and mores. A song which suggests the routine use of drugs is implicitly critical of our society's proscriptions against drug abuse, for example; other songs which state the singer's unwillingness to adhere to generally accepted norms (*e.g.*, obey orders and/or fight in Vietnam) are explicitly critical. A typical example of a popular song lyric which we would code as "social protest" is "Mr. Business Man," recorded by Ray Stevens in 1968:

> Itemize the things you covet
> As you squander through your life,
> Bigger cars, bigger houses,
> Term insurance for your wife,
> Tuesday evenings with your harlot
> And on Wednesdays it's your charlatan analyst
> He's high up on your list
> You better take care of business, Mr. Businessman.

What proportion of popular songs contain "protest" messages? Carey found 35% of popular songs in 1966 unrelated to stages in the courtship process—traditionally the almost-exclusive subject of popular song themes.[17] The great majority of these songs concerned either the relation of the individual to his society or his need for freedom and autonomy in reference to personal affairs. Both themes thus deviate markedly from the set of behavior patterns traditionally reinforced by and associated with popular song lyrics. Cole found that the proportion of hit songs with explicitly "protest" themes among the five most popular songs each *year* between 1960 and 1969 rose from none between 1960 and 1964 to 10% between 1965 and 1969.[18] This estimate excludes hit songs with "borderline," ambiguous or merely implicit "protest" themes; it fails to take into account the sale of long play albums, the airplay of protest songs on the growing number of "underground rock" FM radio stations, and the sale of hit protest singles which did not make their year's Top Five. Ten percent, therefore, is probably a conservative estimate of the proportion of popular songs containing "protest" messages in 1970.[19]

(2) Changing Relations Between the Sexes

The second major shift in the message content of popular songs concerns expressed attitudes towards alternative styles of courtship and boy-girl relations. Hit song lyrics of the early 1950's are filled with romantic images of courtship styles far different from the images presented now by their more recent counterparts. Perhaps the greatest contrast occurs along an "active-passive" dimension, along which the behavior of the actor towards the object of his attentions can be coded and analyzed.

Popular song lyrics through the early 1950's placed love mainly in the hands of fate. The singer played an essentially passive role, waiting for a permanent love relationship to "happen." McLaughlin summarizes her analysis of song lyrics during this time period in these terms:

The most important social relationship depicted in the popular songs of 1952 was that of romantic love. Considered to be the one experience making life worthwhile, love was seen as a matter of complete involvement in a relationship characterized as "magical," blissful, or passionate. Details of the relationship were usually left vague, like the partners who were addressed; but lovers pleaded desperately for acceptance by these generalized persons, offering themselves in total adoration and devotion.[20]

Carey and Horton also find the popular songs of this period to present the singer in the role of passive supplicant.

Since love in the 1955 song lyrics is experienced as externally controlled, it is often perceived as an object or commodity rather than as something the lovers mutually create. Love frequently appears in popular song lyrics [during this time period] as something to be "won" or something which is subject to theft.[21]

By 1959, rock and roll was well on the way to claiming for itself the title of American popular music. "Popular" songs in the ballad style of the early 50's were unable to stem the tide of the newer song styles. McLaughlin notes a corresponding change in the popular song lyrics of this transitional time period:

The songs of 1959 contain much more nearly-explicit mention of sexual matters than would have been allowed in earlier songs.[22]

Like Mooney and Hayakawa, she attributes this change largely to the growing influence of Negro rhythm-and-blues performers and song writers on white musicians and audiences.[23] As we mentioned earlier, songs in this genre by this time were receiving a degree of exposure to mass audiences via Top 40 radio stations unprecedented in the history of broadcasting.

By 1966, the mood of popular music was "sensual, direct, sexual, and 'gutsy'," as compared to the more "languid, searching, 'sweet' " music of the early 1950's:

Romantic love has been rejected as the exclusive requirement for engaging in a sexual relationship....The new outlook on the love affair does not include the expectation of permanence. Freedom is celebrated for both partners....[Today's] rock lyrics reject [the earlier] passive orientation toward the boy-girl relationship....The affair is actively sought by the lovers rather than passively longed for.[24]

In addition, Carey notes a role reversal in the drama of courtship: in actively seeking relationships, males are now able to initiate and terminate the love affair; they are no longer "at the mercy of" the girls. Finally, "love often seems to have been reduced to physical attraction."[25]

These studies demonstrate convincingly that the messages contained in popular song lyrics have undergone radical changes since 1950. Between 68% and 83% of all hit rock and roll songs analyzed by Carey in 1966 either espoused the "new values" of independence and active search in courtship, or freely examined questions previously avoided as "too controversial" by the popular song medium. This finding, taken by itself, is not terribly surprising by this time. It sets the stage, however, to explore a host of related questions—such as:

1) What is the likely "impact" of rock and roll music on American youth?
2) Are the verbal "meanings" of song lyrics an adequate measure of "impact"? If not, what additional measures should be developed?
3) To what extent might the radical changes in the sound and lyrics of popular songs over the last twenty years be due to new arrangements in the music industry, such as:

  a) an increase in the degree of artistic freedom awarded young composers in their contracts with record companies; and

  b) greater receptivity to all rock music by the mass media.

Each of these factors would supplement the more common view that popular music has changed solely because the new youth culture demanded it.

Students of the pop music "phenomenon" are now exploring many questions of this type. Some tentative answers have been suggested by Denisoff and Levine, Peterson and Berger, Hirsch, Mooney, and others.[26] More research, however, into the cause of the changes we have shown, and into their "effects" (if any), could be quite fruitful.

Notes

[1] John Peatman, "Radio and Popular Music," in Paul Lazarsfeld and E. Frank Stanton, eds., *Radio Research 1942-1943* (New York: Duell, Sloan and Pearce, 1944), pp. 335-393; and Donald Horton, "The Dialogue of Courtship in Popular Songs," *American Journal of Sociology* 62 (May, 1957), pp. 569-578.

[2] Richard Peterson and David G. Berger, "The Dollar and Pop Culture: The Influence of Changing Industry Structure on the Control of Social Commentary in Popular Music," in Peter K. Manning, ed., *Deviance and Social Change* (New York: Prentice-Hall (forthcoming), and H.F. Mooney, "Popular Music Since the 1920s: The Significance of Shifting Taste," in Jonathan Eisen, ed., *The Age of Rock* (New York: Vintage Press, 1969), pp. 9-29.

[3] Mooney, *ibid.*, p. 18.

[4] See Andrew Csida, "The 'Hot 100'—How It Is Compiled," *Billboard*, September 13, 1969, p. 60; also "How the Top LP's Chart Is Compiled," *Billboard*, September 20, 1969, p. 34.

[5] Our data indicate that single female vocalists made their best showing in the period 1950-1954. During this time, over 50% of the "hits" were recorded by single male and single female vocalists, the males accounting for an average of 33% of the hits, the females, 30%; instrumentals and songs by male groups made a respectable showing on the charts; hits by female groups were oddities. From 1955-1963, proportionally more hits were recorded by single male vocalists than any other category of singer (in five of the years, single males had at least 50% of the hits); single female vocalists averaged 12% of the hits of this period; instrumentals were somewhat less popular than they had been previously; and hits by female groups were still generally uncommon. With the advent

of the Beatles in 1964, male groups have dominated the charts; the proportion of hits by single males was reduced dramatically in this latter period; female groups were more popular in 1964 and 1965 than at any time previously or since; single female vocalists with hits are rare; and instrumentals have all but disappeared from the charts. In sum, our data show that while there does not seem to have been a preponderance of hits by either sex in the early 1950s, since 1955 males have dominated the charts, first as single vocalists and later in groups. There has been a major shift away from single vocalists, generally accompanied by large studio orchestras, to *male* recording *groups*, who "divide" the song among two or more "lead" singers, and accompany themselves on a variety of instruments, usually featuring electric guitars and drums. Cole and Sitar have traced the course and magnitude of this change in two independent research reports. Sitar indicates that between 1950 and 1961, single male vocalists averaged about 55% per year of all top "hits." Female vocalists averaged about 12% per year, and the remaining 37% was divided between vocal groups and instrumentalists. From 1962 to 1966, however, the proportion of hit records by single male vocalists declined steadily from 52% to 20%; the proportion of hit records by vocal *groups* climbed steadily from 28% to 72%; the proportion of hit records by female vocalists and instrumental groups combined dropped from an unusually high 20% in 1962 to about 8% in 1966 (Sitar, n=550). Dividing his smaller sample of Top 10 hits into fifty from 1960-64 and fifty from 1965-69, Cole arrived at very similar results. See Richard Cole, "Top Songs in the Sixties: A Content Analysis of Popular Lyrics," *American Behavioral Scientist* (January / February, 1971), pp. 390-400; and also William F. Sitar, "A Quantitative Analysis of Hillbilly, Popular, and Rhythm and Blues Recordings and Recording Artists and a Content Analysis of Hillbilly Lyrics." Tampa, Florida: University of South Florida (unpublished paper), 1967.

[6]Numerous "causes" have been suggested by music critics and others, but these are largely speculative. Again, the economics of the industry loom large as a competing or supplementary explanation to that of audience demand. It costs a record company less to record four young singer-musicians than a featured vocalist backed by a large orchestra. Once it became apparent that *either* type of record could be sold in large quantities, the recording industry reduced its output of records involving the higher production costs. Before the advent of "Top 40" radio, most listeners did not have ease of access to these "cheaper" records by recording *groups*, because most radio stations would not play them. Accordingly, before the advent of the "Top 40" format, few record companies were willing to produce this type of record.

[7]Mooney, *op. cit.*, p. 23.

[8]Paul Hirsch, "Sociological Approaches to the Pop Music Phenomenon," *American Behavioral Scientist* 14 (January / February, 1971), pp. 371-387.

[9]Cole, *op. cit.*: Sitar, *op. cit.*; James Carey, "Changing Courtship Patterns in the Popular Song," *American Journal of Sociology* 74 (May, 1969), pp. 720-731; and Mary McLaughlin, "The Social World of American Popular Songs." Unpublished M.A. Thesis. New York: Department of Anthropology, Cornell University, 1968.

[10]Horton, *op. cit.*

[11]Carey, *op. cit.*, p. 730.

[12]*Ibid.*

[13]*Ibid.*

[14]McLaughlin, *op. cit.*

[15]See R. Serge Denisoff, "Protest Songs: Those on the Top 40 and Those of the Streets," *American Quarterly* 22 (Winter, 1970), pp. 807-823; and R. Serge Denisoff and

Mark Levine, "The Popular Protest Song: The Case of "The Eve of Destruction'," *Public Opinion Quarterly* 35 (Spring, 1971), pp. 117-122.

[16]John H. Robinson and Paul Hirsch, "It's the Sound that Does It," *Psychology Today* 3 (October, 1969), pp. 42-45; Denisoff, "Protest Songs," *op. cit.*" and Cole, *op. cit.*

[17]Carey, *op. cit.*

[18]Cole, *op. cit.*

[19]See John H. Robinson and Paul Hirsch, "Teenage Response to Rock and Roll Protest Songs," paper presented to the American Sociological Association meeting at San Francisco, 1969, pp. 4-5; and R. Serge Denisoff, "Songs of Persuasion: A Sociological Analysis of Urban Propaganda Songs," *Journal of American Folklore* 79 (October / December, 1966), pp. 581-189.

[20]McLaughlin, *op. cit.*, p. 55.

[21]Carey, *op. cit.*, p. 729.

[22]McLaughlin, *op. cit.*, p. 64.

[23]S.I. Hayakawa, "Popular Songs vs. the Facts of Life," *ETC: A General Review of Semantics* 12 (1955), pp. 83-95.

[24]Carey, *op. cit.*, pp. 720, 729.

[25]Carey, *ibid.*, p. 728.

[26]See Denisoff and Levine, "Popular Protest Song," *op. cit.*; Peterson and Berger, *op. cit.*; Hirsch, "Sociological Approaches," *op. cit.*; and Mooney, *op. cit.*